SO-AWL-215

ZANE GREY

A Biography

ZANE GREY
A
BIOGRAPHY

BY

FRANK
GRUBER

Reg. U.S. Pat. Off.

WALTER J. BLACK, INC.

ROSLYN, NEW YORK

ZANE GREY

*Copyright © 1969 by Frank Gruber and
Zane Grey, Inc.*

*All rights reserved. No part of this book may be
reproduced in any form without written permission
from the publisher, except for brief passages included in a review appearing in a newspaper or
magazine.*

By arrangement with
THE WORLD PUBLISHING COMPANY

*Library of Congress
Catalog Card Number: 75-75879
Printed in the United States of America*

ACKNOWLEDGMENTS

Grateful acknowledgment is made to William Clark for his assistance in the compilation and checking of the bibliography. Mr. Clark graciously gave his time and effort to make a complete check at the Library of Congress, the New York Public Library, and many editorial offices in New York and Philadelphia.

The gratitude and thanks of the author are extended to the many people in Hollywood who helped with reminiscences of their contacts with Zane Grey: Randolph Scott, Richard Arlen, Harry Joe Brown, Sol Lesser, Jack Karp, A. C. Lyles, Henry Hathaway, Gail Patrick Jackson, James Cagney, and others too numerous to mention.

Especial thanks are also due to Romer Grey, Betty Zane Grosso, and Dr. Loren Grey, as well as to Elenora Evans, the secretary of Zane Grey, Inc.

FRANK GRUBER

FOREWORD

My acquaintance with the books of Zane Grey was made in 1916, when I was twelve years old. In the spring of that year our family moved from Chicago to a farm near Elkton, Michigan. I was already an avid reader and had pretty nearly worked through the juvenile section of the Stanton Park Public Library.

In Michigan I read every circular, every scrap of printed material that came in the mail, but my family subscribed to no publications of any kind.

Nearby, however, was the home of the farmer for whom our family worked. We received our own meager mail in his box, and I saw that he received a copy of the *Michigan Farmer* every week. I would take it out of the box and peruse it, seated on the ground beside the mailbox. The farm articles were deadly dull, but the publication carried a weekly installment of a fiction serial by John Galsworthy, and I read it regularly. I hated every word of it, but it was better than no reading whatever.

After a few weeks the Galsworthy novel ended, and the following week the magazine began publication of a new serial, *The Light of Western Stars* by Zane Grey. I read the first installment and was enthralled. I could scarcely wait for the following Tuesday, when the mailman delivered the new issue, and in the succeeding weeks I would be out on the road an hour before the expected arrival of the R.F.D. mail carrier. I would snatch the mail from his hand and for the next fifteen or twenty minutes I would be lost to the world.

The final installment of *The Light of Western Stars* was printed only a week or two before our family returned to Chicago in November.

We were scarcely settled in our new home when I was off to the library. Having been away for six months, I persuaded the librarian that I was now fourteen years old, which entitled me to an adult card. With this I was able to take out five books at a time instead of the two permitted on the juvenile card.

I found *The Light of Western Stars* in the adult section. I also found *Riders of the Purple Sage*, *The Lone Star Ranger*, *Heritage of the Desert* and *Desert Gold*. I took them all home, and for five, wonderful, glorious days I wallowed in the stories of Zane Grey. I was compelled to go to school, but I read the books in the morning, in the afternoon, in the evening. I took them back to the library and got *Betty Zane*, *The Spirit of the Border*, *The Last Trail*, and a couple of the Ken Ward books that I discovered in the juvenile section.

In two weeks I had read all of the then published books of Zane Grey. I read two or three new ones in the next two years, usually in the magazine version.

Before I discovered Zane Grey I had already read more than a hundred Horatio Alger books, and the reading of these instilled in me the desire to become a writer. This boyhood ambition, acquired when I was only nine or ten, remained steadfast through the years.

I was scribbling by the time I was ten. I did not sell my first story until I was twenty-three and used it as a springboard to get a job as editor of a small farm paper. I worked on farm and business journals until 1934, when I cast the die and went to New York to become established as a writer or forever give up the hope. My main assault was on the detective-story field, but I failed dismally. Leo Margulies, a friendly editor of a chain of magazines, after rejecting my latest story, suggested I try a Western story.

I had absolutely no interest in Western stories. I had not read one since Zane Grey's *The U.P. Trail* in 1918. I had never read a pulp Western story, but Leo Margulies gave me a copy of *Thrilling Western*, and I read it from cover to cover. That same evening I wrote two very short Western stories, which Margulies bought for sixteen and eighteen dollars.

The tide turned overnight, and I began selling everything I produced. During the next year I sold fifty-five stories, of which perhaps fifteen were Westerns.

I began doing well in the pulp magazines and by 1938 was ready to move on to bigger and better fields. I tried some short stories on the "slicks" and found that I could sell them, but they did not satisfy me; after much deliberation I decided to write a Western novel, *Peace Marshal*, which was serialized in *Adventure Magazine* and published in hardcover form in 1939. My next book was a mystery novel, *The French Key*. However, because of the serial money, I went back to Westerns and wrote *Outlaw*. Meanwhile I was writing more mystery novels, selling serial rights to all of them, and they were doing very well as hardcover books. I decided to quit Westerns and concentrate entirely on mysteries.

My eyes were on Hollywood. I had already paid numerous visits to the film capital, to be available for the call when it came. I was counting on the mysteries to bring me that call.

The call finally came in early 1942. But it was not the mysteries that brought it. It was *Peace Marshal*, my first Western, my first book. I sold picture rights to it for one thousand dollars, but got with it a six-week writing contract. I went to Hollywood and am still here.

I knew only vaguely about paper quotas during the war, but when the war was over, the paperback business suddenly exploded. Bantam Books was formed and published four books as their initial offering. The number-two title of the Bantam list was a mystery of mine, *The Gift Horse*, which sold 311,000 copies.

Also on that first Bantam schedule was a Western, *Nevada*, by Zane Grey. It has sold through the years 2,089,000 copies!

In Hollywood, Westerns had been at an all-time low during the war years, but they were beginning to reappear, and with this in mind, as well as the paperback sales, I wrote three new Western novels. I sold all three of them as magazine serials, and all were brought out as hardcover books. They were promptly taken up by paperback companies, and two of them were bought by film companies.

Westerns had become big business.

I rode the outlaw trails very hard during the next few years. I roped horses, hunted buffalo, and donned the uniform of the Seventh Cavalry. I built railroads and established stagecoach lines. I wrote Western books and I wrote screenplays for Western motion pictures.

I had not read a Western story in a dozen years, but one day I picked up *The Thundering Herd* by Zane Grey. I thought the story was only so-so, but the account of the hunting of the buffalo, the life of the buffalo hunters, was the best I had ever read by anyone, and I had read many factual books on the subject in the past.

I picked up a copy of *The U.P. Trail*, which was the last Zane Grey book I had read in 1918. Slowly it seeped through my mind that this was the best Western book I had ever read by anyone. In spite of the dialect, in spite of some plot weaknesses, in spite of a few inconsistencies, it was still *the greatest Western I had ever read*.

But through all these long, long years I had assumed—and even preached—that *Riders of the Purple Sage* was the best Western ever written by anyone! Had I been wrong all these years?

Frantically I started to read *Riders of the Purple Sage*,

and when I finished it I was dumbfounded. I could not determine whether I liked it better than *The U.P. Trail*. I finally decided that these were the *two best Westerns ever written*.

Mind, I now read these books, not as a boy of twelve or fourteen, but as a mature person, a professional writer.

I read a Zane Grey book a day for the next three weeks, and as I read I decided that I wanted to know more about Zane Grey, the Father of the Western Story, perhaps the most popular author of the twentieth century. As I delved into his life, I knew that I had to write the story of Zane Grey.

Zane Grey left a widow, Lina Elise Grey, who has since died, and three children—Romer, Loren, and Elizabeth Grey Grosso. I contacted Dr. Loren Grey, professor of psychology at Valley State College near Los Angeles, and Romer, president of Zane Grey, Inc., the literary estate of his father.

A seed I had cast into the wind some years ago had grown into a flower. In 1958 I had appeared on a television program and declared that *Riders of the Purple Sage* was the greatest Western ever written. Elizabeth Grey Grosso had seen the program and told her brothers about it.

Everything was made available to me—the journals of Zane Grey; the records, anecdotes, and reminiscences of the family; the diaries of both Zane Grey and Mrs. Grey; and the 236-page unfinished autobiography that Zane Grey was working on at the time of his death, which unfortunately ends with his student days at the University of Pennsylvania.

What follows is the story of Zane Grey, the King of the West, and I dedicate it to Elizabeth Grey Grosso, Romer Grey, and Dr. Loren Grey.

                                        Frank Gruber

ZANE GREY

A Biography

In 1920, *This Side of Paradise*, by F. Scott Fitzgerald, burst upon the publishing world and brought its author fame, fortune—and tragedy. In spite of considerable critical applause, however, *This Side of Paradise* sold a meager thirty-five thousand copies and did not even make the best-seller list of the year.

It was a good publishing year. Postwar prosperity enabled people to buy luxuries they had forgone through the war period. Some excellent authors were on the publishers' lists: Peter B. Kyne, Harold Bell Wright, James Oliver Curwood, Joseph C. Lincoln, Ethel Dell, and the marathon best-seller, Kathleen Norris.

But heading the list of these luminaries was Zane Grey, whose *Man of the Forest* was the number-one title of the year.

Zane Grey in 1920 was not a newcomer to the best-seller list. He had been on it since 1915, when *The Lone Star Ranger* was ninth in sales for the year. In 1917 *Wildfire* was third, and in 1918 *The U.P. Trail* was number one. During the ten-year period 1915–24, a Zane Grey book was in the top ten of the best-seller list nine times, missing only one year—1916.

In 1920 there were as yet no book clubs, and the mass-market paperback was still twenty years in the future. To make the top ten on the best-seller list a book had to sell more than one hundred thousand copies. *The Man of the Forest* eventually sold 714,500 copies in the numerous editions, yet it was not the biggest-selling Zane Grey title. That honor goes to *Riders of the Purple Sage*, which has now sold more than 1,215,000 copies in hardcover editions alone. First published in 1912, it is considered by most devotees of the Western novel to be the best ever written.

The name of the New York dentist who "discovered" the West and dug more gold from it than was ever taken from the earth by any single man is synonymous with the American West. He was the favorite author of two generations of Americans. His name is as well known today as it was in his lifetime, and his books are still published and read widely and avidly.

Zane Grey was the people's author. He was read by the masses of his time. He is read by them today, and he will be read a hundred years from now. His popularity in the English-reading world is matched by that in Germany, France, Spain, and even the Iron Curtain countries.

Although Zane Grey began his writing career in 1902 by selling an acticle, "A Day on the Delaware," to *Recreation Magazine*, and then followed with three historical novels, *Betty Zane*, *The Spirit of the Border* and *The Last Trail*, his successful writing period did not begin until 1909. It lasted until his death in 1939, when he was still writing as much as at any time during the thirty-year period.

He produced eighty-nine books in his lifetime. Included in this number were fifty-six novels of the West; one "Eastern" book, *The Day of the Beast*; and three Ohio River-country novels, which brought the total of the regular novels to an even sixty. However, to this should be added two shorter books, novelettes actually, *Don* and *The Wolf Tracker*, and three collections of novelettes and short stories published in book form as *Tappan's Burro*, *The Ranger and Other Stories*, and *Blue Feather and Other Stories*. Two of his books can be classified as "hunting" books, *The Last of the Plainsmen* and *Tales of Lonely Trails*. There were six juvenile books, four featuring Ken Ward and *Roping Lions in the Grand Canyon* and *Zane Grey's Book of Camps and Trails*, plus two books of baseball stories, *The Short Stop* and *The Red-headed Outfield and Other Stories*. And last, but not least, there were eight large fishing books.

Grey's books were rather long. While modern books may be as short as fifty thousand and sixty thousand words, Zane Grey's books, including the few shorter ones, average to one hundred thousand words each. Grey also wrote numerous short articles and fishing serials that appeared in sports magazines, which were never published in book form. Thus his published wordage count probably exceeds nine million—an average of approximately three hundred thousand words a year during his writing career—a prodigious amount of material for one author to produce.

To estimate the total number of readers who enjoyed Zane Grey's work is an impossible task. Forty-nine Zane Grey novels were serialized in magazines of huge circulation. Two of his books ran as serials in the pulp magazine *Popular Magazine*, which had a circulation of roughly three hundred thousand. Four of his books ran in the *Munsey Magazines*, with circulation about the same as *Popular*. One appeared in *Blue Book*, with one-half million circulation. But then Zane Grey moved into the big "slicks": *The Country Gentleman* published thirteen serials and numerous short pieces. The circulation of this biggest and best of the farm papers was seldom less than one and one-half million and at times went over the two-million mark. Nine serials were published by *Ladies' Home Journal*, which was the elite of the women's magazines. Its circulation was never less than two million. Three novels appeared in *McCall's*, five in *Collier's*, four in *American Magazine*, one in *Pictorial Review*, and one in *Cosmopolitan*. The last three Zane Grey books were serialized in the New York *Daily News*, with two million circulation.

Virtually two generations of magazine readers enjoyed the books of Zane Grey, but the circulation of these magazines was not the complete story. Each book, after its hardcover publication by Harper & Brothers, went into syndication, some of them appearing in hundreds of newspapers and smaller magazines. This syndication may have reached from ten to fifteen million readers for each book.

Zane Grey books were tremendous sellers in their original hardcover editions, but the sales were topped then by the cheaper reprint editions put out by Grosset & Dunlap. From the time they began publishing Zane Grey books, Grosset & Dunlap featured them as the "leaders." They sold millions and millions of copies in these reprint editions.

The paperback book had just made its appearance at the time of Zane Grey's death, but later his books went into paperback editions and sold in huge quantities. *Nevada* alone sold more than two million copies in Bantam editions.

In 1950 the Walter J. Black Company, which issued the Classic Book Club editions and the Detective Book Club editions, decided to try out a book club issuing only Zane Grey Westerns. From 1950 until 1968 this company has sold six million Zane Grey books in matching editions.

Hollywood discovered the Zane Grey books very early and based three motion pictures on them in 1918. Since that time forty-six books have been made into pictures, but many of the titles have been remade two, three, or four times, with the result that a staggering total of a hundred and four pictures have been made of Zane Grey books. No other writers' books have had such a wide motion-picture audience.

Zane Grey knew nothing of television, but television, when it came into existence, knew about Zane Grey; the *Zane Grey Western Theatre* appeared on the television screens in 1956 and had a five-year run, during which it screened 145 episodes. At the same time, the Dell Publishing Company put out a monthly magazine, *Zane Grey's Western Stories*, featuring condensed versions of Zane Grey books, plus some stories by other writers of Westerns. It had a ten-year run, when it was discovered that the condensed versions were hurting the sales of the regular full-length titles still being issued.

Zane Grey's books had scarcely become popular in the United States when foreign rights to them were sold, first in England, where they were brought out in huge editions, then in other countries. At the time of Zane Grey's death, his books were issued regularly in twenty countries outside the United States. This declined somewhat during the war, but they are today being actively published in fourteen or fifteen countries throughout the world, some of them for the fourth or fifth time. The Scandinavian countries have always been partial to American Westerns, and Zane Grey books in particular. The books have been huge sellers in Germany, Holland, Italy, Spain, and throughout South America. They have been published in Israel in Hebrew translations. How many millions of people throughout the world have bought, read, and enjoyed Zane Grey books can never be determined. To try to guess how many millions have seen Zane Grey stories on television or on the motion-picture screen would be futile.

CHAPTER **2**

Genealogy has long lost its vogue and is deemed of little importance in these days of equal opportunity for all and the almost fanatical insistence that heredity and ethnic and racial origins are of no consequence and have absolutely no scientific basis.

Yet it is the custom of biographers to trace the lineage of their subjects, and perhaps, in spite of the sociologists, it can be suggested that Zane Grey, who espoused the cause of America so ably in his writings, might indeed have been motivated by the heritage of his forebears.

According to the tradition handed down in the family, the Zanes originated in Denmark. One of them migrated to England, and from him descended Robert Zane, a Quaker and follower of William Penn. He was a maker of serge cloth and in 1678 immigrated to the American colonies. He settled in New Jersey and married. One of his children moved to Virginia.

A grandson of the first Virginia Zane was named Ebenezer. Born in 1746, he left his mark on the colonial history of the fledgling United States. Becoming a militiaman, Ebenezer Zane, accompanied by three brothers and their close friends the McCullochs and Wetzels, plunged into the wilderness and eventually reached the Ohio River.

An island in the river seemed to be an ideal location, and Ebenezer Zane purchased it from an Indian chief. A blockhouse and a few log cabins were built, and then Zane returned

to Hardy County, in western Virginia, gathered together his
wife and the wives of his friends, plus a few recruits, and returned to the island in the Ohio River.

At the outbreak of the Revolutionary War, a stockade
was built on the island and named Fort Henry, in honor of
Patrick Henry. A small detachment of Virginia militia was
sent to man Fort Henry. Ebenezer Zane was commissioned a
colonel and placed in command of the fort, which is today the
site of Wheeling, West Virginia.

The outpost withstood two furious assaults by large combined British-Indian forces. During one of them, the colonel's
young sister, Betty Zane, carried badly needed gunpowder in
her apron, slung over her shoulder, from the arsenal to the
fort amid a hail of bullets. This deed, later used in all the
grammar-school histories, was the basis of the plot of the first
book written by the descendant of Colonel Zane.

Colonel Ebenezer Zane was commended by George
Washington, and the Continental Congress voted him ten
thousand acres of land in the Ohio Valley.

After the hostilities of the Revolution, a wave of settlers,
leading packhorses, wended through the Alleghenies to settle
in the virgin lands of the Ohio Valley. To guide the settlers
and to establish favorable sites for his own land grants, Colonel Ebenezer Zane blazed a road known as Zane's Trace across
the soon-to-become state of Ohio. One of the settlements he
established became Zanesville, Ohio.

In Virginia Ebenezer Zane had been married to a sister
of the McCullochs, his friends and fellow pioneers. The father
of the McCullochs had married the daughter of an Indian
chief, and this Indian blood in the McCullochs may have
imbued his sons and daughter with the pioneering spirit.

Colonel Zane's wife died, and he remarried. He died in
1812; a plaque at Wheeling, West Virginia, commemorates his
founding and defense of the original settlement and fort.

A grandson of the colonel and his first wife, the half-
Indian McCulloch, was named Samuel. Samuel's daughter
Josephine Alice married Lewis M. Gray in Zanesville, Ohio, on

February 5, 1856. Zane Grey, the son of this union, was only one-thirty-second Indian, but he was always proud of the Indian blood that flowed in his veins.

Zane Grey's paternal ancestry was not as distinguished as his maternal background. The first Gray came from a farm in Ireland and settled in Springfield Township, Muskingum County, Ohio, "before 1820." His name was Lewis Gray, and his son Liggett remained to farm the acres his father had cleared.

Liggett's son, Lewis M. Gray, inherited the restlessness of his Irish ancestors. He tried farming but did not like it. He roamed the Ohio countryside as a woodsman and hunter. He became a traveling preacher but was not satisfied. Although he never lost his faith, he decided that the ministry was not for him. The decision may have been influenced by his engagement to Josephine Zane, whose roots were deep in the city founded by her family.

The young preacher became a dentist, which in those days required only a brief apprenticeship with a practicing dentist. He opened an office in Zanesville, hung up a sign, "Dr. Lewis M. Gray," and married Josephine. In the course of time five children were born: two girls, Ella and Ida; and three sons, Lewis Ellsworth, Pearl Zane, and Romer Carl. There is no error in the name "Pearl." In spite of the feminine name, Pearl was definitely a boy. In later years he dropped the "Pearl" and became "Zane Grey," changing the spelling from "Gray" to "Grey."

CHAPTER **3**

A city of some ten thousand people, Zanesville in the 1870's and 1880's was the hub of a large rural area, studded here and there with villages and tiny hamlets. The Muskingum River flowed through the city, and there

were numerous tributary creeks and streams. The outdoors
played a great part in the lives of the Zanesville residents.

The Gray family home was a two-story frame house at
363 Convers Avenue—the number was later changed to 705.
There were vacant lots on both sides, and in the backyard was
an orchard. The open fields were only moments away. Catfish
were plentiful in the Muskingum River.

Pearl was the fourth of the five Gray children. The girls
were five and eight years older than Pearl. Ellsworth was eleven
years older than Pearl and was in high school when Pearl
started grammar school. He had his own friends and could not
be bothered with a kid brother.

Romer was born three years after Pearl, and Pearl took an
interest in him from the time Romer was barely three. As they
grew up they became inseparable, and Pearl's protective attitude toward his brother became known to all who knew them.
If a boy picked on Romer, he had to face Pearl and take the
consequences. The close relationship remained through their
adult lives and during their many hunting, fishing, and exploration trips. Their interests were mutual, and both became outstanding baseball players.

In the last year of his life, Zane Grey worked on an autobiography. He describes some of his earliest memories—the
smell of burning leaves, his running and jumping through the
smoke. He tells of standing on the front porch behind his
father on a Sunday afternoon and fanning his parent, then
running off to play the moment his father fell asleep.

From these reminiscences we learn that his father was a
disciplinarian of the old school, who believed that the father of
a child was entitled to all the respect and services that even the
smallest mind and hands could perform. In spite of having
been a preacher, or perhaps because of it, the father seldom
spared the switch; he was a typical father of the time.

According to Zane Grey, the most unforgettable event in
his young life was the day he saw his first live fish. Mrs. Gray
had decided to take young Pearl, six, to visit his aunt at
Brownsville, thirteen miles away. The trip was made by stage-

coach, and Pearl was given the choice seat beside the driver.
It was a hot July day. There were shade trees along the way
and a tiny stream of water beyond the trees. The stream ran
downhill, and here and there was a small waterfall. The coach
was moving slowly, and Pearl, looking down into the water,
saw something that transfixed him, a finny creature that came
to the surface and snapped up a bug. The creature had a green
back covered with many black spots.

Pearl gripped the driver's arm. "What's that?"

"Just a chub," replied the driver.

"Chub!" cried Pearl. "Could I catch him?"

"You could if we had the time," said the driver. "All you'd
need would be a stick, a piece of cord, a bent pin, and a grass-
hopper for bait."

At the next stop Pearl had to get into the coach and tell
his mother about the marvelous creature he had seen in the
water. He found her unsympathetic. "Pearl," she said severely,
"this little brook runs into Joe's Run, which we crossed at the
foot of the hill. Joe's Run is a bad place for boys."

"Why?" demanded Pearl.

"Because boys play hooky from school to go fishing there,
and then Old Muddy Miser comes and catches the bad boys!"

"What's Old Muddy Miser?" persisted Pearl.

"He's a fisherman, a lazy good-for-nothing fisherman who
lives at Dillon's Falls." Then, to crush the budding interest
that she saw in Pearl's eyes, "A fisherman is a lazy bad boy
grown up. He never helps his mother. He stays away all day and
is never home for supper. He always carries a bottle. You've seen
drunken men. Well, that's what fishing and a bottle does."

The portrait of what fishing and a bottle did to a boy was
a vivid one, but it was not enough.

A fisherman was born that day.

Grey later became the world's most famous fisherman,
holding at one time virtually all records, both freshwater and
saltwater, and fishing played an extremely important role in his
life.

The Gray home on Convers Avenue was in the Terrace section of Zanesville. It was time for Pearl to enroll in grammar school, and the nearest one was the Eighth Ward School. To get there Pearl had to descend the Terrace and cross through a long wooded tract of land with a grassy area for baseball and other games. On the far side of the park was the Muskingum River, which had a strange fascination for Pearl. Almost always he tarried on the bridge to peer down at the murky waters. Often he saw a finny creature, and always it caused a tingle to slither up Pearl's spine.

The Eighth Ward was supposedly an area of poorer homes, and the residents had an antipathy for the snobs on the Terrace. This was especially true of the boys of the ward, the "toughies" of Zanesville. This dislike was demonstrated early in Pearl's schooldays when an Eighth Ward boy, somewhat larger than Pearl, gave him a hard punch in the nose. Forever after, Pearl carried a resentment against the Eighth Ward toughies.

He was not a scholar; he was a dreamer. The lessons were drudgery. Over and over he sat at his desk, chin in his cupped hand, his mind far away. He was always aware of the outdoors. The woods, the fields, and the streams had an abnormal attraction for him.

The school year was a long period of waiting for holidays and the summer vacation. As he learned to read, life became more interesting, but it did not help his schoolwork. He spent his study time reading the forbidden books, and he learned early the knack of concealing the dime novels in the big geography, and although he seemed engrossed in his lessons, he was actually being enthralled with the wild adventures of Buffalo Bill, Deadwood Dick, and Jesse James.

These books were sold by Sam Jenkins in his store in the Schultz Opera Block, a favorite hangout for the young "literary" set. Some of the thrillers of the day were large-format magazines of thirty-two pages. The others were of smaller size, comparable to today's paperbacks but containing only sixty-four pages. Many of Sam Jenkins' customers, including Pearl Gray, would slip three or four of the smaller books into a large one, then hold up the large one and drop a dime on the counter as they went out.

Pearl was ten when a particularly eventful day in his life occurred. His father had promised to take the entire family for an outing to Dillon's Falls on the first Saturday of the summer vacation. Pearl had not forgotten his mother's reference of several years before to Dillon's Falls and the abominable creature who lived there, Old Muddy Miser. He could scarcely sleep the night before the big adventure.

The entire Gray family gathered on the eventful morning, and accompanied by the neighboring Lindsay family and its numerous progeny, the large group set out on the three-mile walk. The road led past the county poorhouse, which Pearl's father saw fit to point out to him, and at the same time administer a general admonition. "If you don't learn to like work and study, that's where you'll wind up, like Old Muddy Miser."

The enchanted spot was soon reached, and Dr. Gray pointed out a huge bank of gray stone that overhung the river. "This is where I fished with my dad when I was a shaver."

Poles and fishhooks had been brought. Bait was soon found, and the fishing began. For hours Pearl and Romer stood on the rock with their lines in the water to no avail; the fish would not accept their bait. Reluctantly they joined the picnic group for lunch.

In the afternoon Dr. Gray led Pearl and Romer along the riverbank to where the water was shallow enough to wade. They tried the deeper pools and muddied them. The father stretched out on the riverbank, and the boys continued their attempts to land just one fish. Suddenly Pearl became aware of a man standing motionless in the middle of the river.

He was an old man, gaunt and bent. His clothes were ragged, and gray hair protruded through a hole in his hat. The old man held a long pole steadily over the swift current and seemed oblivious of everything else.

Pearl retreated to where his father was reclining. "Who is that out there, Pa?" he asked.

Dr. Gray sat up. "Why, that's Old Muddy Miser!" he exclaimed.

Pearl had already guessed that, but the actual picture of the old fisherman was different from what he had expected. He seemed a lonely, pathetic figure.

Neither Dr. Gray nor his son talked to Old Muddy Miser on this occasion. In fact, Pearl was not to become acquainted with him for another three or four years, although he caught a glimpse of him now and then and learned much about him in the ensuing years.

That summer Pearl and Romer were finally permitted by their mother to go fishing alone, and it was little Romer who caught the first chub, a monster almost a foot and a half long. Pearl was soon to become a member of the enchanted fraternity, and before the vacation ended, he counted himself an expert and veteran fisherman.

Pearl played baseball that summer, too. All the boys engaged in this favorite sport, but there were no indications that either Pearl or his brother was better at it than their companions. No one by the wildest stretch of the imagination would have predicted that the roly-poly little Romer Gray would one day become a major-league star or that his older brother would turn down major-league offers to accept an athletic college scholarship based on his baseball skill.

Pearl returned to school that fall with no new resolves to improve in his studies. The principal of the Eighth Ward School, a tall, lean man with a cold, thin face and a sharp voice, took a dislike to Pearl after being hit in the shin by a baseball thrown by him. Pearl was not punished for that, but soon, when there was a fracas during recess, even though Pearl was not involved in it, he was summoned to the principal's office; Zane Grey, more than fifty years later, still recalled the caning he got from the principal that day.

Pearl complained to his father, and he was never again whipped by the principal, but the disciplinary actions against

Pearl continued. Usually they consisted of being locked up in the principal's office for an hour or so after school.

That winter Pearl read *Robinson Crusoe* and *The Last of the Mohicans*. He practically memorized them from continued rereading. Then a friend lent him two books by the popular Harry Castlemon. The books were *Frank in the Mountains* and *Frank at Don Carlos' Rancho*. Pearl read the books and returned them, then borrowed the books again and again, until the boy, Jake Thomas, finally gave them to him as a present and earned Pearl's undying gratitude.

They were perfect choices for young Pearl. Castlemon, the pseudonym for Charles F. Fosdick, was, during the post-Civil War days, one of the Big Four in the field of juvenile writing. The others were the tremendously popular Horatio Alger, Edward S. Ellis, and Oliver Optic, whose real name was W. T. Adams.

These were good books Pearl Gray was reading, and they did much to influence him in his choice of a career.

Later he read a huge volume, *Our Western Border*, an account of the early settlers and Indian fighters of the Ohio River Valley. In this book he became acquainted with Daniel Boone, Simon Kenton, and his own ancestors, the Zanes. He had already been told of the stirring events of Colonel Zane, his sister Betty, and their brother Isaac, who had been saved from burning at the stake by the Wyandotte Indian princess Myeera, whom he married.

CHAPTER **4** ════════════════════════

In maturity Zane Grey was a little under five feet, nine inches in height. He was slightly built, but as a former athlete and one of the world's great sportsmen, he was an unusually strong man. In his youth he was thin and grew slowly. Romer, who was short and pudgy as a small boy, suddenly began to grow, and when he was eleven was almost as tall as Pearl. He was exceptionally strong for his age and extremely adept at baseball.

Pearl had become one of the best baseball players in Zanesville. One Saturday afternoon he was walking toward the ball field on Madden's Hill, where a game was in progress. As he approached he realized that the game had stopped. The yelling and excitement that filled the air could only mean a fight.

Suddenly he saw Romer burst through the crowd, blood streaming from his face. Behind him came Harry Tomans, much older and larger than Romer; he was brandishing a baseball bat and yelling.

Pearl promptly caught up half of a brick and ordered Harry to drop the baseball bat, but Harry turned on Pearl with the bat. Pearl knocked him down with a clean, single blow and turned to face Harry's brother, Jake, older and larger than Pearl.

The fight that ensued was a long, savage one, ending with Jake, unable to get to his feet, panting, "I can lick you—but I've got enough for today."

There was an almost tragic sequel to this fight, but as a result of it Pearl finally became acquainted with Old Muddy Miser.

During the summer Pearl had met the Graves brothers— Ed, Luce, and Crow. Their father was dead, and their uncles were market fishermen, hard-drinking, hard-working men who lived on the outskirts of the Terrace, known as Bold Hill. The oldest of the brothers, Crow, was sixteen, a powerful youth not much inclined to school or work. He was, however, a redoubtable fisherman, and Pearl agreed to go fishing with him and his brothers.

When they reached Dillon's Falls they found a Zanesville contingent already there, including Harry Tomans, who had beaten Romer Gray and had in turn been licked by Pearl. Harry had a rifle with him and promptly began needling Pearl.

Pearl hooked several fish and then caught sight of Old Muddy Miser in the stream. At the same moment a rock flashed over the elderly fisherman's head and splashed near his line.

Harry Tomans stood on the bank yelling derisively. Several other boys began throwing rocks at Old Muddy Miser, and then Harry threw a stone at the old man that struck him on the knee and inflicted a painful wound.

Pearl caught up a chunk of sun-baked mud and threw it at Harry, hitting him. Harry screamed and caught up his rifle. Pointing it at Pearl, he swore that he would kill him.

Shocked and frightened, Pearl did the only thing he could think of. He stooped and pretended to tie a shoelace, expecting any moment to have a slug tear through him.

When he finally looked up, Harry was putting down his rifle. Pearl rushed forward, caught up the rifle, and whirling, hurled it into the river. Harry charged him, and Pearl beat him down and finally knocked him into the river; turning, he found that he now had to fight Ed Graves. While Pearl was beating him, Crow and a couple of others fished Harry out of the water.

The fishing was over. The others left for Zanesville, but Pearl remained behind, and then the old fisherman came up and asked his name.

"Ah, yes, your father is Dr. Lewis Gray, the doctor. He's from near Graytiot and used to come here to fish over forty years ago."

"My father does not approve of my fishing," Pearl told the old man. "It wastes so much time."

"You could waste time in worse ways," said Old Muddy Miser. "There is something fascinating about the study of fish. And to be out in the open, to know the sunshine and the rain and the beauty that is all around you—that is a wonderful thing for anyone."

Although he had been told that Old Muddy Miser was a man who had fallen from high estate, Pearl was surprised to find him to be a man of education. He was a kindly man, and in the days and years that followed, Pearl spent many long hours in his company and learned from him about the ways of fish and animals—and men. Pearl never forgot him.

CHAPTER **5** _____

Pearl graduated from the Moore grammar school when he was fifteen; he had two memorable experiences that summer. One was disastrous, and the other—well, it brought a new element into his life, and while it was frequently disastrous, it sometimes raised him to an exalted state of happiness. He came to know girls.

They had always been around him, of course, but they had not been important before. Fishing, the outdoors, baseball, had always been paramount. Now they were not.

Pearl went to the first party where they played the pillow game. The flushed-faced boys and girls sat about the parlor. The hostess, a girl named Margaret, came to the center of the room carrying a small pillow. Her eyes beamed provocatively as she glanced from boy to boy, evaluating each one.

Finally she came to Pearl, dropped the pillow before him, and knelt upon it. Pearl knew what the game was and what he was supposed to do. But an instant paralysis swept over him.

Amid the twitters of the girls and the catcalls of the boys, Pearl dropped to his knees on the pillow and moved his face toward Margaret's. His lips met hers in the first kiss he had ever experienced from someone not a member of his immediate family.

Blushing merrily, Margaret leaped to her feet and rushed back to her chair, leaving Pearl still kneeling on the pillow. Only the shouting of the boys and the gleeful screaming of the girls brought Pearl to his feet. He was flushed, confused, excited, thrilled, and tingling from the new experience, the new world that had been opened to him.

He dropped the pillow before Daisy Lindsay, the neighbor of the Grays, whom he had known all his life.

She was pleased and kissed him heartily. The game went on. The pillow was not put before Pearl again, but it did not matter.

He had kissed a girl. Two girls. *That* was all that mattered.

The other memorable experience of that summer was the writing of his first story. *That* was the disaster.

There was a ledge of rock at the rear of the Gray home. Underneath it there was a cavity, already enlarged by a previous generation of boys and scooped out still more by Pearl's gang, of which he was the leader. The boys put on a door and decorated the cave with animal skins and weapons, furnishing and equipping it with odds and ends filched chiefly from the Gray home.

Here the boys congregated to read the Beadle dime novels and Harry Castlemon books and eat stolen watermelons.

Pearl had been dreaming of becoming a writer ever since he had discovered the world of books, particularly since he started to read the Castlemon books. This was a deep secret from his family, for his father had long ago decided that Pearl was to follow in his footsteps and become a dentist.

In the cave, by the light of a smoking oil lamp, Pearl wrote his first story, "Jim of the Cave." It was in the Harry Castlemon tradition. The "Jim" in the story was in real life a member of the gang. When the story was completed, the real Jim broke one of the secret laws of the gang and by a vote of the membership was expelled.

In retaliation, Jim went to Dr. Gray and told of the secret cave. Dr. Gray investigated and found numerous utensils in the cave that had mysteriously disappeared from their kitchen. He also came upon the budding author's manuscript.

Pearl came into the cave at that inopportune moment. He saw his manuscript being torn to shreds by his father and was then thrashed soundly with a strip of carpet from the floor, also stolen from the Gray house.

Dr. Gray informed his second son there would be no more scribbling in the family, and Pearl was to put such nonsense from his mind. Furthermore, he would now start learning the trade that would one day support him. The following Saturday he was to report at his father's office.

Never had anything been more distasteful to Pearl than his Saturdays' employment. He had to come in very early and clean the place thoroughly, even wash the windows. Throughout the day he had to perform odd jobs pertaining to dental work. Usually this consisted of removing sets of teeth from vulcanizers and washing and scrubbing the plaster from them.

The plaster of paris, having been subjected to tremendous heat and having assimilated something from the rubber, adhered so tightly to Pearl's hands that it was removed only with difficulty.

Occasionally, however, when Dr. Gray's practice was slack, Pearl would be given a Saturday afternoon off, and he would hurry off to play baseball. If there was no baseball game, he would go for a tramp in the woods. He liked the solitude of the outdoors. He went fishing frequently, but as he grew older the fishing became less frequent, as did the baseball playing.

Pearl fell in love that first year in high school. His walk to school took him past Alice Fell's home. Frequently she was coming from her house as Pearl came along. He carried her books. She told him that her mama considered him a bad boy, but *she* thought that what her mother didn't know wouldn't hurt.

One morning, when Pearl prodded Alice, she admitted that she liked him better than any of the other boys she knew.

Pearl was on Cloud Nine all morning, and the elation carried into the noon recess, when he challenged Bud Crub to play marbles for keeps. Bud was older and much larger than Pearl, and he was, moreover, the champion marble player of the school. Pearl lost his "commies," his agates, and finally his choice Cornelia. A few minutes later he watched Bud use his Cornelia, playing with another boy.

It was too much! In a frenzy Pearl pounced upon his Cornelia and dashed off with it, Bud in enraged pursuit.

Pearl dashed into the school, into a classroom. He caught up a heavy sponge from a desk, soaked with water and ink. As Bud charged down upon him, Pearl threw the sponge. Bud ducked, and Alice Fell, entering the door at that instant, was the recipient of the sponge. It struck her squarely in the breast, and the squishy contents splattered over her entire dress. Alice let out a shriek and dropped to the floor in a dead faint.

The dress was new, given to Alice as a birthday gift by her aunt, and only that morning Pearl had admired it.

He was so appalled now by the catastrophe that he made no attempt whatever to defend himself against Bud. The marble champion knocked him down, and straddling him, pummeled Pearl mercilessly. Pearl did not even resist. When Bud grew tired of pounding, he turned out Pearl's pockets and retrieved the Cornelia marble.

By that time a group of students had gathered around the still-unconscious Alice. The teacher arrived, and the victorious Bud stormed past, announcing at the same time that Pearl Gray had stolen his marble and was the cause of the pandemonium.

The teacher ordered Pearl to go to the washroom and remove the stains of battle from his face. As he was returning, he met Alice being led out by a couple of students. Her dress was stained with ink, as was much of her blond hair.

Pearl knew that it was the end of a beautiful romance. Alice was a proud, sensitive girl, and she would never forgive him.

She never did.

Not long afterward, Pearl spent an entire day with Old Muddy Miser and got his initiation into the fraternity of dedicated fishermen. He learned that Old Muddy Miser was seventy-seven years old. In summer he lived in a cabin by himself and supported himself as a market fisherman, but in the winter he was compelled to take refuge in the county poor-house. He was not bitter about his condition in life. Years later Zane Grey still recalled some of the things that Old Muddy Miser told him on that memorable occasion.

"I've read a good deal about salmon and trout; and you, no doubt, will go far afield from Dillon's Falls someday and catch these fish. I have also read a great deal about the big saltwater fish of the Seven Seas. Nobody seems to have caught these strange, fierce fish of the salty seas, and I wonder why this is so. Surely someday somebody will venture to go after these giant fish. Perhaps you will be the one. I wish I could live to have you tell me about them. You must make fishing a study, a labor of love, no matter what your vocation will be. You must make time for your fishing. Whatever you do, you will do it all the better for the time and thought you give to fishing. And here is the most cardinal and important point. Don't drink. For some strange reason, most fishermen drink, and very many of them are drunkards. Some men fish solely to earn money to buy liquor. Others seem to go fishing to find a time and a place to drink. Whiskey is an abomination for any-one, and especially a fisherman."

Pearl Gray told Old Muddy Miser that he had recently signed a pledge never to drink. His older brother, Ellsworth, had been brought home drunk one night, and the sight of him had shocked Pearl.

Old Muddy Miser talked to Pearl Gray throughout the day, advising him on every step of fishing—beginning with the selection of the proper bait, how to find or catch it, how to put it on a hook, how to cast—and giving him a long lecture on the ways of fish and the waters themselves, so important in the lore of fishermen.

The bitterness of Pearl's first blighted romance slowly faded, but the memory of it never left. There were other girls, however, who were willing to be seen with the handsome youth who was the high school's best athlete. They wrote him notes and met him on his way to and from school. Pearl was quite willing to indulge them, and his schoolwork suffered as a result of it.

It was a long, cold winter. Pearl spent the evenings reading books rather than studying, and it was during this winter that he firmed in his mind the resolution to become a writer. He read and reread his favorite authors, especially Harry Castlemon. He was now working at a shoe store on Saturdays and earned two dollars a week, which he was allowed to keep. He used most of it on dime novels. His favorites were Oll-coombs, Edward L. Wheeler, and Colonel Prentiss Ingraham.

This was a period in Pearl's life when he got into fights at the slightest provocation. He usually won—even when he fought with the older boys.

He acquired a new arrogance, so that it was not too difficult to get the shoe-store owner to tell him that he would no longer need him on Saturdays.

This incurred the wrath of Dr. Gray, and to appease him, Pearl volunteered to go back to work in the dental office on Saturday mornings. Dr. Gray was very busy at the time, and really needing an assistant, accepted.

Since Pearl disliked the mechanical dental work and was not good at it, the doctor started him in the extraction of teeth. Dr. Gray injected a local anesthetic into the gums, and it was then merely a matter of physical strength to extract the tooth.

Pearl's hands had become extremely powerful from his baseball pitching. He had practiced and mastered the art of pitching a curve ball, which required a tight grip. His hands were so strong that he was able to extract the most stubborn tooth without difficulty, and Dr. Gray became greatly pleased with his proficiency. He paid Pearl seventy-five cents for the Saturday morning's work.

Dr. Gray thought it would be a good idea for Pearl to go out into the country and extract teeth for patients who were unable or did not want to come to town. Pearl argued against it, and the doctor did not press the matter at the time, but a seed had been planted that was to grow later on and would

eventually push Pearl up a path that he did not want to travel
—the road to dentistry.

CHAPTER **6**

In 1890 disaster overtook the Gray family. Dr.
Gray had invested a substantial sum of money,
had gone to Washington, D.C., to try to retrieve it, and had
lost everything. He did not want to return to Zanesville, where
news of the calamity had traveled. He arranged for the family
to move to Columbus, Ohio, where he intended to start a new
dental practice and a new life. It upset the entire family, but
they made the move, and Dr. Gray, coming directly from
Washington, a ruined man, in poor health, rented an office on
High Street.

Pearl quickly found a job as a theater usher, and he liked
Columbus. He spent much of his free time in his father's
office watching the crowds and the streetcars go by.

It took time for a new dental office to attract patients.
To help out, Romer went to work driving a delivery wagon
for a grocery. He rose every morning at five o'clock in order
to have the horse hitched to the wagon and ready to ˙start
deliveries at six o'clock. Romer worked uncomplainingly.

Dr. Gray received a letter form a former patient who
lived in Frazeysburg, a small town fourteen miles from Zanesville. She told the doctor that if he would come to Frazeysburg
and extract her bad teeth, she would get him a good deal of
business.

Dr. Gray, who had already toyed with the idea of going
to the rural communities to treat patients, decided to send
Pearl. Pearl was quite willing, especially when his father told
him he could keep the money he earned.

Pearl traveled to Frazeysburg by train and was met by an
aged man who called him "Doctor" and led him to the hotel,

where a dozen patients were already waiting for him. He pulled teeth all that day and the next day up to train time.

Columbus had several baseball teams, on which there were a number of semiprofessional players. Pearl and his brother joined the Capitol team of the City League. In the final game Pearl pitched a shut-out, and the Capitols won the City League pennant. A number of overtures were made to him from both colleges and professional teams, but he could not consider them because of the necessity for earning money to help support the family. Romer, three years younger, was doing his share, and Pearl could not shirk his own duty.

He was still traveling to small towns extracting teeth, and one Saturday he was in Baltimore, Ohio, a rabid baseball town, scheduled that afternoon to play an unbeaten team from nearby Jacktown. Baltimore had a good team but a weak pitcher. During lunch at the hotel, Pearl heard the excited baseball talk; the town would virtually close up for the afternoon, when everyone would attend the game.

It occurred to Pearl that the small-town players would hardly know about the curve ball that was still known only to a limited number of big-league players.

A number of Baltimore players were in the hotel lobby. Pearl tried to resist the temptation but could not, and approaching the the manager of the team, introduced himself.

"I'm Pearl Gray. I was the pitcher for the Capitol Club in the City League at Columbus. We won the pennant. Would you like me to pitch for you today?"

The astonished manager could not believe his good fortune and accepted without delay. It was decided that Pearl's real name would not be used, lest someone recognize it. He was put into the game as a "ringer."

Pearl was told that Jacktown had a belligerent team. They brought along their own umpire and forced him upon the Baltimore team. Their pitcher was a blacksmith named Ben Orth, who had won every game for the Jacktown team that year. He was a noted brawler and had never been licked in a fight.

The biggest crowd Pearl had ever seen for a country baseball game turned out. There were hundreds of vehicles of all kinds, even hay wagons. There was a large contingent from Jacktown.

The Jacktown team turned out to be huge, rough farmers whose custom was to play in their stocking feet. Ben Orth, the pitcher, was a giant weighing over three hundred pounds.

In the first inning Pearl noted that Orth threw with a smooth, easy motion, unusual for so big a man. But his only pitch was a fast ball, thrown waist-high. He struck out the first three Baltimore batters with nine pitched balls.

Pearl took his place on the mound. The first batter was walked, although two of the balls should have been called strikes. Pearl saw what he was up against. The umpire was the Jacktown team's man.

The game went several innings without either side making a hit or getting a run. The situation became explosive.

In the seventh inning the break came. The first batter hit a weak blow that the huge pitcher failed to field quickly enough. Baltimore had a man on base.

The next batter got a single, and the man on first got to third.

The catcher came up and filled the bases.

It was Pearl's turn. He fouled, got a clean strike, then hit a home run. It was minutes before the game could be continued. The Baltimore fans went wild, and the Jacktown people hooted and tried to start a riot.

Two more runs were scored, and the score was six-zero in favor of Baltimore.

The eighth inning began on an ominous note. Pearl struck out the first batter. The second Jacktown man came up, and Pearl threw him a tantalizing curve, so slow you could almost count the stitches in the ball. The batter swung, missed by a yard, and fell over himself.

The entire Jacktown team began to jump up and down and shout: "Ringer! Ringer! Ringer!"

The Jacktown umpire walked out, spread his arms, and motioned for silence. When he finally got it, he bellowed out: "Game called. Nine to nothing. Favor Jacktown. Baltimore's ringer pitcher throws a crooked ball!"

That was the lighted match thrown into the open powder keg. The riot burst out, and the mob started for Pearl Gray. In the confusion and melee he made it to the barn where he had left his clothes, but before he could change, the Baltimore players stormed in. "The Jacktown people are going to ride you on a rail."

Pearl looked through the door and saw the blacksmith Jacktown pitcher with a fence rail on his shoulder, at the head of a wild contingent of Jacktown baseball players and citizens.

Still only half-dressed, Pearl took off. Only his fleetness of foot saved him, but it was a long run and a savage pursuit. Pearl finally found safety in a large cornfield, where he slept through the night. In the morning the farmer gave him a pair of overalls to wear. He had seen the game the day before, and being a Baltimore man, had enjoyed it thoroughly.

CHAPTER **7** ═══════════════

Pearl was making money as a tooth puller. He extended the rural and small-town visits. His brother Ellsworth had enlisted in the Navy, but both Romer and Pearl contributed to the support of the family. Dr. Gray's practice was still very poor, and both Romer's and Pearl's earnings were needed.

Pearl was still a minor and had no license to practice denistry. It began to be rumored about that the state dental board was investigating him, and the rumor was only too true.

An official called on Dr. Lewis Gray. Pearl arrived while

the official was still questioning his father. The result was that both Pearl and his father gave assurance that Pearl would discontinue his illegal practice and go to a recognized dental school and return to dentistry when he graduated.

Pearl's baseball team then played Ohio State and beat the college team. As a result, the team was offered a game with Dennison College, the crack university team of the state. Dennison's great pitcher, Dan Daub, left the college the following year and joined the Brooklyn National team and became one of the best pitchers in the National League.

Before the game, Pearl learned that a scout from the University of Pennsylvania was in the stands. With this to inspire him, he pitched the best game of his life.

His team won four to three, and Pearl was visited by a man named Clark who asked him if he would like to attend the University of Pennsylvania. Pearl frankly told him that he would like it very much, provided he could get some financial aid from the school.

The scout assured him that that would be forthcoming and gave him a card of introduction to the director of athletics at the University of Pennsylvania.

"Get there by October first," he said. "They'll want to try you out for the varsity team before they give you the scholarship."

During the next weeks Pearl received similar offers from the University of Michigan, Chicago Wesleyan, and Vanderbilt in Tennessee. He preferred Pennsylvania because they played Yale, Princeton, and Harvard and had as baseball coach a former coach in the National League. Besides, its dental school was considered the best in the country.

His brother Romer, now sixteen, later known in baseball circles as Reddy because of his flaming hair, left home that summer to begin his long and illustrious career in professional baseball. He joined the Delphos, Ohio, team, where his friend the deaf-mute George Kihm was catching. Kihm also became a famous big-league star.

When it came time for Pearl to leave for Philadelphia, he

had just enough money to buy a day-coach ticket and would arrive in Philadelphia with less than ten dollars.

Pearl slept very little on this trip. He was traveling in country new to him, had cut his family ties, and was venturing upon a life that was different from anything he had ever known.

He watched the mountains of Pennsylvania little dreaming that he would one day hunt here for deer and bear and would fish the mountain streams: he would live in these hills and slave for seven long years while trying to gain recognition as an author. He had already decided on his career. He would be a dentist, but only to support himself until he could win fame and fortune as an author. Nothing would deter him from that.

He arrived in Philadelphia and got a modest room in a cheap hotel on Market Street. Philadelphia was the largest city he had ever seen, and the bustle and commotion of the throngs of people fascinated him.

He went to the university to see the director of athletics and learned that he was away and would not be back for four days. He had so little money that he dared not spend any of it on theaters or amusements.

On Monday he saw the director of athletics, who told him that he would get a scholarship if the baseball coaches approved of him. The varsity team was playing a game the following Saturday, and Pearl was to present himself at that time for a tryout.

The ensuing days were interminable. Pearl roamed the streets of Philadelphia, and when he was hungry he had to content himself with the smallest, cheapest meals.

Saturday came, and he went to the baseball park. He got a uniform and entered the dressing rooms of the Pennsylvania team. He sat to one side and listened to the talk of the players.

He learned that the team was playing the Riverton Club, which was composed almost entirely of former varsity men and was considered the strongest baseball team in that part of the country. It had beaten the Pennsylvania team the previous year. Boswell, Penn's pitcher, the great sprinter Ernie Ramsdell, and Danny Coogan were loud in their insistence that they *must* beat Riverton.

A short, serious player said that he had heard from Madeira, a coach, that they were to try out a pitcher from Ohio.

Coogan and Boswell both let out a roar and cried out angrily that they wanted to *win* against Riverton and not try out new pitchers.

Madeira, the director, came in and asked Hollister, the captain of the team, if the young pitcher had arrived yet.

Hollister said, "I don't know him. You didn't tell me his name."

"It's Pearl Gray," said the director. "He's been highly recommended as the most promising crash player of the West."

Hollister saw Pearl then and approached him. Coogan and Boswell meanwhile beseeched Madeira not to experiment with a new man that afternoon. The game was too important. They wanted to win it.

When the game started Pearl did not yet know if he would get his chance. On the Pennsylvania team were men like the shortstop Ramsdell, first baseman Goekel, Coogan, and center-fielder Thomas, all to make their marks later in the major leagues.

Boswell was the opening pitcher for Penn. It was a hard game, but at the end of the fifth inning Riverton was ahead four to two. Madeira called to Hollister to put in Pearl Gray. A roar of disapproval went up in the varsity team as Pearl walked out to the mound.

Pearl knew that his entire future was at stake. He threw the first ball, which he never saw at all in its flight to home plate. The umpire called it a strike, and confidence swept over Pearl.

He knew that he had everything that day—speed, control, and a wonderful curve ball. The first batter hit up a weak pop fly. Pearl threw out the second on a grounder, and he struck out the third.

At bat, Thomas walked, Goekel hit safely, and Ramsdell scored them both with a double. The score was tied.

Pearl blanked Riverton in the sixth, seventh, and eighth innings without a man reaching first base. The entire team to a man was now behind Pearl.

In the tenth inning, with the score four to four, a Penn man on base, Pearl smacked a two-bagger to center field that won the game. The varsity team and Madeira, the director, all showered praise on him, and Pearl was told to report to Madeira at school on Monday ready to enter the university.

Pearl was granted the scholarship, but he still had to pay for his books, his dental equipment, and his room and board.

He found a room two miles from the college in West Philadelphia with a Catholic family in which there were four grown daughters and two working sons, plus a younger one.

The athletic association offered Pearl a job waiting on tables in the restaurant, but he became stubborn. He would not wait on his fellow baseball players. He did, however, take a job ushering at the football games.

His college prospects were not bright. For a while he attended all classes faithfully, but then he became bored with them. The classes on mechanical and operative dentistry were a trial. He did not like anatomy and physiology. He became interested in therapeutics but found chemistry difficult: it was like mathematics at Zanesville High School, which he had failed dismally. Professor Wormly was crabby and austere, and the freshmen feared him more than all the other professors. Pearl liked him in spite of his faults, but the teacher he was fondest of was Bobby Formad, as the students called him, who taught histology.

Pearl thought the histology class was fun, and when Formad complimented him on his sketches, Pearl decided he would try to excel in this subject.

CHAPTER **8** ━━━━━━━━━━━━━━━━━━━━━━━━

The two-week Christmas vacation was a trial
to Pearl. There was no heat in his attic room,
and it was stay in bed or go out to get warm. Pearl began shooting pool in a West Philadelphia poolroom, a game he had
learned to like in Columbus.

When classes resumed, Pearl had made up his mind to
attend lectures faithfully. His first day he went to attend a
lecture on anatomy in the great amphitheater. The place was
filled with students except for a few rows in the center. By
custom the lower seats were always occupied by upper classmen. The top rows were delegated to the freshmen.

Pearl took a seat in an upper-classman row. There was a
sudden hush about him, then a sophomore yelled loudly,
"Freshman on fifth!"

The call was directed at Pearl but was so loud that the
freshmen far above heard and replied with taunting. The
husky-voiced sophomore bellowed, "Fresh, get off fifth!"

With upper classmen yelling, and derisive taunts coming
from the freshmen above, Pearl refused to budge.

The aggressive sophomore rose to his feet and roared,
"Watch me throw Freshie out!"

He was a big blond chap, and when he approached, Pearl
saw that he was motivated by good spirits rather than malice.
But Pearl had decided that he would not yield, and when the
sophomore reached out for him, Pearl gave him a violent shove
that sent the sophomore backward over a row of seats into the
midst of his classmates.

Pandemonium broke out. The sophomores rose en masse
to get to Pearl, and the freshmen spilled down from their
heights to rescue their champion. The amphitheater became
a scene of riot, and when it was over Pearl was stark naked,
except for one sock. His clothing had all been torn from him,
including his shoes.

A sympathetic freshman lent him an overcoat and took him home in a taxi.

Pearl became a marked freshman, and at times he had to sneak in and out of classes. He longed for February 15 to come, the date for the baseball candidates to report for practice.

He spent his leisure time at the library, reading and day-dreaming. One cold February day he left the library, and to avoid the cold wind, unwisely entered College Hall to take a shortcut across the campus.

He was halfway through when some sophomores spied him. One was the big blond whose assault on Pearl had started the riot in the amphitheater. Pearl had since learned that he was the president of the sophomore class.

He started for Pearl and was followed by four or five other sophomores. Outside, Pearl tried to shake off the pursuit but failed to do so. Attracted by the yells of the sophomores, others joined in the chase, and by the time he left the campus, more than a dozen had joined the hue and cry.

A hundred yards from the campus a high stone stairway led to the street. The pursuers gained as Pearl started his long climb. When he reached the top, he stopped and saw the students charging after him. He looked about for objects to throw down at them, and at that moment a grocer's delivery boy came along carrying a heavy basket of potatoes.

Pearl pounced on the basket and turned to the stairway. The closest pursuers had reached the second landing, and the rest were strung out below.

With two potatoes in his left hand and one in his right, Pearl went into action. The first potato, thrown with all the force and accuracy of his pitching arm, caught the president of the sophomore class in the forehead. The potato smashed to bits, and the class president went down, knocked out cold.

The next potato struck a sophomore in the stomach, and the third bowled one over like a tenpin. Pearl continued to pour down potatoes with all his strength and all the accuracy of which he was capable.

Injured sophomores were scattered up and down the

staircase, and when it was over, Pearl was in command of the staircase, the sophomores in complete rout.

A crowd had gathered to watch the fracas, among them Riemold, a Pinkerton detective assigned to the university to watch the students. Pearl knew that he was recognized but was too angry to care.

He paid the delivery boy a dollar for the potatoes and went to his lodgings.

That evening there was a knock on his door. Expecting his caller to be a policeman, and resigned to his fate, Pearl opened the door.

A short, derby-hatted man with a huge cigar in his mouth entered and sized up Pearl.

"Where'd you get the whip?" he demanded.

Pearl could only stare at him.

The little man chuckled. "Pearl Gray, I know all about you. I've had a report about your pitching in Ohio from one of our alumni scouts. I'm Arthur Irwin of the Philadelphia National League team, but I'm also the varsity baseball coach at the university. Now, keep it under your hat, but that potato stunt of yours has made you a member of the Pennsylvania varsity!" Overnight the attitude of the sophomores changed. They began to cultivate Pearl.

The baseball players reported to "the cage" in small groups, skipping their classes, and many were eliminated in the try-outs. Those who survived, including Pearl, moved to the baseball field when the weather became warmer. Even the crack varsity hitters, Thomas, Goekel, and Coogan, could do little against Pearl's pitching, and Pearl began to see that he would have a fine career as a college pitcher.

Came the thunderbolt that shattered Pearl's hopes and dreams! The National League had just passed a rule moving the pitcher's mound back to sixty feet from the home plate, and the college baseball teams were compelled to follow the new rule.

The years of Pearl's practice throwing the curve ball were

all for the shorter distance of fifty feet, and the new rule was a disaster to him. The curve ball was his chief stock in trade, and now he was put out of business!

However, the coach decided to keep him on the team because of his hitting, and he was moved to the outfield.

As if this blow were not enough, the University of Pennsylvania now decided that a student had to pass his first year's examinations before he could play on a team. Pearl was compelled to take the examinations two months ahead of the regular classes. He was not prepared for them.

Dr. Truman gave him a passing grade in therapeutics. He went before Old Pop Wormly in chemistry, who asked Pearl a few simple questions. Pearl had to guess at the answers. Wormly then asked him about baseball. He was curious about the game's attraction, although he had never attended a single game. When Pearl finished, Wormly drawled, "Well, Mr. Gray, you know a good deal more about baseball than you do about chemistry." He gave Pearl the lowest possible passing grade.

His grades so far were all under sixty. Only one more extremely high grade could bring up Pearl's average.

The last examination was to be given by Dr. Formad in histology. Dr. Formad refused to give him a test. "You are one of the best students in histology I have ever had," he told Pearl. "However, I have never given a student a hundred percent, so I will give you only ninety-nine."

The grade lifted Pearl beyond the "passing" average. This single grade made possible the continuing of Pearl Gray's education and his baseball career, and it put him on the road that eventually led to Zane Grey's literary success. Zane Grey was always grateful to Professor Formad.

Pearl Gray's years at the University of Pennsylvania were not altogether happy. Because of his athletic prowess, he was much sought after, but he was by inclination a "loner." The convivial gatherings of the upper classmen were inspired by, or became the result of, the college man's propensity for drinking. Pearl had promised his mother that he would not drink while he was in college, and he kept that promise. As a matter of fact, he did not drink for the rest of his life. After his early wild years in Zanesville and Columbus, he never tasted another drop of spirits. He was a complete teetotaler, a species the rarest of the rare among sportsmen.

A teetotaler at a drunken brawl is a complete misfit, the stranger at a wedding feast, and Pearl Gray withdrew to himself more and more. Only on the baseball field was he one of the crowd.

Baseball kept him from becoming a good scholar. He received passing grades, but he knew it was because of his athletic fame.

Only in the college library was Pearl Gray really content. He read all the adventure writers of the day, and he read the classics. Whenever he was despondent he went to the library, and by the time he left his spirits had been lifted.

In his final year at Penn the baseball team defeated the New York Giants in an exhibition game at the Polo Grounds in New York. They defeated the teams of Cornell, Johns Hopkins, Lehigh, and Harvard.

The game with the University of Virginia was the last of the schedule; Virginia was ahead in the ninth with two Penn men out and one on second. As Pearl came to bat, a professor shouted, "Gray, the honor of the University of Pennsylvania rests with you!"

Pearl hit a home run and won the game. The crowd covered him with roses, and the papers called him the real-life Frank Merriwell, the popular fiction character who always came up to bat in the last half of the ninth and won the game.

And then Pearl Gray was graduated and faced a grimmer world. He had a diploma in dentistry and hated it. He did not want to be a dentist. He could not escape it: it was the only vocation he was trained for.

CHAPTER

Pearl Gray went to New York City in 1896 because it was the center of the writing and publishing world. It was a difficult place for a new dentist. New York already had thousands of dentists.

He rented an office at 100 West 74th Street and got a cheap room nearby. It was at this time that Pearl changed the spelling of his name from "Gray" to "Grey," for the sign outside the dental office read "Dr. P. Zane Grey, D.D.S."

Patients came, but they were few and far between. He was great on extractions, not so good at drilling teeth or making inlays and bridges. He preferred the pulling of teeth, but he had to take any and all dental work that came his way.

He was a reluctant dentist at best, and his attitude did not endear him to the average patient. He existed on a minimal income and lived on a diet that was slow starvation.

His reputation as a college baseball star did not die out upon his graduation in 1896. Sportswriters continued to mention him in their articles, and this publicity brought him his first patients.

Because of this and his utter boredom of the humdrum New York life, he joined the Orange Athletic Club in East Orange, New Jersey.

The Orange Athletic Club had a baseball team composed entirely of former college baseball players. This was the inducement that caused Grey to travel every weekend to New Jersey. Many of the players on the team were men he had played against while at the University of Pennsylvania. Most of them had turned down offers from the professional teams because they had gone into professions and businesses and wanted to play baseball only for pleasure. The team played many professional big-league and minor-league teams during the spring-training periods and had the reputation of being one of the finest baseball teams in the country.

Grey was considered one of the best players on the team. A sportswriter wrote of him: ". . . Gray is probably the most valuable accession to the team this year."

In 1900 another writer declared, "Doc Gray is famous for making home runs when needed."

Pearl was sorely tempted to turn professional, but he knew it would be the end of his dream of becoming a writer.

He thought of it when he smelled the foul odor from a mouthful of infected teeth; it was with him when he drilled a molar, when he scraped and ground and polished vulcanized plates.

It was with him during all the long, lonely nights at his miserable lodgings.

He wrote. He wrote badly and wished that he could live over the days of his youth. He regretted the lessons he had not studied, the grammar and the English that he had so carelessly glossed over. He blamed no one but himself. He had been a heller in high school. He had spent too much time in playing baseball, getting into trouble. He had fished too much. He had neglected his studies.

He wished that he could relive the days of his boyhood, but there is no going back. One can only live the present and hope for the future.

Winters were the worst in New York. During the day he worked at his dental office, but the evenings were long, and for a man in his financial circumstances, there were not too many things to do. He could afford the theater only once in a while. He could not stay in his dingy room night after night. And there were the weekends.

He met girls, and he went out with many, but he did not become attached to any of them. His dating was a hit-or-miss thing.

His brother R. C. (Romer) came to New York. He had followed Pearl and his father into dentistry, but he was no more enthusiastic about the profession than Pearl was. He played baseball in summer, and that used up much of his physical energy. Although he did not earn much from dentistry, he had a good income during the summer.

For a time his salary in baseball was six hundred dollars a month, which was an exceedingly good income for those days. It enabled him to be a "man about town." But he and his brother Pearl were very close, and they spent much leisure time together. They got away on weekends for fishing excursions. They found that their favorite spot was along the Delaware River, which separated New Jersey and Pennsylvania. When R. C. was affluent they stayed at the Delaware House on the New Jersey side, directly across from the tiny hamlet of Lackawaxen.

When funds were low, they camped out. They actually preferred the camping out, but when they spent more than a day on the Delaware they sometimes wanted the convivial atmosphere of the Delaware House, much patronized by residents of New York City, who came out for weekends or to spend a week or two in the summer.

Both Pearl and his brother were camera enthusiasts, and from early times they took a camera with them on their trips to photograph their catches and each other. There was a strong fishing rivalry between the two, each trying to outdo the other in the size and number of their catches.

Sometimes Dr. P. Zane Grey locked his dental office in the middle of the week and took a train to the Delaware River. He did that in August, 1900, and over the weekend was joined by R. C.

They were paddling along the river a short distance from the Delaware House. Three girls were camping out in a cabin on the bank of the river. The Grey brothers paddled close to the shore and began a flirtation with the girls. Not being instantly rebuffed, the men landed on shore and continued their bantering flirtation. They snapped pictures of the girls with the old Brownie camera that Grey owned at the time.

One of the girls was Maddie Ulrich. Another was Lina Elise Roth. She was the daughter of a successful New York

doctor who had recently died. He had long suffered from
Bright's disease and had succumbed at the age of forty-three.
His widow was at the Delaware House on this occasion, and
Lina was staying in a nearby cabin with her friends.

Lina Roth, in 1900, was seventeen years old. She was a
student at the Normal School of the City of New York (later
called Hunter College) and intended to go on to Columbia
University and eventually become a teacher. Lina was extremely interested in books and literature, and she and Dr.
P. Zane Grey hit it off immediately, in spite of the eleven
years difference in their ages. Lina was brown-eyed, dark-com-
plexioned, and about five feet, four inches tall. She weighed a
hundred and ten pounds. She had extremely fine features, clear-
cut, almost cameolike in quality. In the talk between the girls,
Dr. Grey was discussed at length, and the other girls expressed
their preference for him, which intrigued Lina even more.
Later, at the Delaware House, she was fully aware of the attention he received from passing girls and women.

On Labor Day there was an exodus from the Delaware
House. The business and professional men had to get back to
New York, and their wives and families either went with them
or remained for a few days and then followed. Lina Roth and
her mother remained for another week.

In later years Zane Grey, on several occasions, gave the
date of his first meeting with Lina Elise Grey as 1902, but the
actual year was 1900, for on October 3, 1900, Lina wrote to
Dr. Grey in New York:

Dear Dr. Grey,

I would have written before to thank you for those
delightful pictures, had I not waited to hear from
Maddie. She will come Saturday evening, so we shall be
pleased to see you and your brother.

I have enclosed the picture for which you asked me,
although I don't consider it worth having. It was
taken almost a year ago, and I have changed since that

time. I really don't know why I am giving it to you.
Do you?

Sincerely yours,
Lina Roth

It was the first of some hundreds of letters that Lina
"Dolly" Roth wrote to Dr. P. Zane Grey, Dr. Zane Grey, Pearl
Grey, during the next five years. Dr. Grey saved them all, and
Dolly Grey, in turn, saved all the letters that he wrote to her
during this five-year courtship period.

From the formal tone of Lina Roth's first note to Zane
Grey it would appear that their relationship was still a rather
casual one, based on perhaps a single brief meeting in the
company of others. Such was not really the case, however, for
in 1917, after they had been married for twelve years and when
their son Romer was already eight years old, Dolly Grey, in
writing her daily letters to her husband, who was at the time
fishing at Long Key, Florida, says:

Romer asked me tonight when I first kissed his father.
I promptly told him August 29, 1900. Now, could *you*
have remembered that date after all these years?

Their first meeting was on August 28, 1900, but there
was more than one meeting, and some of them were not in the
company of others. At this time Dolly also met R. C., and
now, in October, 1900, she was arranging a double date between herself and Dr. Grey and R. C. and Maddie, the girl
friend who was with her at Lackawaxen during August.

Although there is no evidence to substantiate it, the formal tone of the note may have been because of Dolly's mother,
who did not entirely approve, in the early days, of the relationship between her daughter, who was only seventeen, and Dr.
Zane Grey, who was already twenty-eight.

In a later letter Dolly again invited Dr. Grey to visit at

her home, preferably after three o'clock, at which time her
mother was to be away.

Most of their later dates would be at her mother's home.
The Roths resided at the time at 38 Edgemont Avenue, al-
though in 1902 they moved to 701 St. Nicholas Avenue.
Neither of the addresses was too far from Dr. Grey's office on
West 74th Street or the dingy room nearby in which he lived.
There is never any mention in any of the many, many letters
that were exchanged between Zane and Dolly during the years
of their courtship that Dolly ever visited him at his lodgings.
They met at Dolly's home, at his office, or in places about
midtown New York.

Dolly considered herself a "modern" girl, about which
Zane Grey frequently chided her in his letters, but "modern"
meant something entirely different in the years 1900–1905
than it does in 1969.

Zane Grey himself in 1900 was decidedly not a "modern"
man, any more than he was twenty-five years later, when he
railed continuously about "flappers" and the wild youth of
the early 1920's. His novel *The Day of the Beast* is a virtual
tirade against the modern youth of the period. In 1922 he considered dancing immoral because the close contact between
the body of a male and female stimulated sexual desire. He
was even more of a moralist in 1900. He would kiss a girl he
liked, but he would not condone "necking" for himself any
more than he would for anyone else.

There are continual references in his letters to these subjects. At the same time, he admitted that he liked girls, and
he went out of his way at times to tell Dolly of girls who
had "made passes" at him. He never failed to get a prompt,
stinging reply from Dolly.

In 1925, the grandmother of Lina Roth Grey, then aged
eighty-four, wrote down for her daughter and her daughter's
children as much of her family history as she could recall. The
document, dated October 22, 1925, remains a family heir-
loom. It is written in a clear, exquisite handwriting and indicates that it is the work of an intelligent, well-educated

woman. Mrs. Caroline Baettenhausen, who was born in 1841, lived until 1933 and was in excellent health until her very last years.

Her reminiscences go back to her own grandmother, Caroline Spangenberg, who was born in Göttingen, Germany, on February 1, 1792. She relates some encounters with soldiers of Napoleon's conquering armies, then goes on to say that her grandmother was married at the age of fifteen to a musician and bore twelve children, nine of whom survived childhood.

One of the daughters of Caroline Spangenberg married H. N. Wilhelm, who graduated from the famous university at Göttingen and became a doctor. They decided to try their luck in America, and in August, 1840, arrived in New York. There Caroline was born. Her father prospered as a doctor and gradually sent to Germany for his relatives. All of the Wilhelm children attended private schools.

Caroline Wilhelm married William Baettenhausen in 1858. Baettenhausen was a fairly recent immigrant from Cassel-Germany. Mrs. Baettenhausen had six children. One of the daughters married a young doctor of German descent, Dr. Julius Roth, who was Lina Roth's father. His own father was a successful businessman and when he died in 1905 he bequeathed about six thousand dollars to each of his grandchildren, Lina Roth and her brother, Julius.

In March, 1901, Zane Grey and Lina Roth were already in love and had had their first quarrel. There were to be many. But there were always periods of making up. When they met, Lina was only seventeen; they were writing love letters by the time she was eighteen. Grey's letters, at twenty-eight, indicate a mature man, her early ones show her youth, but she matured rapidly, and during the ensuing five years some of her letters indicate the writing and thoughts of a much older girl.

It was Grey who caused most of the quarrels during the period. He apologizes over and over for the black moods from which he suffered at times, during which he frequently said things to Lina that he regretted immediately afterward and

for which he sometimes apologized for two or three days.
There were periods when there were daily letters between the
two, yet they sometimes saw each other on the days that
the letters were written.

Grey's letters were usually shorter than Lina's, but long,
eloquent, eight-page letters from him are not uncommon.

Although he teased her a great deal and now and then
tossed in mention of other girls, it is doubtful that he actually
went out with other girls during this five-year period. The
girls were usually imaginary, mentioned merely to make Lina
jealous.

They saw each other two or three times a week. Frequently Grey went to the Roth home on Sundays for dinner.
There is sometimes a bantering note in Grey's letters, but often
he writes with passion and anger. During this period Grey and
R. C. spent much time during the summer fishing at Lackawaxen, and frequently Grey wrote to Dolly asking her to
come there. She went often, staying at the Delaware House.
When Dolly was at Lackawaxen, Grey usually also stayed at
the hotel, but when he and R. C. were alone they camped out.
Several Delaware House postcards written by Grey from the
hotel give the rates, two dollars per day.

Once, while Grey was fishing, he became ill and checked
into the Delaware House, then wrote Dolly a detailed account
of his illness and larded it with remarks that the women
employees of the hotel were coming in and out of his room
continuously, sighing, and giving him affectionate looks. This
drew a heated reply from Dolly, and Grey became well
very quickly and returned to New York.

After meeting Dolly Roth in 1900, Grey apparently gave
up playing baseball in Orange, New Jersey. He never once refers to it in the letters of the next few years. He took numerous
trips to Lackawaxen, but the only other trip he made
during the next five years was a brief visit to Columbus,
Ohio, at Christmastime in 1901. He wrote Dolly daily while
he was away on this trip.

There are few references in the letters to Grey's writing during this period; the contents of their correspondence is chiefly romantic. But early in 1903 he tells her in one note that an editor named Lanier had rejected "the book"—title not given. He makes a cynical comment about it and says that he is going to send it out to another editor. These things were probably discussed, however, in their frequent meetings, for Dolly always went over his stories and helped him with them.

Dolly was going to college during these years, and her letters have frequent references to the fact. Once or twice she mentions coming examinations and has doubts about passing them, but she always did. Her handwriting on occasion was beautiful, but at other times it was a virtual scrawl, especially when she was angry at Grey.

They called each other by nicknames, many and varied, but nicknames should remain in love letters. The name Dolly, by which Zane called her more than any other, persisted, however, and she was called Dolly for the rest of her life. It was a long courtship, steadfast, but sometimes stormy.

But the storminess disappeared in 1905. The letters that went back and forth are longer, more serious, especially on Grey's side. He no longer chided her, he no longer criticized or teased. The tone of the letters is that of a man very deeply in love, a man suddenly become impatient, who wants to be married as soon as possible.

In New York Zane Grey had joined the Campfire Club as its youngest member. The club was composed mostly of big-game hunters. Its luminaries were Ernest Thompson Seton and Dan Beard. At the club Pearl related an incident he had experienced while fishing with his brother, R. C.

Boardman, a member of the club who was a publisher, suggested that Pearl write down the incident and submit it to a magazine.

Dr. Grey was willing to do just that and was elated when he sold it to Shields' *Recreation*. It was published in the May, 1902, issue, and Dr. Grey bought a large number of copies,

which he kept in his office and gave to patients. He did not
tell them that he had been paid only ten dollars for the article.

"A Day on the Delaware" was Grey's first published
writing. The article was reprinted in 1919 in a collection,
Tales of Fishes. It is a simple, uncomplicated article on the
rivalry between Pearl and his brother R. C. as they fished along
the Delaware, one on each side of the river, with taunts and
calls of triumph back and forth as the day's fishing progressed.

It is a surprisingly well written human-interest story.
Since he was able to write so well in this first published piece,
it is difficult to understand why he had so much trouble later
on, why it took him so long to become established. He wrote
and submitted many articles during the intervening years.

But in the spring of 1902, Dr. P. Zane Grey was an author.
Of sorts.

A few months after the article was published in *Recreation*, Dr. Grey made his second sale, an article entitled "Camping Out." It was bought by *Field & Stream* and published in
the February, 1903, issue under the byline, "Dr. P. Zane Grey."

He continued to write articles, but "Camping Out" was
the last one he sold until 1906, more than three years later.

Still, Grey had proved to himself that he *could* get something published, and the first published piece is an author's
most important milestone. Until then there is always a vast
uncertainty. It is a mental block that some would-be writers
can never break down.

Millions and millions of people have thought they could
write, and millions have tried it and failed. Only thousands
have ever made that first story sale, and many could not make
the second, third, or fourth. Zane Grey had made his first sale
and his second. It was the third one that he could not make.

Yet, spurred by that first and second success, Dr. Grey
poured it on. He spent more and more of his time at his writing. He wrote and he rewrote.

Perhaps, because of these first sales, fishing stories would
be his specialty. If so, he had to stimulate himself, become

steeped in the subject, so that he could write authoritatively and enthusiastically. He took more to the woods and rivers of New Jersey and Pennsylvania.

Dr. P. Zane Grey had his inspiration, and he battened down his hatches, determined to become an established author by the time Lina finished college.

A novel would do it. A successful novel would solve all the problems of social status, of finances.

Pearl would write a novel during the winter of 1902–1903. The plot was ready-made for him; so were the characters and the situations, the glamor and the excitement—the story of his ancestor Colonel Ebenezer Zane and his sister Betty. It was in the fourth-grade school readers. He would blow it up and embellish it, and his own family, steeped in tradition, would love it. And so would others.

He wrote that winter. He sat at a kitchen table in his old dingy room. His only light was a flickering oil lamp.

He wrote and he rewrote. He was raised to the heights and plunged into the depths of despair. The novel went well, it went badly.

In the spring the novel was finished. Grey did not know if it was good or bad. He hated it, yet at times he loved it. It was his brainchild, his creation.

He submitted it to Harper & Brothers, and it was rejected. Dr. Grey was stunned into despair.

CHAPTER **10** ─────────────────────

Dr. Grey carried the book to a second publisher. It was rejected, and he submitted it to a third, a fourth, and a fifth. Only a person who has yearned to be a writer all his life, who has hoped and dreamed of it, who has agonized and labored for hours and days and months, can truly understand the emotions of a person who has had his creation rejected with the damning finality of a printed rejection slip.

In several interviews and even in articles he wrote about this trying period, Zane Grey tells that a wealthy patient offered to lend him the money to have the book printed and that he accepted the offer and then found a printer of his own who agreed to print the book. Though he repeated this story often, he never gave the name of the patient.

The name can now be told. It was a young female patient, Lina Elise Roth. When Lina required dental work, she naturally went to the office of Dr. P. Zane Grey. She went there frequently when she had no appointment for dental work.

Her interests were literary, and one of the things that attracted Lina to Dr. Grey in the beginning was the fact that he intended to become a writer.

Like many later successful writers, Grey had not done well in the subjects he should have been most interested in in high school and college: grammar, English, rhetoric. He had spent too much time on athletics. The subjects in which he was deficient, however, were the ones in which Lina Roth excelled. She saw the weakness in his early writing and she tried to coach Grey in the subjects that he lacked. She brought him books, and they discussed the lessons during the winter of 1902–1903. It was Lina who encouraged him to write his first novel.

During the winter Lina saw the growing pile of manuscript. At least once a week she read what Grey had written. She was clever enough not to criticize any of it. She did not call attention to errors in punctuation, in grammar. She praised Pearl's work, she lauded the good scenes and glossed over the bad ones. She was in love with him, and she told him the things he wanted to hear, that he *had* to be told. Her enthusiasm and encouragement never flagged. She copied the completed manuscript in full, and the manuscript that the editors were to read was in Lina's handwriting.

When editor after editor rejected *Betty Zane*, Lina saw the tenseness increasing in Grey. In her presence he pretended indifference. He had had other things rejected. It was all part of the game. But Lina knew that the cheerfulness was forced. She knew how *she* felt after every rejection, and there grew within her a determination that *Betty Zane* would be published. Lina insisted that publishers could be mistaken. Grey had sold two articles to magazines. He had proved that he could write. *Betty Zane* was a fine novel. It was an excellent piece of craftsmanship. She was proud of it, and she was proud of Dr. Pearl Grey.

She was in love with him.

At last, she offered to pay the cost of having the book printed. Grey demurred, but Lina was insistent, and he finally consented.

The book was printed and bound, and at last the author held his first book in his hands. It was a thrilling moment. The custom of an author paying to have his book published was not unknown in 1903.

Zane Grey was his own publisher, and he would be his own distributor. He took the books to the bookstores in New York, and he got a few of them on display tables. He gave out review copies to literary critics and bookstores.

The few reviews that were published weren't too bad. One or two of them were actually quite good. Zane Grey was proud of these. He clipped them and carried the little pieces with him. He showed them to his dental patients and told them where the book could be purchased.

He haunted the bookstores, and to humor him the booksellers gave *Betty Zane* prominent space on the tables.

The book sold, but only in the New York area, where Grey himself had placed the books. *Betty Zane* would never, never earn back the money it had cost to print it.

Grey minimized this, and during these years of fluctuating ups and downs Lina Roth remained steadfast. His next book would be better, she told Zane. He had mastered the technique of the novel. The first novels of new writers never sold well. The second would do better; and the third—*that* would be the *big* one.

Grey had already planned his next book. Even while writing *Betty Zane* he knew that he must tell the story of his great-great-uncle Jonathan Zane, the brother of Colonel Ebenezer Zane. In it he would relate more fully the exploits of the famous scout Lew Wetzel.

He began to write, and soon he was in the deep throes of creation. He drilled teeth and made inlays during the day, and in the evenings he wrote. Lina went over the pages and corrected them. They discussed the scenes he had written, the ones he would work on next. The manuscript grew page by page, and by early fall of 1904 it was completed.

Zane Grey called it *The Spirit of the Border*. Carefully copied by Lina Roth, it was delivered to the offices of Harper & Brothers. In due time it was rejected, and the agony that he had endured when *Betty Zane* made the rounds began all over again.

There was one difference, however. Zane Grey had committed himself totally. Discouragement, temporary setbacks, delays, he could accept, but not total defeat. He was learning his craft. The writing in *The Spirit of the Border* was better than that of *Betty Zane*.

His third book would be even better. He began writing it while the second one was making the rounds.

He worked on the third novel throughout the winter of 1904–1905, and by spring it was completed. The book was *The Last Trail*, and again it was delivered to Harper. For the third time, Harper rejected a novel by Zane Grey. *The Spirit of the Border* was still making the rounds, and now *The Last Trail* began going to publishers.

Zane Grey had worked hard that winter. His dental practice had grown, and he was saving some money. While in New York he lived economically, but he felt the need of getting outdoors at times, and he continued to make occasional trips to Lackawaxen. Sometimes he stayed at the Delaware House across the river from Lackawaxen, but more often he pitched a tent on the outskirts of the small Pennsylvania village.

R. C. was usually with Zane on these weekend trips, and

the two often discussed the possibility of moving permanently to Lackawaxen someday. Romer still played baseball in the summer, but in a few years he would be quitting baseball and then he would become a full-time dentist.

Lina Roth also liked Lackawaxen. It had been a favorite vacation spot for her parents, who came often to spend a weekend or a full week or two at the Delaware House.

Lina and Zane had met five years before at Lackawaxen. Their engagement had been a long one; it was time they were married. They had talked about it many times. Zane had always been a reluctant dentist. It was a means of making a living, that was all. His future would be as a writer; both Lina and Zane were dedicated to that.

Why not make the break now? As long as he continued to practice dentistry, he would be a part-time writer. It was too difficult, practicing dentistry during the day, writing at night. Zane did not mind hard work, but he would mind it less if the work was the kind he wanted to do.

A. L. Burt & Company accepted *The Spirit of the Border* that eventful summer. Burt was chiefly a reprint house, but occasionally printed original juvenile books. They thought that the book would have a modest continuing sale. They would not pay an advance on the book, but there would be royalties after the book went on sale.

The acceptance of a book by a publisher was the deciding factor. The decision was made. Zane Grey would quit dentistry and devote his full time to writing.

A family conclave was held that summer. The Gray clan gathered at the Delaware House. The now-widowed Mrs. Lewis Gray came from Columbus, Ohio, accompanied by Ida (Ella had died at an early age). Ellsworth and his wife came from New York City, where Ellsworth had been working as an artist and illustrator.

Romer came from a nearby city where he had been playing baseball. Zane told the assembled family of his plan. A five-acre tract of land at the confluence of the Delaware and Lackawaxen rivers was for sale. It was actually a tongue of land that reached into the rivers. At the very tip of it was a two-story cottage.

The cottage faced south. On the left was the Lackawaxen, on the right the Delaware. Both rivers were within thirty feet of the cottage. A fishing enthusiast, living in the cottage, could step to the east end of the porch and cast a line into the Delaware River, or he could walk to the west end of the porch and fish in the Lackawaxen. Zane Grey was to do exactly that many, many times in the future.

In spite of occasional differences, the Gray family was a close-knit one. Zane told the assembled family that he intended to purchase this five-acre tongue of land. He and Lina would live in the cottage now on the land, and the other members of the family could, if they wished, build homes on the tract. Romer promptly threw in his lot. During the summer he had met Reba and they had already decided to be married in September, as soon as the baseball season was over. They would start building their own house immediately.

Ellsworth voted in favor, saying that he too would build a house on the point of land. That left Mrs. Gray and Ida. They decided that each of the three brothers would contribute a certain amount of money for the fourth house, in which Mrs. Gray would live with Ida.

The marriage of Zane and Dolly had already been agreed upon, but it would not take place until late November. Zane, however, decided to close his dental office and get things in shape at Lackawaxen and start full time on his writing. Two or three months more in the city would not be worthwhile. Mrs. Gray and Ida moved into the cottage with Zane while their house was being built. By the time it was completed, Zane and Dolly would be married, and they would take over the house.

Purchase of the property at Lackawaxen took all of Zane's savings, but Dolly's inheritance from her grandfather would be their reserve if Grey's writings did not earn him enough in the near future.

Some 1905 letters between Dolly and Zane Grey are of interest:

May 3, 1905

Dear Pearl:

I won't have time to write at home today, so I'll write in my off intervals here at college. The model is just taking a rest between poses. We are illustrating a story of Mary Wilkins.

I believe I must be crazy or something. I just realized this morning what a process your letters always went through. When I receive them I read them at least three times with various emotions. Then they travel around with me all day long, being read at intervals. Before I go to sleep at night I read them once or twice more, put them under the pillow, and read them again in the morning before I put them away. Then I usually take out all the recent ones about once a week and read them. Don't you think there must be something the matter with me?

There is a constant change for the better going on in you. I can feel it all the time. When I compared the difference in you now and two, three, even one year ago, it makes me very happy, and very confident that you will accomplish something in the literary field. As you know, there can be no standing still. It must be either advance or retardation, and in you it is mostly advance now. I say mostly—there are some slips still, but I think they're getting fewer and not so serious. I never know of the actions these slips result in but I always know the state of mind they cause in you.

There are some days when I feel I could write volumes to you, and today is one. Yesterday, I didn't write because I didn't know what to say. Your letter stimulated me.

Love, from your
Dolly

On September 4, 1905, Grey wrote to Dolly from Lack-awaxen:

My dear Dolly,
    Come on Number 1 Saturday unless I write or wire
you otherwise. Be sure and have a comfortable time on
the train.
    I enclose a paragraph I want you to *study* in view
of making it the opening one for my novel *Lethe*. I
woke up in the night, and the words came almost as you
have them.
    Good-bye for today, I may not write again, especially
as I expect to see you Saturday.

                                                              Yours,
                                                              Pearl

Here is the paragraph referred to in Grey's letter, still in
the original envelope, in which it was mailed to Dolly Roth
in 1905.

    Folly, thou has cost me dear; the light of woman's eye
—Ah! Wine—thou mocker! Outcast am I, thrown from
my father's house hard upon the world, after an idle,
luxurious, improvident youth. Better surely, to yield to
the strain of suicide blood in me and seek forgetfulness
in the embrace of cold dark death. What makes life worth
living? Indefinable, for me, as the unpardonable sin. Yet
to give it up, at twenty-five, when the blood burns, for
the unknown—No. I will see this game of life out to its
bitter end. I will try again, and yet again. Men may rise
on stepping stones of their dead selves to higher things.

At this time Zane Grey had already written *Betty Zane*
and *The Spirit of the Border* and was working on *The Last
Trail*. He had also had two articles published in sports magazines. A quick glance at the foregoing indicates that he still

suffered from what Dolly called in her previous letter "periods
of retardation," for it is hard to conceive how a serious student
of literature could, even in 1905, use such stilted phrases.
Perhaps the reason this paragraph remained in the envelope
was that Dolly did not like it and preferred not to discuss it
with her soon-to-be husband.

An interesting note, however, is the proposed title, *Lethe*.
This remained in Zane Grey's mind until 1921, when he
wrote *Shores of Lethe*, only to have the title changed before
publication to *The Day of the Beast*.

On September 7, 1905, three days after he sent Dolly the
paragraph on *Lethe*, he wrote to her again:

Most Charming of Maidens!

Your letter came at noon. Reddy [R. C.], who arrived
last night at one-thirty, said the same things of N.Y.
that you did.

I guess I'm pretty well satisfied to stay here for a while.

Mother and Ida are crazy about the stuff Red brought
home. He gave me two dandy books and mother a
canary bird, and underclothes at $5 per suit, besides lots
of other things from Reba.

Reba gave Red a ring, and say! Dolly, I wish you
could see it. Two large diamonds and a ruby. It cost
$750.00 if it cost a dollar.

Red and Reba will spend a little time here after they
get spliced.

Betty had her kittens, three black and one Stubbs. I
don't know who to blame for the others. You ought to
have seen Stubbs when he saw that canary-bird. He was
in my arms and he growled, but I didn't think much
about it. I let him down and by Jiminy! he jumped
ten feet right upon the cage and if Red hadn't grabbed
him he'd have torn the cage to pieces. I licked him like
the dickens and he never batted an eye. Oh, he's a wonder.

Remember to think about me and take care of your
health.

I finished Chapter 4 last night.

Yours devotedly,
Pearl

R. C. had played his last season of baseball. He and Reba,
a wealthy young woman, were married in September, 1905.
On September 14, 1905, Dolly wrote to Grey:

My Dear Boy,

Your letter wasn't silly, but a dear. Only I fail to
understand such hieroglyphics as ————. What can you
possibly mean? Perhaps in the long while that we have
been parted you have bent your energies to acquiring
some new language.

You must be working faster than a steam engine to
have already begun Chapter Seven. I am very anxious to
read of the course of Miss Helen's love-making. I suppose
like the proverbial course of true love it is far from
smooth. Make it as rough and exciting as possible for that
stimulates interest and makes people rejoice so much
more when they do get each other.

Yesterday I took a walk and passed Teacher's College
and I was surprised at the feeling I had. I didn't
care even to look at it. I was thoroughly sick and tired of
it and thankful that I wasn't going to return. I want now
to live and love and what I learn henceforth I will learn
from the point of view of life. All our knowledge counts
for nothing if we cannot apply it to our daily lives.

I had a very nice little note from Janie today inviting
Mama and myself to come over Sunday afternoon. She
writes that she saw Rome [R. C.] on Sunday for the
last time and she says, "Don't let's talk very much about
it, Doll," in her letter. I think that is dead game and I
admire her a great deal for it. Of course, Janie is young

and she'll get over it easily, but I know she cared a great
deal for Rome. She is now looking for a position as
stenographer.

Good-bye, now. Don't stop writing to me, and I'm
living in anticipation of the 23rd.

Your own,
Dolly

Late in November, 1905, Lina's mother sent out the
announcement:

Mrs. Lina Roth
announces the marriage of her daughter
Lina Elise

to

Dr. Zane Grey
on Tuesday, November the twenty-first
nineteen hundred and five,
New York City

A friend gave Lina Roth a beautiful leather diary as a
wedding gift, and the newly married Dolly Grey decided to
become a diarist. For some months she kept a meticulous
record of the day-by-day events of interest. After some months
the entries became briefer and briefer and stopped altogether
within a year. But the habit of recording things, once instilled
in Dolly, remained with her, and periodically she began a
diary anew. She would keep it up a year or two, stop for a
year or so, then resume again. She continued the practice
until 1942, when she apparently discontinued it entirely. To
her diaries we are indebted for some interesting insights into
the lives of the entire Gray family.

Zane Grey himself kept a diary at times. It was often
very detailed, but he was a spasmodic diarist at best. He began
a daily journal in 1917 and continued it regularly until 1923,

then did not keep one again until 1928, when Dolly presented him with a handsome diary. He wrote in this briefly for a year or so, then dropped out and did not resume again until 1931, when he thought his affairs were at their worst. He continued until 1933, then ceased writing a diary altogether.

From the diaries of both Dolly and Zane Grey and from their letters to each other it is possible to re-create some of the most vivid events of their lives and to gain an insight into some of the "deals" that were entered into for Zane Grey's works.

The diaries of husband and wife are vastly different in content and tone. From the early days Dolly was the steady one of the family. Her diaries frequently show a placid outlook on life, sometimes even a humorous one. As late as 1937 she reread the diaries of the early years, and here and there inserted a pithy comment, which she dated. She usually tried to cover up her real emotions by writing wryly of certain events. Tragic things were touched upon very briefly, whereas her husband anguished over each setback, each crisis.

Zane Grey had his ups and downs. He agonized when he was down, he exulted when he was up. Dolly's accounts are on a much more even keel.

The first entry in Dolly Grey's diary is: "Married November 21, 1905."

The actual diary, however, begins on January 1, 1906, and is headed "Our Honeymoon." This is followed, in Dolly's beautiful handwriting:

> Instead of making the usual New Year's resolutions, I think I can do no better than to quote part of Wordsworth's poem and try to live up to it.

> > I saw her upon nearer view,
> > A Spirit, yet a Woman, too,
> > Her household motions light and free,
> > And steps of virgin liberty;
> > A countenance in which did meet,

Sweet records, promises as sweet;
A creature not too bright or good,
For Human nature's daily food;
For transient sorrows, simple wiles,
Praise, blame, love, kisses, tears and smiles.

And now I see with eye serene,
The very pulse of the machine;
A being breathing thoughtful breath,
A traveller between life and death,
The reason firm, the temperate will,
Endurance, foresight, strength or skill,
A perfect woman, nobly planned,
To earn, to comfort and command,
And yet, a Spirit still and bright,
With something of an angel light.

Today, Pearl went to New York to buy the tickets for California. In about a week we'll be "over the hills and far away." What a new experience that will be for me, who have done absolutely no traveling. Of course, there was work and preparation, so that kept me so busy all day that I scarcely had time to miss Z. G. In the evening I read Balzac. His toils are upon me and I can feel his fascination, but it extends no farther than my imagination.

Jan. 3, 1906:
Worked pretty hard all day. Pearl came back.
Contents of trunk: first tray, hats, collar, linen shawl, books, fishing tackle, etc.
Second tray: Gray suit, short skirt, red waist, white jacket, sachet, combing jacket.
Third tray: pink dress, tan, two white skirts, white petticoat, chemise, c.c. stockings.

Jan. 6, 1906:
Received today balance of money willed to me by my grandfather in the following amounts:

$1,000 to be sent to G. Roth in Detroit, as per agreement.

$947.97 due me after deduction.

$73.80 interest due on trust fund of G. Roth.

$500 due from Julius.

January 8:

Went to New York on No. 30. Met Mama at Mr. Librischer's office and turned over $1,000 check for George Roth. Deposited $1581.81 in German Savings Bank. Shopped at Wanamaker's. Grandma's for dinner.

January 9:

Returned home on #1 with Mrs. Gray.

January 11:

Left on #3 for Chicago. First experience on a sleeper. Train steadily losing time.

January 12:

This morning we are over three hours late and it's nip and tuck whether we catch the California Limited. We are flying through level and monotonous lands of Ohio, with dingy-looking towns at short distances from one another. At Mansfield Doc met Sandy McDermott. Indiana only differs from Ohio in that the towns are fewer and smaller. We arrived in Chicago with just enough time to catch the California Limited. Five minutes lost would have made us too late.

January 13:

Last night we went to sleep outside of Chicago. This morning we are flying over long stretches of Missouri and Kansas. Made Kansas City about 9:30. The Missouri River is wide and muddy with numerous islands of alluvial deposits. In Kansas we saw some wonderful orchards, miles and miles in area. But the dry, unbroken stretches of perfectly level and flat farmlands are the most astonishing.

January 15:

Arrived at El Tovar this morning, finding the canyon lost to view in clouds. Towards evening it revealed itself in the glory of the sunset. It is a second inferno, stupendous, awe-inspiring, glowing with fiery colors.

January 16:

Today we took the never-to-be-forgotten trip down into the Canyon. Mounted astride horses and mules the party started out with two guides. Down the trail, ice-covered for a mile and growing steeper and steeper we rode with great precipices yawning before and beside us. Down the very face of the cliff the path wound its tortuous way.

January 17:

All that I wanted to do today was rest up. Every bone in my body ached as if it were going to break. Caught cold.

January 18:

Took pictures, walked, rested. Not yet recovered from the effects of the ride.

January 19 [back on the train]:

This morning we left the Canyon in a snowstorm but outrode it. Passed Williams and a number of towns. Ate at lunch counters. Cold bad. Felt very sick and had a bad night. Caught our first glimpse of California.

January 20:

Arrived in Los Angeles. On the way passed through San Bernardino, where we observed our first glimpse of beautiful orange and lemon groves against a background of snow-clad mountains. The country is like a garden. Arrived in Los Angeles about 8:30 and drove to the Westminster. Clanging trolley cars drove us away in a half-hour, determined to go right to Coronado. Waited in Station. Saw dying consumptive woman.

Ride to San Diego was charming. High hills covered with fresh green grass. Sheep grazing. Old mission.

January 21:

Coronado is the most beautiful place I've ever seen. On a sandy peninsula between ocean and bay . . . abundantly covered with great palms and flowering plants and trees; it is semitropical in its character.

January 22:

Went over to San Diego. Bought fishing tackle. In afternoon Doc caught a shark off the end of the pier. I had gone out with him in the morning, but went back as I felt chilly, so missed it.

To this is written the comment by Dolly Grey, dated 1937: "This was the beginning of Z. G.'s sea fishing. How mountainous it became!"

January 23:

This morning we arose early and went out to fish, but the fish didn't seem to bite. In the P.M. we went over to San Diego, invested in some more tackle, and got a good idea of the town. An old man, evidently taking us for the degenerate rich, handed us a paper, denouncing fashion. As I happened to be dressed up considerably, he probably thought he was hitting the mark. Perhaps he was. Confession is good for the soul.

January 24:

Today I am a grass widow. Doc went out on an all-day fishing trip and I did not feel sufficiently well to accompany him. Took walks after breakfast and after lunch. I never get tired of seeing the ocean and hearing the boom of the surf. Did some sewing and reading and except for my walks remained in my room, for I do not like to be alone among so many people as there are here. I have no self-confidence.

January 27:

Today we took the trip to Old Mexico and Tiajuana.

January 28:

Nothing of especial interest happened today. Doc fished from the end of the pier and I walked a little, sat on the beach, etc.

January 29:

We started out early today on a fishing trip.

January 31:

Pearl's birthday. The Clausens were leaving today and we very suddenly made up our minds to go also. Trunks were packed in two hours and off we went.

Dolly's 1937 note on this reads, "Main reason for the sudden departure was that Z. G. couldn't get any bait!"

February 1:

This morning early we left Los Angeles for Santa Catalina. First we took the train for San Pedro, then a really fine-looking boat for the island.

February 2:

This morning Doc went fishing on the ocean, but I, dreading my first experience, remained here. At noon the fishing boats began to come in and all seemed to have had pretty good luck.

February 3:

Today we took another fishing trip, but with no material luck.

February 4:

Doc went fishing but I remained at the hotel.

February 5:

Today I caught my big albacore.

February 6:

This morning Doc took Mr. Clausen out fishing.

February 8:

Today we left Catalina Island. Doc went out and attempted to catch a yellow tail.

Dolly's 1937 comment on this: "Notice—*attempt*. That's why we left."

Returning to Los Angeles, the Greys took a trip to Mt. Lowe, passing the exact spot on Mariposa Avenue where they would have their big home in 1920. They intended to go to Redlands, but it was raining, so they started up the coast, stopping off at Santa Barbara, then continued on to San Francisco. They remained there only one day, then took the train to Salt Lake City, which Dolly noted as "a dirty, disagreeable place." At Salt Lake City they boarded the Denver & Rio Grande train, which was so crowded that they were unable to get a Pullman berth. They had to sit in a tourist car all the way to Colorado Springs. They remained only one day in Colorado Springs, and the next day were on the eastbound train, rolling through Kansas. In Chicago they had only three hours' stopover before boarding the Erie train which took them back to Lackawaxen. The honeymoon trip was over.

The succeeding entries in the diary are more sparse, with many days skipped. One recounts a trip of Dolly's to New York, where she got a check and deposited it in the Bowery Bank. On April 4 there is a single-line entry: "Cat house finished." This entry is significant in the later revelation that Zane Grey was a lifelong lover of cats. His daughter Betty provided the information that at one time there were nineteen cats (all Persian) in the Lackawaxen home, and then Z. G. went on a long fishing trip, leaving the cats in Dolly's care—and Dolly was not as fond of cats as was Z. G.

For May 8, 1906, there is an interesting note: "Doc and I went to N.Y. Surprised the folks.

Interest $45.00
    "   8.75"

And the following day: "Doc, Mr. James and myself went to theater, then home for dinner." This is the Alvah James who later introduced Z. G. to Buffalo Jones.

For May 10, Dolly records: "Went shopping. Bought desk

for $10.96, piano $165. Drew $400 from bank. Deposited $50 at Macy's, gave rest to Doc. Lunch at the Astor."

In 1906 Zane Grey was a full-time writer, and he plunged into his work with renewed zest. He wrote short stories, verse, articles. He mailed them to magazines in New York, Boston, and Philadelphia. They were returned, and he mailed them out again.

The Last Trail was still making the rounds. Once in a while Zane Grey traveled to New York City to pick up the manuscript from a publisher who had rejected it, and then he would deliver it to another publisher. On these trips he would also visit magazine editors, those who had rejected his stories and others to whom he wanted to submit material. He called at the offices of Street & Smith on Seventh Avenue, near Fourteenth Street. He visited the offices of the Munsey Company at 280 Broadway. He read their magazines, *Munsey's, All-Story, Argosy, Cavalier.* He submitted stories to them. None was accepted.

There were sports magazines all around New York. Zane called at their offices, discussed hunting and fishing articles with the editors.

The train trip from Lackawaxen to New York required more than three hours; if Grey took an early-morning train, it was noon when he arrived in the city. That gave him only a few hours before he had to take the evening train home. Sometimes he decided to stay over until the next day, in which case he always wrote Dolly. He would be home frequently before the letter arrived, but it did not matter.

This is the sort of letter Grey wrote to Dolly in 1906 while in New York:

Dearest Mushy,

If it's a bad day here tomorrow I'll be home as soon as I can get there, but if it's pleasant I'll stay a day longer.

I purchased a suit and two hats. I got to thinking
that as you love me so much and think me so handsome
it is certainly my duty to look right.

I took Mr. Murphy to lunch and we arranged for him
to come up about the 12th of October.

I am anxious to get back, the same as I always am
when I get away. . . . I don't appreciate you half as much
when I'm there with you as when I'm away. But then
you're so mushy all the time, you just look at me and
then with a whoop you grab me and yell, "He's mine!
He's mine!" Now the way you won such a nice husband
was by saying fine, intellectual things and looking pale
and interesting. I've been goldbricked, that's all.

Well, that's enough nonsense. I am dissatisfied with
my efforts toward work these last two weeks. It seems
slow; steady is not my way. I must fire up and go off or
loaf. Be good and don't take walks except to the village.

Dolly also went to New York; sometimes Zane went
with her, sometimes she went alone. She visited her mother two
and three days at a time. When she remained more than one
day she never failed to write to Zane.

In 1906 he sold but one story, a four-page fishing piece,
"James' Waterloo." *Field & Stream* bought it.

It was an unsuccessful year as far as writing was con-
cerned, but it was a happy year personally for Zane Grey. He
spent hours fishing, hunting, tramping through the woods
and fields. He was happy at his work, and he enjoyed the re-
laxed, married life. His savings were gone, and they had to
draw on Lina's reserve to keep them going, but soon the tide
would turn. Zane Grey believed it, and Dolly had no doubts
whatever.

The year 1907 was more promising. In the spring Grey
sold an article on fishing to *Shield's Magazine*; only a few
days later *Field & Stream*, one of the best of the outdoors
magazines, bought a baseball story from him.

During his residence in New York Grey had attended occasional meetings of the Campfire Club and had become friendly with a number of the members. On one of his visits to the club he met Alvah James, who had made a reputation as a South American explorer. James invited him to attend a lecture by J. C. Jones.

Better known as Buffalo Jones, the plainsman had been a buffalo hunter in the 1870's, a game warden at Yellowstone, and in more recent years an ardent champion of the buffalo, which was being threatened with extinction. He had a small ranch on the rim of the Grand Canyon in Arizona where he was experimenting with the hybridization of buffalo and black Galloway cattle, hoping to produce a breed capable of subsisting on the natural vegetation of the desert and a minimal amount of water.

Jones claimed that his experiment was succeeding but that he required capital to carry on. This inspired him to embark on an eastern lecture tour. He had taken some motion pictures of wild animals he had captured with a lasso, and with the lure of these he hoped to draw audiences.

James and Grey attended the lecture, which turned out disastrously for Jones. His stories were just too incredible for the eastern audience, and they hooted and called him a liar.

One of the few who believed Jones, however, was Zane Grey. Alvah James introduced them.

An idea began to grow in Grey's mind. Heretofore he had written only fishing stories and the three novels of Colonial times. He was groping for a new type of story. He had read *The Virginian* and knew of its great success. He thought he might get some background information from Buffalo Jones.

He called on the old man at his hotel and found him ill, discouraged, and in a foul temper. He talked to him, cleaned up his room, ran some errands for Jones, and brought him his food. The Colonel complained vociferously about the treatment he had received at his lecture.

Grey assured him that *he* believed the Colonel. Moreover,

he had a proposal to make. He would accompany Jones to his ranch in Arizona, stay with him awhile, see everything at first hand, then return and write a book about Colonel Jones's work. The book would influence people to finance Jones's experiments.

Jones liked the idea, but scowling at Grey, said, "All I know about you is that you're good at pulling teeth. How do I know you can write?"

Grey just happened to have a copy of *Betty Zane* with him. He left it with the Colonel.

Two days later he returned to the hotel. He was inquiring for the Colonel at the desk when Jones came up from behind and clapped Grey on the shoulder with a huge hand.

"Where'd you learn to write like that?" he cried. Then and there he invited Grey to come to Arizona, but Zane would have to pay for the trip himself. There would be other expenses. Wranglers would have to be hired, dogs purchased, food.

Grey returned to Lackawaxen and told Dolly of the proposed venture. An inventory of the family assets was taken, and it was discovered that the trip would require virtually every dollar they had, including the last of Dolly's inheritance.

Grey promptly decided against the trip. It was a foolhardy thing at best. Grey had lived long enough on his wife's money. He had dreamed too long about the foolish notion of earning money and finding fame as a writer. His scribbling had cost them too much. It was time he returned to his dental practice and faced the realities of life.

Dolly would have none of it. "It would be unfair to Colonel Jones if you were to back out now," she declared. "Don't worry about me. I'll get along somehow." Then she added with all the assuredness she could manage, "I've got a hunch that this trip to the West will be the turning point in your career."

Grey demurred. It wasn't right for him to risk everything at this time, but Dolly remained adamant. She prodded him relentlessly, and Grey finally gave in.

The Colonel returned to Arizona to make arrangements, and Grey followed a few days later.

Grey was thirty-five years old. He was in good physical condition as a result of his baseball-playing days and his continual hunting and fishing in the Lackawaxen area, but he was not a Westerner, and a horse to him was something that you hitched to a plow or buggy.

Dolly and Zane Grey had been in Arizona only a year and four months earlier. They had stopped off at Grand Canyon, stayed at the El Tovar Hotel at the edge of the canyon, and made the trip down the canyon on muleback. Dolly had written vividly of it in her honeymoon diary. At the time, Zane Grey had no idea that he would ever return to Arizona for the sole purpose of writing a book about it. When he bought his ticket in New York, he bought it with a stopover privilege in Grand Canyon. He wanted to relive, if possible, the days of the honeymoon, and secondly, he wanted to study the canyon now with the enlightened eyes of a writer.

Dolly knew of the proposed stopover, and she wrote to him at El Tovar. It was a poignant letter, and it seemed to Zane Grey that she had already regretted permitting, rather urging, him to make this prolonged trip away from her. In their brief marriage he had been away several times, but they were only short trips to New York.

Now, however, he was twenty-five hundred miles from home and intended to remain away for several weeks.

He arrived at the El Tovar on the rim of the Grand Canyon on March 27, 1907, and promptly sat down to write to Dolly:

My dear little lonely wife,

I arrived at six P.M. in a blinding blizzard. The hotel is crowded, and me in my tough clothes! Dear, your two letters broke me all up. I am about sick and wish I were home with you.

We have had pretty hard luck in the way of dogs.

Colonel Jones is getting them. I'll write you tomorrow
about our plans and I do hope you will get the letter. If
you don't I'm afraid you will have a fit.

My dear, I'm much surprised at the tone of your letters
and very sorry. If I thought you meant all you wrote, I'd
give up my trip. Your letters were splendid but they made
me unhappy. I know I shall come back to you loving you
more than ever and I shall be much better every way.

Good night now, Dolly. Remember you are in my
room, with all that is dear to me, and you are my wife.

Always yours,
Pearl

The next letter from Zane to Dolly is written on the sta-
tionery of the Commercial Hotel in Flagstaff. It is dated
April 8:

My dearest Dolly,

Not a line from my girl since I left Grand Canyon! I
know you've written and it's not your fault I have not
heard from you.

Jones and Mr. Wooley are here with the dogs. Oh,
you ought to see these dogs! I intend to bring one home
with me.

We shall start in a day or two. We travel with the
Mormons for a hundred and eighty miles. I'll get to study
them and get to go into the Moki and Indian towns. This
ought to make great material for the occasional short
story I want to write. We reach Jones's ranch in four
days. Then we work around the north rim of the
Canyon, where we shall camp. The snow is going off.
San Francisco Peak is still white, but we expect only a
foot or so of snow over there.

That is the best I can tell you of our whereabouts. I
cannot hear from you until I reach El Tovar and that
will be three to four weeks.

Of course I'll be busy and shall not miss hearing
from you so badly as you will miss not hearing from me.

I am positively quivering with joy at the prospect of the
trip. I have lost all my blues and I'm actually happy. I
need this wild life, this freedom and I'll come back to
love you to death.

> Good-bye little wife, with love,
> Pearl

The party did not get off quite as soon as Zane had expected, for on April 12, still in Flagstaff, he wrote:

Dear Sweetheart Dolly,

We get away right after noon today. I am writing
you a little consolation note but I haven't any news. I
hear the Little Colorado is coming up and we'll have
trouble there.

You ought to see this crowd of Mormons I'm
going with. If they aren't a tough bunch I never saw
one. They all pack guns. But they're nice fellows.

Mr. Wooley wants me to go to Kanab to study the
Mormons. He has two families and fifteen handsome
unmarried girls. I guess I won't go. I really would be
afraid of so many.

Tonight I'll see the stars on the desert.

> Good-bye, with kisses and things,
> Pearl

The delay in Flagstaff was chiefly because Jones wanted
to wait for a man named Wallace, who was coming from
California to join the party. Meanwhile, he introduced Grey to
the men who would go with them to Jones's ranch, Jim Emmett, his two sons, and two hired men. All were Mormons, the
first Mormons Grey had ever met. They were quiet, hard-working men, completely self-sufficient in a harsh land. In the days
to come Grey would learn to appreciate these men. No job

was too difficult for them, no hazard too risky to undertake. They were desert men, the third generation to eke out a livelihood from this bleak and arid country.

Mules had already been bought for the trip, and Jones had two hunting dogs with him and was expecting three bloodhounds to come from California.

The dogs arrived, but Wallace failed to show up, and Jones came to the conclusion that the man had backed out. It was decided that they would start without him the next morning.

The pack saddles were on the mules when Grey joined the expedition. A fight among the dogs was stopped, and then Grey mounted the first horse he had been on in many years. To put it bluntly, Grey had never ridden anything but a farm plug back in Ohio.

They covered twenty-five miles the first day, climbing to circle the high San Francisco peaks in the north. By noon it was agony for Grey to remain in the saddle, and it was even worse to mount his mustang again after the short halt for the midday lunch.

He gritted his teeth and clung to the pommel throughout the long afternoon, and when the Mormons finally chose a camping spot, Grey could barely dismount from the saddle. A Mormon unsaddled his horse for him and hobbled it, so that it could graze during the night but not stray too far away.

Grey ate a small supper and rolled himself up in a blanket. He was asleep in an instant.

He was awakened at dawn by the sound of the Mormons moving around. They were early risers and were already performing the camp chores, bringing in the horses, putting the packs on the mules, and preparing breakfast.

It was sheer agony climbing into the saddle, but after a while his muscles limbered up and Grey found the going much easier than he had the day before. They were descending into the desert now, and as the scrubby cedars failed and the bunches of sage grew smaller and fewer, the day became quite warm. The Mormon leader, Jim Emmett, pointed to a low ridge of sand dunes in the distance. "The Little Colorado runs there; how far would you say it was?"

"Thirty miles," guessed Zane Grey.

"It's seventy-five. We'll get there day after tomorrow."

Emmett had advised him correctly, and when they reached the Little Colorado they drank the first fresh water since leaving Flagstaff.

The river bottom was dangerous quicksand, but the Mormons had had experience with it, and the crossing was made safely. It was another seventy-five miles to the Big Colorado, and by the time they reached it the barrels and kegs of water they carried with them were empty.

The Colorado River was high and swift, and Grey did not think they would be able to cross it, but they soon reached a cable strung across the river. Under it ran a rope.

Across the river an old flat scow was moored to the bank. Jim Emmett fired his rifle, and a man appeared and got into a small skiff. He rowed upstream for a considerable distance, then swung into the current. The little skiff was twice turned around but reached the near bank safely. Two Mormons got in, recrossed the river, and got into the scow. They grasped the rope overhead and began to pull. Slowly the scow came across the swift-running river.

Jones, looking at Grey's taut face, said that they should get the agony over quickly. Horses were loaded aboard, the men climbed on, and the hazardous crossing was begun. Two or three times the scow was virtually swamped. Emmett was wet to the waist from trying to hold the horses and gear, which were in danger of being lost several times. Grey remarked that he must be a splendid swimmer or he would not take such chances. Emmett told him that he couldn't swim a stroke, and even if he could, it would not save him if he fell into the torrent.

Emmett's supreme confidence reassured Grey, and he felt better during the rest of the trip.

Emmett's ranch was not far north of the Colorado, and

he and his party left the group there. The somewhat reduced cavalcade continued on.

A few hours later, descending into a canyon, Zane Grey saw his first buffalo; he thought it was a tremendous herd, but Jones, whose herd it was, told him that there were only two hundred head in it.

From the next ridge they could see a cabin in a rolling valley and in half an hour they had reached their destination.

They were warmly greeted by Buffalo Jones's two hands, Frank and Jim, who had joined Jones in this lonely existence several years before.

Twenty new cattalo calves—worth ten thousand dollars— had been born during Jones's absence, and he was exultant. He questioned Jim and Frank about every detail of what had happened while he was away.

Frank said that he had seen cougar tracks two days before near the Siwash; they were the biggest tracks he had ever seen and could have been made only by Old Tom, a tremendous cougar that had caused immense loss of livestock for years.

Jones immediately began making plans for a cougar hunt but said that they would need some more men. One came the next day, Grant Wallace, for whom they had waited in Flagstaff. He had arrived a day late and had followed the Jones entourage, one day behind them all the way.

The next day Grey was given a horse to ride, to replace the mustang he had ridden from Flagstaff. It was a white horse called Spot, and there was a gleam in the eyes of the two wranglers as they led the horse out of the corral and got him saddled for Grey.

"Of course you can ride?" asked Frank.

Grey knew that he was in for something, but assured the two men that he was an old hand with horses and climbed into the saddle. The white horse promptly took off at a speed that had Grey gasping, but he clung to the saddle pommel and let the horse have his way until it had run itself out. When he finally brought the animal back to the corral, Jones praised him for his magnificent handling of the white mustang and swore that he would skin Frank and Jim for trying to work off such a mean mount on a tenderfoot.

It was several days before they were ready for the hunt. Requiring horses, they rode to Buffalo Jones's closest neighbor, who lived thirty miles away and whose business was catching wild horses and breaking them. On the way back they were caught in a sandstorm and had to stop for several hours until the storm blew itself out.

From the new batch of horses Grey selected one that was called Satan, a large black who was faster and better suited to the task ahead than the white. Jones claimed that white horses frightened buffalo.

Three wild-horse hunters were at Jones's cabin when they returned. They were eager to go along on the hunt, for the cougars had destroyed a number of horses that the men had caught and tamed.

The hunting party started out the next morning with seven dogs, among them one named Don, who was later to become the hero of Zane Grey's famous story *Don*.

The dogs promptly flushed a jackrabbit and started after him, but Jones whipped out a double-barreled shotgun from a saddle scabbard, and aiming it at the dogs, let go with both barrels. It was his way of training dogs. The fine shot merely stung them at a range of seventy-five yards.

The hunters covered thirty miles the first day, then camped and the next day climbed up onto the Buckskin Range. Coming down into a wild canyon, the dogs picked up the trail of a cougar. Grey saw the tracks and marveled at their size. Jones and his men were sure that it was Old Tom.

There was wild riding for an hour or more. A pair of dogs treed Old Tom. He got down and bounded away, and the dogs followed and crossed a fresh deer trail and went off after the deer. It was the following morning when the weary dogs found their way back to camp.

It was several days before they got back on the trail of Old Tom. During that time Zane Grey saw his first herd of wild horses, led by a magnificent white stallion. They also discovered some ancient Indian cliff dwellings. Grey was fascinated with them and insisted on exploring them and copying the pictographs on the walls.

The horsemen followed the baying dogs at a furious pace, and soon the tone of the dogs' barking changed. They had treed the cougar.

Grey, coming up to the dogs, directly behind Jones, saw the animals below a scrubby piñon tree. Twenty feet from the ground was an enormous mountain lion, who was quickly identified as Old Tom. One of the dogs was climbing up into the tree, working his way from limb to limb.

Jones climbed the tree behind the dog and pulled him away, even as Old Tom was moving down to swipe the dog with his huge claws. Jones carried the dog back to the ground, and suddenly Old Tom hit the ground near them and was off once more.

The mountain lion was not treed again for almost a mile. Jones, with lasso in hand, began to climb the tree, after cautioning those below to shoot the lion instantly if he leaped in their direction. Jones swung his lasso at the cougar; the animal leaped to the ground and headed directly for Zane Grey.

Grey was ready; he fired. The animal in his death leap hit the edge of a long slide and went down two hundred yards, where he was picked up, dead.

CHAPTER

Grey remained with Buffalo Jones for several weeks. He asked Jones the name of every plant. He absorbed the Western dialect of Jones and his friends. He listened to the innumerable tales that were told around the campfires. He learned of the outlaws, the rangers, the wild-horse hunters. He absorbed the lore of the Indians. He took copious notes and forgot nothing.

He returned to Lackawaxen glowing from the experiences he had had, with a burning desire to weave them into stories. His forte from here on would be the Western story. He had learned to love the West and he wanted to write about it.

When she saw her husband's enthusiasm, Dolly Grey knew that she had been right. The privations she had endured during his absence were unimportant. A new life had been opened for Zane; he had acquired a new zest for his writing. He would succeed now; Dolly Grey knew it.

Zane Grey took up his writing pad, and words streamed from his pen. He relived the thrilling adventures he had had with Buffalo Jones and his men. He described the vastness of the land he had visited, the loneliness of it, and because his love of it had become so great, that too was revealed in his writing.

It was good work, Grey knew, the best thing he had yet written. He poured it out, working early and late. He wrote and rewrote. It was not an easy task that he had set for himself; he wanted to impart all that he had learned of this Western country, and he was inclined to overwrite. There could be no long, dull passages in this book. It had to move swiftly, it had to catch the reader's interest and keep him entertained and at the same time educate him in things he had never known about the West and its way of life.

The original intent of the book had been to convince Easterners that Buffalo Jones's project of saving the buffalo from extinction—the hybridization he was engaged in—was a worthy cause that should be subsidized financially.

As the book progressed, however, this theme became gradually submerged, and the final story was much, much more than that. It was an epic of the West.

Zane Grey thought so, and Dolly Grey was convinced of it.

Buffalo Jones believed it was the greatest document he had read in his entire lifetime.

Grey had been in correspondence with the old plainsman. He had advised him when the book would be finished, and

Jones came East. He read the manuscript in the cottage on the
Delaware, and his enthusiasm and praise of it warmed the
heart of Zane Grey.

Jones had become acquainted with Ripley Hitchcock at
the publishing house of Harper & Brothers. They would both
go to Harper's and talk to Hitchcock and accept the money
that the editor would give to them.

Mention of Harper's caused Zane Grey momentary concern.
Harper's had rejected, in turn, all three of the books he had
written so far. This was different, however. This book was
better than his previous ones. It was a biography of a living
American, a stirring adventure tale, and it was laid in the
great American West that Owen Wister had depicted so well
in *The Virginian*.

The Virginian was still a big seller. *The Last of The Plainsmen*, which title was the choice of both Jones and Grey,
would take up where *The Virginian* had left off. It would make
a fortune for them.

They took the train to New York. They went to the offices
of Harper & Brothers on Franklin Square. There was no difficulty about getting in to see the editor Ripley Hitchcock.

Hitchcock greeted Buffalo Jones warmly. He was cordial
to Zane Grey and reacted to the enthusiasm of Jones and Grey
when they described the content of the manuscript. Harper's
would certainly be interested in publishing a book of this kind.
He, Hitchcock, would give it priority and his personal attention. It would take a few days. Hitchcock would, after all,
have to read it, and he thought it only fair that some of his
associates should read it too.

Buffalo Jones could not remain in New York. Grey could
handle the details of contracts and publishing.

Grey returned to Lackawaxen. Impatiently he waited for
the mail every morning. The letter from Hitchcock was not
too long in coming. It was brief, laconical. It simply asked
Grey to come to the office to discuss his manuscript.

Grey hurried back to New York and after a considerable

wait in the reception room was ushered into the office of Ripley Hitchcock.

It was a different Hitchcock that Grey now faced. When he had been here before with Buffalo Jones, the editor had been warm, enthusiastic about the story. He picked up the heavy manuscript from his desk. "I've read this," he told Grey, "and some of the people in the office have gone through it. I'm sorry to have to tell you that the decision is that we should not publish it."

Zane Grey was stunned. Why had he been summoned from Lackawaxen? Could not Harper's have written him of their decision? Could they not have mailed the manuscript?

What was Ripley Hitchcock saying?

"I do not see anything in this to convince me you can write either narrative or fiction."

Silently Zane Grey repeated the words to himself, and they burned so deeply that they seemed to become etched in his brain. He never forgot them; he repeated them aloud a hundred times in the future, a thousand times. Sometimes in moments of great despair he sobbed them aloud.

He left the editor's office and walked stiffly down the stairs to Franklin Square. Only when he reached the sidewalk did the full impact overwhelm him, and he had to clutch at the lamppost to keep from falling to the pavement.

He had worked so long and so hard to reach his goal. His hopes had been so high, his dreams so magnificent.

How could he tell Dolly? She had sacrificed so much for his sake. Her belief in him had been magnificent. To top it all, she had thrown away her own security. She had given him the last of her money, had forced him to take it on the final gamble that she hoped would turn the tide.

He had failed. He had let her down. He had taken her love, her vast courage, her money. He had gambled it—and lost.

He would stifle the dream he had nurtured for so long. He would give it up. He would start anew. He would devote himself completely to the one thing he *could* do. He would drill teeth, he would yank them from their roots. He would make the finest inlays and plates.

The trip back to Lackawaxen was not too long for Grey. Stonily he stared through the window at the passing countryside. The turmoil, the chaos that was in him, began to sift itself out. His brain became clear, sharp—and cold.

Ripley Hitchcock could be wrong. Those assistant editors, the readers, who were they? Underpaid clerks, sycophants. What did they know about writing? Were they authors themselves? Could they write a short story, a novel?

If they could, they would be doing it.

Could Ripley Hitchcock write a novel?

Zane Grey had written three novels. He had published articles in magazines. He had been paid for them. He was an author. He had *proved* it!

Dolly was entitled to the fulfillment of her dreams. Zane Grey owed *her* that much. He would give it to her.

By the time he reached Lackawaxen the decision had been made. There would be no turning back. There would be no more wavering, no more doubts or half-doubts. He would go on, he *would* be a writer.

He had made his final decision on that subject.

He arrived at his home. He told Dolly of the rejection by Harper's. He told her flatly, in a matter-of-fact tone. He told her of his travail on the train, of his determination to continue on, and when she saw the steel in Zane Grey's eyes and felt the assurance of his words, his tone, Dolly knew that he had won his greatest victory, and she was happy for him, for herself.

No matter the trials, the hard work that lay ahead, the privations, they would conquer them one by one.

Her confidence had always been strong. She had always believed in her husband, and now that he had found this belief in himself, they would fight and they would win together.

Why *The Last of the Plainsmen* was rejected by a dozen publishers is one of the mysteries of the publishing business.

A reading of the book reveals an astonishing fact: it is an excellent adventure book, which even today would receive top ratings from the book reviewers and critics.

At the time it was written, in 1907, it should have been snapped up by any publisher. It might have become a bestseller. Never before had the West been so brilliantly described.

Although the book proved such a great disappointment to Zane Grey at the time, it nevertheless served its purpose. The trip itself and the recounting of it instilled in him such a great love of the country where he had had these adventures that he was inspired to write more and more about it. The experience of writing this book contributed greatly to his later success as a writer of Western novels.

CHAPTER **12**

It was winter now. Grey remained in Lackawaxen throughout the long months. He could not afford the trips to New York.

He arose early every morning to start the fire in the kitchen stove. Frequently he had to sweep out the snow that had sifted into the room from the too large cracks in the doors and windows.

He had to shovel a path to the woodpile, where he worked briskly to saw and split the stove wood that would be required throughout the day.

The kitchen was only sparsely furnished—a table, a few chairs, a stove, and a cupboard. Often Grey moved the table close to the stove. The room was a difficult one to keep warm.

He wrote on the table, seated on a kitchen chair. Frequently his hands became numb, and he would open the stove door to thaw them out. He spent long hours every day at his writing.

He wrote articles on hunting and fishing, stories on baseball. He drew heavily on his own experiences, on those of R. C.

—Reddy Gray, who spent the winters in his nearby home. If it had not been for loans from R. C., the entire Gray clan would have fared badly indeed during that winter.

Dolly's money was gone. She had given the last of it to finance Zane's trip to Arizona. Reddy's faith in the eventual success of his brother was as great as Dolly Grey's.

In the early spring Grey traveled to New York. The Outing Publishing Company, which published a sports magazine or two, had read the manuscript of *The Last of the Plainsmen* and wanted to talk to Grey about it.

The company had put out a few sporting books. They were willing to bring out *The Last of the Plainsmen*, but they believed that it would have only a modest sale. They could not pay the author for it.

The frustrations of this book had been too many. Most of all, Grey felt that he had let down his plainsman friend Buffalo Jones. Jones was an old man; he deserved to see this book about him in print.

Grey told the Outing Publishing Company that they could have the book. Perhaps it would go into a second printing, in which case Grey would receive a few dollars.

He returned to Lackawaxen. He took long walks in the woods. Sometimes he would go hunting and fishing with his brother.

Grey wrote every day. The sheets piled up; the manuscripts went out and came back. Once in a great while there was a small check. *Field & Stream* bought two articles from him in 1908, and *Everybody's Magazine* bought one. The checks were infinitesimally small. The family still had to depend on the loans from R. C.

Grey had sent several short stories to *The American Boy* in Detroit. The associate editor, Clarence Budington Kelland, had written him some encouraging letters. Kelland himself was at the beginning of his great writing career, at this time writing the famous Mark Tidd juvenile books that were serialized first in *The American Boy*.

Grey read these stories, thought he could write a serial

around baseball, which he certainly knew well enough. He wrote a long story, *The Short Stop*. Its hero was Chase Alloway, who played baseball in the Zanesville-Columbus region. One of the highlights of the story was when Alloway, playing as a "ringer," used his curve ball against a team with the same results as Zane Grey's own playing against the Jacktown team.

The American Boy rejected *The Short Stop*. Grey sent it to other juvenile magazines, but none seemed to want it. Late in the year, however, the book-publishing company A. C. McClurg of Chicago accepted it.

It was Zane Grey's first substantial sale. He had written four books previously. He had had to pay to have one of them published, had given another to a publisher, and the royalties of the other had been virtually nil. Now, at last, a publisher paid Zane Grey an advance on a book. It was not a great amount of money at the time, but it was the largest single check he had received in the six years since he had been a writer.

McClurg was essentially a reprint house, bringing out editions of books that had been first printed by other publishers. The only originals they published were juvenile books, which the company's sales force was well organized to sell. They had done very well with the Horatio Alger books. Since they reprinted books of other publishers and since Grey had now established a beachhead, it occurred to him that McClurg might be interested in reprinting *The Last of the Plainsmen*.

Outing agreed to give the plates to Grey for a very nominal sum, plus the first publishing rights to *The Last Trail*.

McClurg decided in favor of *The Last of the Plainsmen* and brought it out in a low-priced edition. It earned about two hundred dollars for Grey, as did *The Short Stop*, over and above the hundred-dollar advance.

Victory, final and sweeping victory, was only a short distance ahead. Grey sold five articles in 1909, and editors were becoming more friendly to him.

The editor of Street & Smith's *Popular Magazine* had almost bought a story from him. Zane Grey could virtually taste success. He had five of his books on his bookshelf, and soon there would be a sixth and a seventh.

He wrote another juvenile book, *The Young Forester*, and while he was working on it, he was laying out the plot of a novel of the West, his most ambitious work to date. He completed the juvenile and sent it to Harper rather than McClurg. Without pause he plunged into the big book. He had had this book in mind ever since 1907, when he had returned from his Arizona trip. It had seemed too ambitious a project at the time, especially after the resounding failure of *The Last of the Plainsmen*, but he knew that he was ready for it now, and the words streamed from his pen.

This was what he wanted to write, a romance of the far West. All that he wrote before had been the preparation—*Betty Zane, The Last of the Plainsmen*, the juveniles, the hunting and fishing articles. They had served their purpose by teaching him his craft.

In 1909 he was thirty-seven years old. It was time for his first *big* book.

He had learned much about the Mormons during the days with Buffalo Jones. He had absorbed the atmosphere of the Utah country, the philosophy of the hardy people who had accepted their faith, their way of life. He put it all down on paper. He wrote and he rewrote. The lessons he had had from Dolly in rhetoric and grammar stood him in good stead.

Dolly read the pages, made suggestions in structure. She did not criticize the story. She praised him continuously, told him that it was marvelous.

The manuscript grew. It was by far the longest that he had ever written. He was still working on it when Harper & Brothers accepted *The Young Forester* for their juvenile series of books. Grey took it in his stride. He was not even too elated when *Popular Magazine* accepted a short story that had been written for another magazine and had been making the rounds.

The long story was finally completed. Zane Grey knew that it was good. Dolly Grey knew it. The last thing he did on the book was to write a title page: *The Heritage of the Desert*, by Zane Grey.

Grey went to New York. The receptionist at Harper & Brothers knew him as the author of one of their juveniles to be published that fall. She sent in word to Ripley Hitchcock, and Grey was summoned into the chief editor's office.

Hitchcock remembered Grey and was courteous. Grey placed the heavy manuscript on the editor's desk and earnestly addressed him with the words he had rehearsed during the train ride: "Mr. Hitchcock, I know you are convinced that I cannot write fiction, but this is the type of book I have always wanted to write. I have worked harder on it than on any other book I have done. I believe it is a *good* book. I will never bother you again. I only ask as a personal favor that you read this manuscript yourself."

Hitchcock may have been persuaded by the author's earnestness, but he knew that the company had accepted a juvenile book by Grey, and he assured him that he would, indeed, read this book himself—and quickly.

Dolly Grey had painstakingly made a second copy of *The Heritage of the Desert*, and Grey now delivered this second copy to the editor of *Popular Magazine* at Street & Smith's. They had only recently bought the baseball story from him, and they promised to give the longer manuscript their serious consideration.

Grey went back to Lackawaxen. These were anxious days. Dolly Grey was pregnant. Their first child would soon be born, and the responsibility under which they already labored would become even greater.

The days passed, and a letter came from Hitchcock. As the fateful letter of two years ago, this also told nothing of the publisher's intentions. It was equally laconic: "Please drop into the office for the purpose of discussing your manuscript, *The Heritage of the Desert*."

Grey took the morning train to New York. A feeling of gloom hung heavy over him. Was this to be a repetition of the scene of two years ago? Was Ripley Hitchcock going to give him back the manuscript and again tell him that he could not write fiction?

No, he could not do that! Even if he did, it would merely mean that Hitchcock would be the loser. Grey had proved himself. The steel was in him now. He could no longer be discouraged. Hitchcock could not stop him more than momentarily.

Grey entered the office of Harper's executive editor. The broad smile on Hitchcock's face and the hearty handshake telegraphed the contents of Hitchcock's speech. "Grey," he said, "I've read *The Heritage of the Desert*. You've done it. You've made me eat my words. It's a fine novel, and here's the proof of it."

He picked up the famous blue contract that Grey was to become so familiar with through the years. He sat by the desk now and was so filled with emotion that he could scarcely write his name.

He was vindicated. So were Dolly and R. C., who had paid for his belief with hard cash.

When Grey left the office he went to the nearest telegraph office to send a telegram to Dolly. There was no telephone in the cottage at Lackawaxen, or he would have telephoned her. He should have waited another hour, for Grey decided to go over to the offices of Street & Smith, who published *Popular Magazine*. When he entered the editor's office he was greeted with: "I just wrote you yesterday that we were accepting *The Heritage of the Desert!*"

This was what he and Dolly had hoped for. He had conquered both citadels in a single day. He listened to the editor. "Our regular rate is one cent a word, and your story is at least a hundred thousand words in length, so we're going to mail you a check for one thousand dollars on Friday."

The restraint that had been hovering over the house on the Delaware was gone when Grey returned. The last lingering doubts of which no one spoke openly had been dispelled.

The house of Harper, which Grey had assailed since 1903, had been conquered. So had the formidable house of

Street & Smith. With a serial! From here on it would be smooth sailing.

CHAPTER **13** ═══════════════════════

The juvenile department of Harper's preferred that their juvenile books be issued in series, a custom established even before the Civil War. They wanted from four to six books based on the same characters. When one was published, they liked to announce the title of the next. Horatio Alger had thus written his books, as had Harry Castlemon.

Grey could write another Ken Ward book as soon as he wished. He preferred to get at another adult Western, but he had no plot in mind. He had thought so long, had worked so hard on *The Heritage of the Desert*, that he had given no thought to anything else.

A juvenile would be a good change of pace. He would have time to think of his next Western.

He launched into *The Young Lion Hunter*, again drawing upon his own experiences. He had already depicted his hunting experiences with Buffalo Jones, but that had been a factual biography. He could write a juvenile story about it, a fictional piece.

He completed the book, and galley proofs came from McClurg on *The Short Stop*. He read and corrected them with Dolly's excellent help.

The galleys arrived for *The Heritage of the Desert*. Harper's had scheduled it for early publication.

Grey pored over the galley proofs, and as he worked he felt even more certain that at last he had found his métier. Dolly was more quiet, thoughtful. She had a baby to take care of now. Her husband did not need her as much as before his vindication.

The Heritage of the Desert was published in September,

1910. It was a beautiful book; the illustrations were excellent. The book was priced at $1.35, an average price for the time.

The reviews in general were favorable, and the sales were brisk from the start. They passed the thirty-one thousand mark, and Zane Grey was elated.

The publication of *The Short Stop* a month later was almost an anticlimax. In its own field it received good reviews, but its sales were modest.

The Heritage of the Desert was the forerunner of all of Zane Grey's Western novels. In it he set the pattern that he was to follow for so many years. It is the story of John Hare, an Easterner, suffering from tuberculosis, who has gone West, hoping to cure his tuberculosis—or die. As the story opens, Hare, after wandering from village to village in southern Utah, has taken the wrong trail and has collapsed, suffering from his illness, from exhaustion, and from hunger and thirst.

He is found by the Mormon patriarch August Naab and some members of his family, which includes a half-Indian girl, Mescal, whom the patriarch has adopted and raised as a Mormon. Naab lives in a stronghold in the mountains; he has large herds of cattle and sheep, but his domain is being encroached upon by the Gentile cattleman-rustler Holderness, whose ally is the outlaw Dene.

Hare's wanderings have been noted by the outlaws, and he has become a marked man; he is known as "Dene's spy," and the outlaws believe him to be a spy for the government. They are determined to kill him, and soon Dene rides up and searches for Hare; Naab hides Hare and outwits Dene, but the outlaw vows that he will get Hare sooner or later, and Naab will suffer for it.

Naab nurses Hare to health, accepts him as a member of his family, and teaches him things about the West, the use of weapons, horsemanship, how to exist in the arid country. He sends him into a valley with Mescal to herd sheep. Slowly Hare recovers from his illness, becomes robust and educated in the ways of the West. He falls in love with Mescal and then learns that she has been pledged to become the second wife of August Naab's eldest son, the savage, wayward one of the family.

As the story progresses, the outlaws move in and steal openly from Naab, his waterholes, his cattle; they kill his sheep, but Naab's religion will not permit him to fight back. On the day of the wedding, Mescal flees, goes into the wilderness with her trusted Navajo aide. It causes the breaking-up of the wild Mormon son. He joins the outlaws openly and aids them in their depredations against his father.

After a long search for Mescal, Hare finds her, but by this time the climax has been reached in the affairs of the outlaws and August Naab. Naab's favorite son is killed by the outlaws, whose crimes against the Mormons in the country have become so widespread and savage that the Mormons must rise against them. Naab finally realizes that they must be exterminated, and in spite of the tenets of his church, knows that he must become the leader in the coming war. But Hare slips away, seeks out Holderness, and kills him, almost immediately after Holderness himself kills the eldest Naab son. The story ends with Hare marrying the girl, Mescal, and accepting a share of the Naab empire, where he will live out his life as a friend and "son" of the old Mormon patriarch.

The story has in it all of the elements for which Zane Grey became famous later, including a magnificent wild horse, Silvermane, who is caught and tamed and helps Hare and Mescal several times. The color and atmosphere are as beautifully drawn in this book as they were later in *Riders of the Purple Sage* and other Grey novels. It is as strongly pro-Mormon as some critics later said *Riders of the Purple Sage* was anti-Mormon. The writing is excellent, the dialogue is modern; reissued today, the book would be as up to date as any historical novel just written. It is to the credit of Ripley Hitchcock and the editors of Harper's that they recognized the excellence of this novel after having previously rejected four of Zane Grey's books. The story is so good, and in 1910 must have been so unusual and outstanding that it would have been an appalling error of judgment for an editor not to have recognized its merit. It is still one of the best novels of the West ever to be published.

Success wore well with Zane Grey. His immediate income was ample for his modest means, but he could not live on the juveniles alone. He had to start a new book, and he had only a vague idea of what he wanted to write. It would be a romance of the West, of course, but it had to be an entirely different story from *The Heritage of the Desert*. And it had to be *better*. Harper's would expect that—and so would the thousands of readers of *The Heritage of the Desert*. If it did not come up to the standard of his first important book, they would call him a one-book author. His third book would find the going very rough. Zane Grey knew that there *would* be a third book, a fourth, and many more.

He wrote some short stories for the McClure Syndicate. Baseball stuff. He got going on the third Ken Ward juvenile, *The Young Pitcher*. Once more he drew heavily on his own life, using in toto the potato-throwing incident from his early days at the University of Pennsylvania.

By the time he had completed *The Young Pitcher* he was ready for his next big book.

The background would be the wild southeastern corner of Utah, in the same general area in which he had placed *The Heritage of the Desert*. There would be Mormons in this one too. The Mormons he had met while with Buffalo Jones had been fine people, but he had heard things about them, how their faith in their beliefs was the dominant factor in their lives. That dedication to their church and its tenets had caused them to be driven from their original homes in Missouri and Illinois. It had set them against the United States government, forcing the government to send a great military expedition against them.

And the whole country knew of the Mountain Meadows Massacre. In 1857 a California-bound wagon train had taken the overland route across southern Utah. It had been attacked by Indians, then supposedly rescued by a detachment of militant Mormons known as the Avenging Angels. Every man, woman, and child had been brutally murdered by the Avenging Angels and their Indian allies. Seventeen years later the leader of the Avenging Angels had been executed by the United States government, but there had been a highly publicized trial before the execution, and to the average American citizen it seemed that the Mormon Church had been behind the Mountain Meadows Massacre.

The struggle of the Mormon Church to preserve its polygamy, later so well depicted by Zane Grey in *The Rainbow Trail,* had also done much to generate a national hostility against the Mormons.

Actually, Grey had respected Mormons highly since his acquaintance with them in 1907. He used Mormon characters frequently and always treated them with dignity.

In *Riders of the Purple Sage* he attacked the institution of polygamy and the blind faith in certain tenets of the church that had caused much of the trouble in the early frontier days. But there were good Mormons in the book as well as "bad." The heroine herself was a Mormon and did not lose her faith. She rebelled only against certain individual Mormons, who she believed had overstepped and distorted the principles of her religion.

Some readers of *Riders of the Purple Sage* thought that the book was a general attack on the Mormon Church itself, and they were afraid that it would offend the Mormon people. Opposed to the general theme of man's inhumanity to man was the universal theme of man's fight against the baser elements of man, the age-old instinct of man's struggle against nature and the elements; self-determination of the individual from which all progress in the world has sprung. The novel was, actually, a glorification of the Mormon struggle for existence against a hostile people and country. Their comparatively recent migration, involving incredible hardships, and their settlement in and conquest of a bleak and desolate land were a testimonial to their courage and faith.

Certain critics overlooked all of this and completely

ignored the fact that *Riders of the Purple Sage* was a magnificent epic story of a land, a people, a way of life. Read as entertainment alone, it is a powerful story against an awesome background, never depicted before and never again so well. Zane Grey's love of this country shows in every phrase of his description. His main characters are magnificently drawn. Almost "stealing the show" are the two horses, Black Star and Night. Zane Grey's admiration for these animals had no limit; over and over in later novels, notably *Wildfire*, he revealed his understanding of and fondness for the equine species.

As a study in human emotions, the novel is superb; judged strictly for action and violence alone, it has no peer.

The plot of *Riders of the Purple Sage* is a rather complex one. Jane Withersteen, twenty-eight, has inherited from her father the largest ranch in southeastern Utah. It includes most of the great valley, the hills and canyons, the town of Cottonwoods. She has also inherited her father's faith, a complete belief in the tenets of the Mormon Church.

Cottonwoods is a Mormon community. It was established by Jane's father in 1851, when Brigham Young sent legions of his people in all directions from the main settlement at Salt Lake. They were to settle any land in which they could possibly eke out a living. They were to grow and multiply, and plural marriage was not only encouraged but insisted upon. The Mormon Church had to become strong enough to resist the eventual encroachments of the Gentiles.

Jane Withersteen's father had found a giant spring in the arid country. It was the key to his later prosperity. He was a strong man, and he built well, basing his success upon the strength of his church.

He has now died, and Jane is still unmarried and a tempting prize to all Mormons, those who are single, those who are married.

Elder Tull, already married, would like to make her one of his multiple wives, but Jane, although a stout believer in the tenets of her church, has balked on that one single point:

she will not be the second, third, fourth, or fifth wife of any man. When she marries it will be for love only.

A few Gentiles have drifted into the community. They are outsiders and do not fare well against the combined hostility and pressure of the Mormons. Bern Venters, a young man from Illinois, has been in this country for eight years. He had his own small ranch for a while, but as a result of depredations committed against him by Mormons, he has lost his property and become a hired cowhand for Jane Withersteen.

He is attracted to her, and she to him; they even think they are in love, but this love is not a blind passion and may not be real. It is more sympathy for each other than actual love. Jane is being harried by Elder Tull; she needs a loyal man to work for her and defend her. Venters needs a strong protector.

In the opening scene, perhaps the greatest first chapter in any novel of the West, Elder Tull and six of his Mormon associates ride up to the ranch and demand of Jane that her Gentile hand be turned over to them for punishment. His attentions to Jane Withersteen have been noted by the Elder, and the decision has been reached to drive the man from the country. Since he has refused to leave of his own accord, the Mormons are now going to whip him and drive him off forcibly.

The whipping, according to Mormon custom, will be a savage one, delivered with rawhide whips that will leave Venters a mass of raw flesh. He may not survive it, especially if he is driven into the desert without treatment.

Venters is unarmed. He has given his guns to Jane so that he will not use them against the Mormons under provocation. He is seized and bound, and in his agony Venters warns the Mormons that they may make another Lassiter of him, a man more dreaded by the Mormons than the Devil himself.

The lashing is about to commence when a rider is sighted bearing swiftly down on the ranch headquarters. The lathered horse comes up panting, and the rider dismounts and asks Jane if he can water his horse. He wants nothing for himself, will not ask for water for himself, just for his horse. Jane grants it, of course, and the rider sizes up the situation. Elder Tull blusters and tells the man to ride on, that none of this concerns him.

The new arrival makes no attempt to conceal his contempt or hostility for these people, and the Mormons, gaunt, hard-bitten men, show their belligerence toward the new arrival. They have noted the two guns slung low on his thighs, but they have guns themselves, and they are seven to one.

Tull snarls that the Gentile Venters must leave this ranch, this country. The stranger bluntly tells the Elder: "Mormon, the young man stays."

The Mormons reach for their guns and begin to converge upon the new arrival. The stranger goes into a gunfighter's crouch, and Venters cries out: "*Lassiter!*"

The hands of the Mormons, already touching their weapons, freeze into immobility. A stunned silence falls upon the group. The name of Lassiter is known throughout the Mormon country; he is a legendary will-o'-the-wisp who appears here and there, kills, then disappears into the wild country. His special, and only, targets are Mormons.

Elder Tull finally moves. He turns, reels toward his horse, and mounting, rides off. He is swiftly followed by the other Mormons.

The dreaded mysterious gunfighter, whose name is a legend, has become the leading man of a thousand Western novels, but it was Zane Grey who first used him so well in *Riders of the Purple Sage*, and he wrote his scene and depicted his character so well that no one has been able to better it through the succeeding years.

Thwarted by the presence of Lassiter, Elder Tull uses his influence with the Mormons, with the church. He appeals to Bishop Dyer, the elder statesman of the church. Dyer visits Jane. He was a close friend of her father's. Together they founded and opened up this far outpost of the Mormon Church. Dyer chides Jane, tells her it is her duty to marry and procreate for the faith. Elder Tull is a staunch pillar of the church. He will make Jane the foremost of his wives.

The matter is unresolved. Elder Tull's pressure grows. Jane's hands, threatened, leave the ranch. Her women will no longer work for her. Her herds disappear. Only Venters and Lassiter remain on the ranch to take care of the dwindling herds. Away from the ranch, Venters and Lassiter have a talk, and part of Lassiter's past is revealed. He had been a Ranger in Texas when his sister, married to his best friend, Frank Erne, had met a proselyting Mormon, who had in the end forced Milly Erne to go with him, even though she had already borne a child to Frank Erne.

Lassiter started out on the search to find his sister, return her and her child to her rightful husband, Erne. The pursuit led into the Mormon country, where all lips were sealed, where all hands were against Lassiter. He refused to give up the search, and the years rolled by. By a process of elimination he had finally come to believe that the end of the trail would be at Cottonwoods.

Venters quickly verifies Lassiter's belief. He had actually known Milly Erne. She had been befriended by Jane Withersteen. But the name of the man who had brought her here, the man whose forced mistress she had been—that remains a secret. Milly had turned against the Mormons, against the man who had forced her into her captivity. In retaliation her child had been stolen from her . . . and then Milly had withered away and died. Only Jane Withersteen knew where her grave was. Jane, too, knew the name of the man who had ruined Milly, but she will not tell.

Lassiter prevails upon Jane to show him his sister's unmarked grave, but that is as far as she will go. She will not, cannot, reveal the name of the man Lassiter has been seeking so long, whom he will surely kill when he finds him.

Venters trails the stolen herd of Withersteen cattle. He finds that the Mormons are in league with the notorious bandit and outlaw Oldring, whose name has become a scourge on the border. With Oldring always is a younger, masked bandit, who is even more feared than Oldring himself.

Venters comes across the Masked Rider, shoots him, then discovers that the masked one is actually a girl, Oldring's daughter, Bess. She is badly wounded, and Venters cannot leave her. He finds a landlocked valley, reached only by ancient steps carved in the rock by prehistoric Indians. At the top of the steps is an enormous rock, worn away by erosion of the winds and sands through the centuries, so that it actually balances on a tiny perch. He tries his strength against the rock, moves it, and realizes that a strong man can roll it down the slope—although the rolling of it will destroy the only access to the valley and lock up whoever is in it forever.

There is game in the tiny valley, grass, a stream. A person could live there for years.

Venters moves Bess Oldring into a cave in the valley, nurses her, and falls in love with her. She returns the love.

Already introduced are the two magnificent horses of Jane Withersteen, Black Star and Night. They are Jane's greatest love, and under the hands of Zane Grey, who loved horses more than any other animals, these noble steeds become alive. When everything else has been stolen from Jane, she still retains these closely guarded animals. And then they are stolen by Jerry Card, the finest horseman among the Mormons.

Jerry Card gets the two horses into the valley controlled by Oldring and is spotted by Venters, who is riding his huge, half-wild horse, Wrangle, who can run down any creature on four legs.

There now ensues the most magnificent race ever portrayed in any novel of the West, Venters astride Wrangle and Jerry Card riding one of the horses, leading the other. The race is a long, killing one. Venters knows that the stamina of his huge wild mount will kill the two race horses, and eventually he does almost that. Jerry Card, the great rider, moves from one horse to the other, but he cannot elude Wrangle and the determined Venters.

Jane Witheersteen is at the end of her tether. Her ranch has been denuded of livestock. A woman she has befriended is dying, and Jane takes her seven-year-old daughter, Fay, to live with her. The woman dies, the last friend Jane has. The Mormons are closing the noose about her, now boldly led by Bishop Dyer, with the villainous Elder Tull the activist.

In a poignant scene between Lassiter and Jane, when they are ready to flee the ranch, Jane reveals that it was her father who years ago was the proselyting Mormon who had stolen Milly Erne from her husband—at the behest of the man who is now Bishop Dyer, who had seen Milly Erne and fallen in love with her. Her father was as guilty as Bishop Dyer, she declares, but it is Bishop Dyer who ruined and punished Lassiter's sister—by having her daughter abducted and given to the outlaw Oldring to live a life of baseness. Oldring had actually tried to protect his ward and had incurred the enmity of the Bishop because of it.

Lassiter must now kill Bishop Dyer. It is the inevitable end. He goes to the Bishop's church and before the entire congregation kills him brutally, shooting first one kneecap, then the other, one elbow, then the other, and finally sending a bullet through the Bishop's skull.

Lassiter is only moments ahead of the pursuing Mormon posse. He makes his getaway with Jane, knowing that neither one can ever return to Cottonwoods.

Along the trail they encounter Venters and Bess, now recovered enough to escape from the valley. Astride the fleet horses, Black Star and Night, they know that they can outrun any Mormon posse. Lassiter tells Venters and his newfound niece, Bess, that he can look out for Jane and little Fay. It is up to Venters and the girl to make their getaway and go to Illinois, where Venters has a family, never to return to this bleak land.

The young couple go off, and Lassiter starts with Fay and Jane for the hidden valley. They are pursued up the trail by the Mormon posse, headed by Elder Tull. When they reach the top of it, Lassiter is faced with a fearful decision. He cannot withstand the large posse. They will kill him and take Jane into a life worse than death. Lassiter, however, can roll down the rock, kill the vengeful pursuers . . . and doom himself and his party to eternal captivity in the valley.

Jane makes the decision: *"Roll the rock, Lassiter!"*

The Mormons are coming close. Lassiter still hesitates. Again Jane beseeches him to roll the rock. He does. The Mormons are killed, and Lassiter, Jane, and Fay go into the valley to remain there forever, an idyllic existence in a Utopia of their own, but cut off forever from other human life.

Like the magnificent opening chapter of *Riders of the Purple Sage*, this final chapter is one of the greatest chapters of any adventure novel ever published.

The book itself, with its plot and subplots, is a fine one. The writing, especially the scenes with the horses and the descriptions of the bleak country, is superb.

Zane Grey in this book used some of the dialect for which he was later frequently condemned by many critics, but it is not so broad as it became later, and it helps here to give an authentic flavor to the Western characters. Jane and Lassiter both speak as educated people, however. Only the other characters fall into dialect.

All of the characters are superbly drawn, even to Jerry Card, who speaks less than a half-dozen sentences in the novel but is a memorable character because of his magnificent horsemanship. He is described as a froglike man, and when he is pursued by Venters, that is the only way you can recall him—a human frog astride a horse.

Riders of the Purple Sage well deserves the accolade it has received through the years, "the best Western novel ever published."

CHAPTER **14** ═══════════════════════════════

When Zane Grey had completed *Riders of the Purple Sage* he felt that he had given everything to it of which he was capable. He was physically exhausted and emotionally drained.

Dolly Grey had read the story during its creation. She read it page by page, scene by scene. She corrected minor errors in grammar and punctuation. She reread the chapters, and when the novel was completed she read it again in its entirety, slowly, carefully. When she came to the final page, a feeling of rapture and awe swept over her. She thought that *Riders of the Purple Sage* was the finest novel she had ever read by anyone, and she knew that it was not just because of her closeness to the author.

It was, in Dolly Grey's opinion, a masterpiece. She told her husband so.

And then it began—all over. Zane Grey delivered the manuscript to Ripley Hitchcock at Harper's. Their relations had become very warm. Hitchcock had liked *The Heritage of the Desert*, and its sales had been gratifying. Besides, the juvenile department had now published three of Grey's books and were loud in their praise of him.

The firm of Harper & Brothers was friendly and receptive to any new offering by Zane Grey. Grey himself had no qualms about *Riders of the Purple Sage*. If *The Heritage of the Desert* was a successful book, this one should be twice as successful.

Grey left the manuscript with Ripley Hitchcock and made the trip downtown to the Frank A. Munsey Company. Bob Davis had written him a letter after the publication of *The Heritage of the Desert*. Grey had met him on numerous trips downtown before, when he submitted his short stories and articles.

Bob Davis was at the height of his fame. He was the best-known, the shrewdest of all magazine editors. He was ever on

the alert to discover new talent, and when he found one, he
aided and encouraged him. He had done much to develop O.
Henry. He had published *The Circular Staircase* by Mary
Roberts Rinehart, which had catapulted her to fame.

He had been watching Zane Grey. He had read his short
material and had seen promise. That promise had been ful-
filled in *The Heritage of the Desert*. He had written, asking
to see Grey's next novel, with a view to serializing it in one of
the Munsey magazines.

Dolly Grey had made a copy of *Riders of the Purple Sage*.
Grey gave it to Davis, and the editor was delighted. He would
read it himself immediately.

Grey remained in New York. Ripley Hitchcock had also
promised to give him a speedy report.

The call from Munsey's came first. Bob Davis was profuse
in his praise of *Riders of the Purple Sage*. It was a spendid
work, a greater novel even than *The Heritage of the Desert*.
But—Davis was afraid to publish it. His magazines had a
wide circulation. Thousands of Mormons subscribed to them
or purchased copies on the newsstands. They would be of-
fended by the story and possibly boycott the Munsey magazines in general.

The feudal lord, Frank A. Munsey, was still ruling his
domain with an iron fist, and he was not too busy with his
newspapers and trying to help Teddy Roosevelt establish the
Bull Moose party to neglect the reading of the monthly financial statements of his magazines. If there were a sudden drop
in the sales of one of them, the luckless editor would be
summoned to the throne room and dressed down with the acid
tones for which Munsey was famous.

However, Bob Davis was sure that another magazine would
welcome the novel and he dashed off a letter, which he gave
to Grey.

Grey kept the letter in his pocket and delivered the manuscript to Street & Smith's *Popular Magazine*, which had serialized *The Heritage of the Desert*. He should have taken
Riders of the Purple Sage there in the first place.

Within a day or two Grey received the phone call from Ripley Hitchcock. When he entered Hitchcock's office, it was like a plunge into a polar sea. Ripley Hitchcock was profuse in his praise of *Riders of the Purple Sage*. It was a better novel than *The Heritage of the Desert*, but he did not think that Harper's should publish it. It would be offensive to too many people, not just Mormons, but to broadminded people who did not believe it was wise to criticize any one denomination or religious belief.

However, Hitchcock intended to be fair about it. He would not be adamant. Even though he was the senior editor of Harper's, there were others on the staff who should have an opportunity to give their views. If the consensus was in favor of it, Harper's might still publish it. Give them a few weeks.

The black days had returned. When Zane Grey had already tasted the sweet fruits of victory, the final triumph was about to be snatched from him. He had to go home and learn, all over again, to live with adversity.

Gloom hung over the cottage on the Delaware River. Grey could not write. He had to start all over again, come up with an entirely new book that would pick up where *The Heritage of the Desert* had left off. Could he do it, knowing that his hardest work, his magnificent effort, had just gone for naught?

Dolly Grey suggested a trip, another visit to the Southwest with which he had fallen so deeply in love. It would clear her husband's mind of its doubts; it would renew his inspiration.

The suggestion fell upon receptive ears, but in the end Zane Grey decided upon a change of locale. Harper's had asked him for a fourth Ken Ward book, and he had been thinking of a new setting for this one. The trip would give him the background for it.

In a few weeks Harper's would have the final word on *Riders of the Purple Sage*. Whatever the result, Grey would then be able to cope with the problem of the next novel, and he would have the juvenile book out of the way.

CHAPTER **15** ───────────────────────

As an avid reader of all the fishing magazines,
Zane Grey was aware of the best places for
every kind of fish. Chiefly a freshwater fisherman, he had long
had an ambition to try his luck at tarpon fishing, but these
lived only in the great saltwater seas. From correspondence
with fishing-magazine editors, readers of the magazines, and
contributors, Grey had formed the opinion that there were
four areas in the Western Hemisphere where the great tarpon
could be found: off the coast of Nova Scotia, along the Florida
keys, off southern California, and in the warm waters of the
Gulf of Mexico, near Tampico. The fish moved, however;
although fishing for them at one spot was excellent at a certain time of the year, it was not good at another time.

The season for tarpon was now in full swing at Tampico,
in Mexico. He decided to go there, but because he wanted to
see the Southwest again, he took the train to Arizona. He
stopped off at Flagstaff and went on a short trip with the
famous guide Al Doyle.

Returning to Flagstaff, he boarded a train for Douglas,
Arizona, and crossing the border to Agua Prieta, of which he
was to write later, he boarded a Mexican Central train. After
a brief pause in Mexico City he embarked on another train
for the seaport of Tampico.

He watched the barren wastes of yucca and rocks on the
long trip from the American border turn into the fresh and
green forests of the tropical jungles. Near the base of a tower-
ing mountain he saw a deep canyon and caught a glimpse of
Micas Falls, more beautiful than any he had ever seen.

At a little station called Valles the train crossed the river,
and Grey learned from a native that this was the Santa Rosa
River, whose origin was unknown. Much of this country
was unexplored.

Before he reached Tampico, Grey had made up his mind to learn more about this unknown river.

At Tampico Grey was in his element. There were hotels along the wharves in which virtually all the guests were fishing enthusiasts who had come here from countries thousands of miles away. The tarpon season was on, and the talk at the hotels and docks was of fish and fishing. A few of the enthusiasts were men whose reputations as fishermen Grey was familiar with. He had corresponded with some of them.

He could have gone tarpon fishing with others, and from watching them he could have learned the ways of the big-game fish. But he had read so much about tarpon that he thought he could manage by himself. Besides, he did not want to reveal his ineptness to other fishermen.

He engaged a Mexican Indian who had a small boat that had to be rowed. They went back and forth across the mouth of the Panuco River, Grey trolling all the time. For hours he saw no signs of the big fish, but when the tide began to come in the tarpon began to splash, to roll. The rolling indicated that they were not hungry and would take no bait.

They went ashore and ate their lunch, then suddenly saw a school of tarpon feeding on a huge school of mullet that had been cut off from their river haunts.

Grey and his guide quickly boarded the little boat and went out toward the tarpon. A sudden strike was made by a big fish, and when Grey was pulled up from his seat he knew that the things he had read about tarpon were all too true. The fish made five great leaps out of the water. He seemed to stand on his tail, on his head; he dived to the bottom and reappeared covered with mud.

The tarpon pulled the boat clear of the river, then returned. The fight went on for more than an hour; then Grey began to reel in the fish. He was a seven-foot giant, and Grey pulled him along to the shore. Then the tarpon gave a gasp and a huge lunge that carried him back into the water and to freedom.

Grey had lost his first tarpon.

He was soon to land one, however. Gradually he learned the art of tarpon fishing. He had first learned his fishing lore in the streams and ponds near his Zanesville, Ohio, home. He had learned patience from the best fisherman he had known as a boy, Old Muddy Miser.

Grey wrote of his failure on his first tarpon-fishing day in an article, which he sold to a magazine. He was soon to have another experience that he also wrote about.

Grey had heard much about the mysterious Santa Rosa River. Indians of the interior told of the waterfalls on it, which were a barrier to navigation.

It was the sort of adventure that appealed to Zane Grey, a search into the unknown. He wanted a companion and questioned many of his new-made friends. They had heard of the Santa Rosa River and wanted no part of it.

By chance he encountered a young man named George Allen, an American who had been two years at Tampico in the employ of a railroad company. Allen had a vacation coming, and the Santa Rosa exploration project appealed to him.

They needed an expert canoeman, and it had to be an Indian who could speak the languages of the interior. Pepe was mentioned by one of the boatmen in the region; he was currently out of favor because of his excessive craving for the native pulque. Pepe's wife and children were in dire need, and influenced by this, Grey offered Pepe three times the ordinary wage on condition that he promise to remain sober.

Pepe called upon all the saints he could name as witness that he had tasted the last pulque.

Grey bought guns and ammunition, tents and blankets, utensils, provisions, everything that would be needed on a jungle trip. He found a boat that he believed would fill their needs.

Everything was shipped by train to a village upriver, from which the expedition would take off. Grey, Allen, and Pepe rode the rickety cars to the village.

Then began the most arduous trip Grey had ever embarked upon. The river was a roaring torrent, the reason for which was soon learned. It consisted of a series of rapids and waterfalls. They forced their way through some of the rapids, pulled the boat through more difficult ones. When they reached a waterfall, they had to unload the boat and carry the contents above the falls, then go back and carry the boat. Frequently there was a second waterfall only a half-mile or a mile beyond, and the process would have to be repeated.

Zane Grey related it all in *Ken Ward in the Jungle*. In it he became the youthful Ken Ward, his companion, George Allen, became George Alling, Ken Ward's friend who shared the adventure.

They encountered the wild boar of the jungle, snakes ten feet long, the deadly jaguar, but their biggest problem was an insect tick which buried its head in the skin of the adventurers and could be removed only by putting a lighted cigarette to the insect. Zane Grey, who did not ordinarily smoke, was glad to accept cigarillos from Pepe, the guide, and he puffed on them to keep the fire going.

Years later Grey told of the expedition in detail in "Down an Unknown Jungle River," a feature of the large illustrated edition of *Tales of Southern Rivers*. This was the true account of the fictional *Ken Ward in the Jungle*.

CHAPTER **16**

Zane Grey returned to Lackawaxen refreshed and invigorated. He had made copious notes in Mexico and was already hard at work on his fourth juvenile book.

Bad news awaited him at home. Harper's, after several readings, had decided against *Riders of the Purple Sage*. The second copy of the story had been rejected by *Popular Magazine*. Dolly had mailed it to a third magazine, which had also rejected it.

Grey was not satisfied, and barely pausing in Lackawaxen, he went off to New York. This time he went over Ripley Hitchcock's head to Mr. Duneka, the vice-president and executive officer of Harper's.

Bluntly, Grey asked him if he had read *Riders of the Purple Sage*. Duneka said that he had not, but he had read the reports of several of the readers and editors. They were unanimous in their opinion not to publish it.

Grey pleaded with Duneka that he read it himself. He did not want to go to another publisher with the book. The company had done well with his first novel and had published three of his juveniles. He was writing a fourth even now.

The vice-president promised to read the book. Grey took a second copy to a fourth magazine editor. He returned to Lackawaxen, but within a week he was back in New York. Mr. Duneka had promised him a fast reading.

He went into the vice-president's office, and Duneka greeted him warmly. He had read *Riders of the Purple Sage*, and so had his wife. Both of them considered it one of the greatest reading pleasures of their lives. Harper's would publish the book, and would give it all the promotion that such a fine novel demanded.

Ripley Hitchcock did not complain because Grey had gone over his head. He had himself liked the novel. It was merely a question of policy, but if Mr. Duneka was willing to accept that responsibility, it was all right with Hitchcock.

From that day Hitchcock never wavered in his support of Grey. Zane Grey could do no wrong.

Back in Lackawaxen, Grey completed *Ken Ward in the Jungle* and began to think of his next adult book for Harper's.

The money from *The Heritage of the Desert* was gone. The smaller amounts from the juvenile books were not enough to support the family. Their second child was expected in the spring.

The long-awaited day in 1912 finally came—publication day of *Riders of the Purple Sage*. The New York bookstores had huge stacks of them. The book sold briskly at once and

was talked about everywhere. Soon there was a stampede
for it.

The reviews were excellent; many of them would now be
called "rave." Criticism of the subject matter was minimal.
The book's impact on the publishing world was tremendous,
but it was the readers themselves who talked it up—and made
it the most successful Western novel ever published.

CHAPTER **17** ══════════════════════

The Western story has had a long and honor-
able history. Its origin cannot be dated with
calendar precision. You could make a case for James Fenimore
Cooper's Leatherstocking Tales as being the first Westerns.

Certainly they were stories of the West—the West as it
was in the early eighteenth century. The western New York
locale was not as remote to the early readers of Cooper as the
great American West is to the devotee of the Western story
circa 1969.

James Fenimore Cooper had gone to England to become
the darling of the tea-and-crumpet set when another American
took up the burden and thrilled and horrified his readers with
tales of hard fighting, riding, and deeds of derring-do, set
against the wild frontiers of Kentucky and Missouri.

This scribe was Joseph Holt Ingraham, and he was
prodigious indeed with his pen all through the 1830's, and
1840's, and into the 1850's. Then he "got religion," and handing
his steel pen to his son, ascended the pulpit to become a
preacher.

The son of Joseph Holt Ingraham, writing as "Colonel"
Prentiss Ingraham, outdid his sire in volume as well as in
violence. The dime novel came into existence in 1860, and
Colonel Ingraham was one of the foremost dime-novel writers for four decades.

Ingraham was rivaled only by "Colonel" E. C. Z. Judson,

who wrote chiefly under the pseudonym of Ned Buntline and glorified and made famous Buffalo Bill, Wild Bill Hickok, Wyatt Earp, and other brawny lads of the 1870's and 1880's; and while Buntline was making these frontiersmen famous, he was, as Colonel Judson, living a life of his own that made the adventures of his heroes seem like ladyfingers with tea and milk.

As a midshipman in the U.S. Navy, Judson fought seven duels. That he won them all is attested by the fact that he continued among the living, for the duels were fought with pistols at twenty paces.

He was also the only literary figure ever to have been lynched. In 1849, while publishing his own magazine in Nashville, Tennessee, he was lynched by a mob and left hanging from a lamppost. Friends cut him down before life expired totally. The lynching mob had been led by the husband of the lady with whom Judson had carried on a clandestine affair.

After his flight from Nashville, Judson made his way to New York, where he organized the Know-Nothing political party, which carried two states in the national elections in 1856.

Judson spent most of the Civil War in a New York City prison because of his subversive activities. He was accused of being a Copperhead and, worse, was embroiled in the antidraft riots. His rioting proclivities continued after the war, when he was the leader of an anti-British mob that stormed a theater where a British production was being given. A number of persons were killed in this riot, but Judson escaped serious punishment.

The exploits of Buffalo Bill, Wild Bill Hickok, Texas Jack, Deadwood Dick, and other dime-novel heroes entertained millions of readers into the 1890's, when the dime novel became more frankly juvenile than in the preceding decades. Frank Merriwell and the younger heroes took over, and the dime novels began to taper off in the early 1900's. For four decades they had kept alive the Western story.

In 1902 a new type of Western was published. It exploded

on the American literary scene with the power of an atomic bomb.

This was *The Virginian*, written by an Easterner whose entire Western experience consisted of a few trips to Wyoming and Idaho. He was a close personal friend of Theodore Roosevelt, and the President, always an advocate of the outdoor life, "plugged" the book on numerous occasions, which certainly helped its sales.

The Virginian was the number-one best-seller of 1902, and the fame of its author, Owen Wister, is still ringing down the twentieth century. Wister wrote other novels, including *Lady Baltimore*, which was the number-two best-seller of 1908, but only *The Virginian* has endured.

The Virginian brought the Western story from the woodshed into the parlor, and the form sprang back into greater popularity than ever. Every writer in the country who had seen a horse was soon writing Westerns, but during the next decade none came within a lariat's throw of *The Virginian*.

William MacLeod Raine, a Denver-transplanted young Englishman, was publishing Western novels in 1905. He wrote more than a hundred books during the next fifty years, but was better known for quantity than quality. His books had only modest sales and never approached best-seller status.

A young man in Brooklyn, Clarence E. Mulford, published a book in 1907, *Bar 20*, that sold very well, and his succeeding novels enjoyed considerable popularity. In later years the Hopalong Cassidy motion pictures, based on his books, were popular; subsequently shown on television, they were a sensation with young children.

A woman in North Dakota, hiding behind the masculine initials of B. M. (*B* for Bertha) Bower had a considerable success with her Chip of the Flying U stories, but these were overshadowed by the spectacular success of Zane Grey.

If *The Virginian* was a five-megaton bomb, then *Riders of the Purple Sage* had a fifty-megaton impact. When Grey continued with *Desert Gold*, *Wildfire*, and *The U.P. Trail*, all best-sellers, the Western story rose to its greatest heights.

When Zane Grey had become a household name, publishers sent out the word, "Let's find another Zane Grey." Everybody was writing Westerns; all the publishers were publishing Westerns. The pulp magazines had come into a flourishing existence, and magazines like *Western Story* and *Argosy* exerted themselves to find a potential Zane Grey and develop him.

The Munsey editor Bob Davis published some of Zane Grey's serials, although he had rejected *Riders of the Purple Sage*, but when Grey began selling his serials to higher-paying magazines, Davis looked for a writer to take his place.

In 1917 a very lean and hungry young man of twenty-five was living in a cold-water flat with two friends. He was writing poetry but not selling it.

Tired of eating only beans, the young writer, Frederick S. Faust, wrote a short story. He sent it to Davis, who bought it. Faust wrote another story, and Davis bought it and summoned the author to his office.

Davis told Faust of the tremendous popularity of Zane Grey. He was frank in admitting that he was looking for "another Zane Grey." He gave Faust a copy of *Riders of the Purple Sage* and urged him to read it and then try to write a Western novel in a similar vein.

Faust wrote a novel in less than ten days and submitted it to Davis. It was titled *The Untamed*. Davis read it and sent for Faust.

"This is it," he told the young writer. "I think you can be the new Zane Grey." Musing aloud, he thought that Frederick Schiller Faust was too German (it was during World War I), too literary a name. "What you ought to have is a short, easy-to-remember name, with a Western flavor to it."

"Max Brand" was thus born.

Faust was launched on his fabulous career, and in the next twenty-seven years he wrote more than twenty-five million words, perhaps more words than were ever written by any other writer. He published, under fourteen pseudonyms, well over two hundred novels and a considerable amount of shorter material. He was a pulp-magazine writer, known in his heyday as the King of the Pulps. A vast amount of his material appeared in Street & Smith's *Western Story* magazine, but he was a regular contributor to *Argosy* and virtually all of the magazines that were willing to pay his high word rate. For twelve years he lived in Italy and ground out his Western stories. Born in Seattle and raised in central California, where he graduated from the University of California at Berkeley, he was, however, decidedly not a Westerner. He never explored the West, he did not ride horses, he had no interest in the West whatever.

The West of which Max Brand and his numerous pseudonyms wrote was a fantasy West, "a Max Brand Western world." His characters were as fantastic as his West, but he was a beautiful, sensitive writer, and his myriad of fans preferred him to all other writers.

Since his untimely death as a war correspondent in 1944, a cult has sprung up around Max Brand. There are Faust fan clubs, Faust fan magazines, Faust collectors.

A scholar all of his life, Faust's specialty was the Italian Renaissance period. He made his living from writing Western stories, but his name became well known in another field entirely. One of his side products featured a character called Dr. Kildare, who became famous in motion pictures and later on television.

More than 170 of Faust's magazine serials have been printed in hardcover books. The sales have been modest, seldom exceeding twenty thousand copies. In paperback editions they have fared better. His production was vastly greater than that of Zane Grey, but his sales and popularity never reached that of the man he had tried to imitate with his first novel.

In 1917 Ernest Haycox, a youth of eighteen, was preparing to enter the University of Oregon. He had already made up his mind to become a writer. He studied journalism, worked for a short period on a Portland newspaper, and began writing short stories, sea stories, Revolutionary War stories, anything that he thought or hoped he could sell. He was not very successful, but he began to read some of the Zane Grey and Max Brand books and tried a Western or two. He sold them and wrote more and more Westerns. He moved to New York to be closer to his markets, and soon he was the sensation of the Western pulp magazines. His stories were more adult than the average pulp Western.

A short, slight man, he never thought of himself as a Westerner, but he realized the vast potentials of this field and determined to make himself an authority on the subject. He read every book he could find on the West, factual books, histories, books on Indians and gunfighters, on the flora and fauna of the West. He became an expert in Western history and Western lore, and it began to show in his writings. He married a young artist then living in New York whom he had met at school in Oregon, and with his future well established in the pulp magazines, he moved back to Portland, Oregon. His pulp serials were issued as hardcover books. They received excellent reviews, and soon Haycox was selling his stories to the smooth-paper magazines. He wrote twenty-four novels in his short writing career (he died in 1950, at age fifty-one), but he produced almost two hundred short stories, most of which appeared in *Collier's*, *The Saturday Evening Post*, and other magazines of that class. He received as much as five thousand dollars for a short story and thirty thousand dollars for magazine serials.

He was probably the best Western *writer* of all. His prose was sparse and beautiful. His pages rang with authenticity. As a craftsman he was greatly admired and imitated by his fellow writers.

The sales of Ernest Haycox's books never reached the astronomical figures of those of Zane Grey. He was never as popular with the masses, but if one had to name a Big Three of the Western story, they would have to be Zane Grey, Max Brand, and Ernest Haycox.

Alan LeMay had been writing for the pulps in the late twenties. He was an excellent writer and highly regarded. He went on to the slicks in the early thirties, but then Hollywood called him, and he spent most of the rest of his life doing scenarios for motion pictures, although later he returned to his first love and wrote two memorable Westerns, *The Searchers* and *The Unforgiven*.

A new name began to appear in the pulp magazines in the middle thirties, Luke Short, an Illinoisan by birth. He chose the name of a frontier gambler and gunfighter as a pseudonym; his real name was Frederick Glidden. He was a fine writer, and his stories and books were popular. He has continued through the years and has racked up a reputation as an excellent craftsman.

During the heyday of the pulp magazines in the 1920's and 1930's a vast number of writers appeared in the magazines who had varying success. Some left their mark and went on to books and other fields. Some remained in the pulps, contributed to the growth of the Westerns, but never really hit the top rungs. Among them were fine craftsmen such as H. Bedford Jones, Jackson Gregory, Stephen Payne, S. Omar Barker, William Colt MacDonald, Frank C. Robertson, W. C. Tuttle, Walt Coburn, Harry F. Olmsted, Charles Alden Seltzer, Kenneth Perkins, Gordon Young, and Johnston McCulley.

Came the Depression, and the pulps shuddered and gasped, and many of them expired. New publishers entered the field; there were new editors and lower word rates. A new type of Western story came into existence, a more realistic, modern Western, although it still had to retain the flavor and the events of the Old West. Better writing was required by the magazines. The basic word rate was one cent per word, and only a very few of the better names received more than that. Competition was keener than it had ever been, and many writers of the 1920's were pinched out.

By the late 1930's things had been pretty well sifted out, and the new luminaries of the Western story were firmly established. Among these now were Luke Short; his brother Jonathan, writing under the name Peter Dawson; Thomas Thompson; Dwight Newton; Jack Schaefer; Tom Blackburn; Les Savage, Jr.; Steve Frazee; the brother team of John and Ward Hawkins; W. T. Ballard; and Harry Sinclair Drago.

Then came the paperback.

A man named Robert deGraff issued a modest line of little books in 1939 that were beautifully printed and had laminated covers. They were sold for twenty-five cents, a fairly high price at a time when *The Saturday Evening Post* was still selling for five cents and the average pulp magazine, much thicker and larger, sold for ten or fifteen cents.

DeGraff brought out only fifty thousand copies of a title. The books sold well, and he issued them in hundred-thousand editions. At the beginning his list was top-heavy with mystery novels, but he tried a few Westerns by Zane Grey, Ernest Haycox, and Max Brand. They sold almost as well as the mysteries.

Soon there were a number of imitators, chief among them the books put out by Ian Ballantine, who came from England and established the American editions of Penguin Books, already a flourishing item in the British Isles.

The war came, and paper quotas were rigidly enforced. Paperback editions of a hundred thousand copies were published and were sellouts. The established pulp magazines were sellouts throughout the war, but there were few innovations in publishing, except that the government established a publishing unit that printed small paperback books of popular authors to be given free to the armed forces.

The moment the war ended, paper quotas were lifted, and the paperback business exploded. Editions of two hundred and fifty thousand and more were quick sellouts. Bantam Books was established in 1945, Penguin Books had become the New American Library of World Literature.

Mystery novels were enormous sellers, but the publishers began to scrape the bottom of the mystery barrels and were compelled to try some Westerns. They found that Westerns sold as well as mysteries and were soon outselling them.

The new Western boom was on, and it was very, very big.

A brand new crop of Western writers made their appearance. Some were holdovers from the pulps, although some of the better-known names from the pulps failed miserably in the new paperback field.

Will Henry and Clay Fisher (both pseudonyms of Henry S. Allen) were new names, as were Wayne D. Overholser, Lewis S. Patten, Nelson C. Nye, Noel M. Loomis, William R. Cox, Louis L'Amour, Bill Gulick, and Sam Peeples.

Writers who had written for the pulps for one cent a word and had had hardcover Western books published in the 1930's for from one hundred and fifty to four hundred dollars were now writing paperback Westerns and earning between two and five thousand dollars per book.

Hollywood rediscovered the Westerns and began to push them out in ever-increasing numbers. The Western story reached its apogee in 1958, when one-third of all the feature motion pictures were Westerns, when there were thirty-seven Western television series on the air, when paperbacks sold three hundred million copies—one hundred and ten million of them Westerns.

The American public became surfeited with Westerns, and the bubble burst. Western pictures plummeted in popularity, Western TV series dropped to three or four, and the Western paperback fell upon lean days.

But the Western story had had its fallow periods before. It never died out completely, and it did not die out now. It simmered, and by 1965 it began to sprout all over again. It grew more sprightly in 1966 and 1967, and by 1969 had almost returned to its 1958 peak popularity.

The new Western, however, has undergone some tremendous changes, although basically it is the same story it has always been, of escapism and entertainment, of strong, silent heroes, of dastardly villains, of gunfights and action.

The first motion picture with a story line was *The Great Train Robbery*. It was made in 1902 and starred the later famous Broncho Billy Anderson. This was the same year that Zane Grey first saw his name in print with his fishing story, "A Day on the Delaware."

The script of *The Great Train Robbery* was written on the director's cuff, and for a number of years the Western silent pictures that were made had only brief story outlines. The director created scenes from these, and the results satisfied the primitive motion-picture audiences. But when more money was spent on pictures, better stories were required. Producers experimented by buying a few stage plays, notably *The Squaw Man*, the first picture filmed in Hollywood. Zane Grey was the first really popular Western writer whose works were bought by Hollywood. Three of his novels were filmed in 1918, and Grey established a motion-picture price of twenty-five thousand dollars per book, from which he never deviated for years, although later he was to get as high as twice that. The price was an exceptionally high one for those days, but Zane Grey was America's most famous writer, and the producers paid what he asked.

Few other writers got such high prices for their books, certainly not Western writers. During the depression days of the 1930's, Grey still got his twenty-five-thousand-dollar price, but other Western pictures were written by staff writers who received as little as thirty-five dollars per week. Only a few published stories were bought, and they were usually purchased for between two hundred and fifty, and five hundred dollars. Ernest Haycox, however, received five thousand dollars for his short story "Stage to Lordsburg," which became the film *Stagecoach*. Some people regard this as the best Western motion picture ever filmed. He received only the same amount from RKO for *Trail Town* in 1944. In 1945 Walter Wanger paid him thirty-five thousand dollars for *Canyon Passage*.

When the Western boom came in the late forties, the prices for motion-picture properties began to rise. Twenty-five thousand dollars became a common figure.

In 1967 an original motion picture screenplay, based on *Butch Cassidy and The Sundance Kid*, sold for the record price of four hundred thousand dollars.

The Western story has become Big Business.

Dr. Lewis M. Gray, father of Zane Grey (1896).

Mrs. Lewis Gray, mother of Zane Grey, with grandson Loren (1916).

(Above) Dr. P. Zane Grey, while practicing dentistry in New York City (1904).

Pearl Gray, dental student and baseball star, at the University of Pennsylvania (1895).

Zane Grey roping lions in the Grand Canyon (1908).

With his horse Don Carlos, in Arizona (1918).

He wrote *The Heritage of the Desert* and *Riders of the Purple Sage* in this cottage at Lackawaxen (1912).

At Tonto Basin, with his horse Brutus (1929).

The brothers Gray, Zane, R.C., and Lewis Ellsworth, at Lackawaxen (1917).

With bear cubs at his Tonto Basin ranch (1922).

Once a "humble cottage"—the Zane Grey home at Lackawaxen (1918).

The Zane Grey home at Altadena.

In New Zealand (1927)

Zane Grey with a record Grey Nurse shark
off Sydney, Australia (1936).

Fisherman II

"The World's Most Successful Author"—
Zane and Dolly Grey at Avalon (1930).

In Australia (1938).

Betty Zane, Z. G., Mrs. Z. G., Loren, and
Romer—the Zane Grey family at Altadena
(1927).

Mrs. Zane Grey in Z. G.'s studio (1955).

At the inception of the Zane Grey television series—Loren Grey, Betty Zane Grosso, Mrs. Zane Grey, actor Dick Powell, and Romer Grey.

The Zane Grey home at Avalon (left, on hilltop).

During the filming of *Riders of the Purple Sage* (1918).

CHAPTER **18** _____

With the success of *Riders of the Purple Sage* assured, Zane Grey plunged into another novel. He shifted his background farther south and used as a theme an extremely modern one, the revolution in Mexico. The long-time dictator of Mexico, Porfirio Díaz, had been deposed in 1911, and anarchy had swept over that hapless country. One general after another seized power and found that he could not hold it; armies in the south won victories, armies in the north and west won victories but found them slipping through their hands.

The man of the people, Francisco (Pancho) Villa, for a time had an unbroken series of victories. Nominally only a bandit, Villa had caught the imagination of the unlettered peasants, and he found enthusiastic supporters wherever he went. He made a bold dash across the border, raided the town of Columbus, New Mexico, and incurred the wrath of the United States government, which eventually led to his downfall.

In 1912 and 1913, it was still anyone's ball game in Mexico, and Zane Grey chose this chaotic situation as the theme for his novel *Desert Gold*. The story is laid in the desolate land that borders Mexico and Arizona from midwestern Arizona on the American side, into California. It is, with the exception perhaps of Death Valley, the most desolate and dreary land on the North American continent.

In *Desert Gold* Zane Grey reveals his fascination with the arid wastes that he was to write about so vividly in *Wanderer of the Wasteland*. He also reveals his liking for Indians.

Desert Gold suffers by comparison with the superb *Riders of the Purple Sage*, but it was nevertheless an excellent book, one of Grey's best.

Serial rights to *Desert Gold* were purchased by Street & Smith's most successful magazine, *Popular*, which had also published *The Heritage of the Desert*. *Popular* was edited by Charles Agnew MacLean, who was at the helm of the magazine until the late 1920's. He was one of the most famous editors in New York, second only, perhaps, to Bob Davis at Munsey's. The magazine published some outstanding stories, and MacLean himself was responsible for launching many writers who later became famous. Since he bought Grey's first Western novel, much credit goes to him for having "discovered" Zane Grey, at least in the magazine field.

There were now two children in the Grey household, Romer, almost three and one-half, and Betty Zane, less than a year old. The household distractions had made Zane Grey irritable. He felt that he had to get away for a while. He had long thought of going to Florida to try his hand at tarpon fishing and had even selected the place, Long Key, halfway down the Florida keys. It was a famous place, drawing fishermen from all over the world.

He told Dolly, and she was not too happy about it. She had not complained about any of his previous trips, to Arizona, to Mexico, and had in fact encouraged him to make those trips. They had been important for background material in his writing, but just a plain fishing trip was another matter.

She was aware of his periods of depression. They would sometimes last for days. He could not write. He tried to shake off the black moods by taking long walks in the fields, by fishing in the Delaware. He had to get at a new book; he had it partly worked out in his mind, but he could not concentrate. He wrote a few pages, tore them up, brooded for days, and made new starts. Dolly knew then that he *had* to get away for a while. She began to pack his things.

Grey went to Long Key. He wrote to Dolly every day, sometimes twice a day. She wrote to him as many letters as she received from him. All the letters that went back and forth during his stay at Long Key are extant. In the first few letters

Dolly Grey could not quite conceal her annoyance at her husband's "vacation," but she was now becoming initiated into the intricacies of handling his business affairs, and she soon lost herself in that. Along with her housework and the care of the children, she had plenty to occupy her time. Yet she spent an hour and sometimes two hours every day writing to Zane.

Zane, in Long Key, was now establishing a routine that he followed in the many, long years when he was away on a hunting, fishing, or exploring trip. He rose early every morning and spent an hour or two writing. Then he would go fishing, putting in as many as eight or ten hours at it. In the evening he wrote letters to Dolly and spent another hour or two writing. He had few periods of depression while on these trips—except when he got a letter from Dolly the tone of which upset him. He read the letters carefully several times. He studied her words, looking for hidden meanings. Sometimes he thought he found them, and then he became depressed. When her letters were cheerful, he was happy.

The physical exertion of fishing was good for him. The long hours trolling in the Gulf Stream enabled him to think clearly of his stories, so that when he sat down with his writing pad in the evening the words came easily and the narrative flowed smoothly.

He reported almost daily to Dolly on the progress of his work.

When Zane Grey arrived at Long Key he discovered that he was a famous author—among people who mattered to him. Almost all the fishermen knew of him from his frequent contributions to the sporting magazines, but, more pleasing to Zane Grey was the knowledge that, almost to a man, the fishermen had read *Riders of the Purple Sage. Desert Gold* was also running serially in *Popular,* and some of the fishermen were reading the installments.

Desert Gold was published by Harper's immediately after it ceased running in *Popular.* The momentum from *Riders of the Purple Sage* held over, and the book sold briskly from the start, threatening for a while to surpass the sale of

Riders. But *Riders of the Purple Sage*, although published a year before, had a continuing sale throughout 1913.

The novel he was working on at Long Key was *The Light of Western Stars*. The background was New Mexico this time. The story is totally different from the three he had written before. The time again was the present—1913.

Serial rights to *The Light of Western Stars* were promptly bought by *Munsey's Magazine*, and the book was issued in January, 1914. Its success was gratifying. The Mexican troubles were still front-page news. The United States had already sent a naval and marine expedition to Veracruz, with a notable cast of attending war correspondents, including such luminaries as Richard Harding Davis and Jack London.

CHAPTER **19**

Mrs. Frances Grundy, a sprightly woman who looks much younger than her eighty years, lives today near the Zane Grey home in Altadena, California. Her father, a New York businessman, retired very early, and the family moved to Lackawaxen. She first met the Zane Greys in 1909 and has maintained a close relationship with the family ever since. Mrs. Grundy was only twenty in 1909, still unmarried, but she became very friendly with Dolly Grey, then twenty-six. Dolly was pregnant with Romer at the time.

"She was a vivacious young woman," recalls Mrs. Grundy. "She could have passed for my own age at the time. She had the cleanest-cut features of any girl I knew—cameolike, I guess you'd say. A real beauty. After Romer's birth she weighed less than one hundred and ten pounds. She held that weight for many years, growing heavier only in her thirties. She was devoted to the children, but her life was her husband, Zane Grey. She never stopped encouraging him, and after he had written the first drafts, she went over them, correcting English, gram-

mar, punctuation. She had majored in English in college, and
Zane was always more interested in setting down his ideas on
paper than in polishing. Dolly would spend days and days going over the stories, and finally she would copy the entire manuscript in her own hand. It was her handwritten manuscripts
that the editors read. In later years the manuscripts were typed
by a stenographer, relieving Dolly of that tedious job, but
Dolly never stopped correcting the stories. This began even
before they were married. It was Dolly who corrected and
copied the manuscript of Zane's first book, *Betty Zane*."

Lina Elise (Dolly) Grey was totally committed to helping
her husband become a famous writer. Their courtship had
been a long one, over five years, and the couple grew to know
each other well. Dolly knew of her husband's love of the outdoors. She knew that he would be only a shell of a man without his hunting, fishing, and exploration trips. She joined him
in many of the early, shorter trips, but when the children came
she had to remain with them. She would not hear of his curtail-
ing his own outdoor activities. He had to live that kind of life
in order to write what he did.

When he made his first long trip away from home, to
Arizona to be with Buffalo Jones, Dolly knew that a new world
had opened for him, and when she saw how well he had used
the material gathered on that trip in *The Heritage of the
Desert* and *Riders of the Purple Sage*, she knew that he had to
continue his trips to renew and add to his knowledge of the
West.

Dolly never regretted her decision. She encouraged Zane
to make the trip to Mexico in 1911, and when Zane wrote her
from Long Key, after having already been away from home for
several weeks, that he wanted to go from Long Key to Arizona,
she did not protest.

Grey arrived in Flagstaff, Arizona, in April, 1913, and immediately looked up the famous guide Al Doyle, whom he had
first met in 1907. Grey had heard of the great natural bridge that
had only recently been discovered by the Indian trader John

Wetherill, the first white man ever to have viewed it, although it was long known to the Indians of the wilder, more remote sections.

The Wetherill brothers had an Indian trading post at Kayenta, and John's wife, who had learned the Paiute and Navajo languages, was highly regarded by the Indians. She was told of the great bridge and passed on the information to her husband. The Indians were reluctant to lead the trader to it but finally agreed.

Wetherill had conducted only one previous party to the bridge, but later in the year, after the Grey expedition, he took President Theodore Roosevelt to it.

Al Doyle agreed to take Grey to Kayenta, and there they made arrangements with Wetherill, who was fortunate enough to locate Nas ta Bega, the Paiute Indian who had first led Wetherill to Nonnezosche.

Cautioned that the trip would be a long, rigorous one, the expedition set out. Grey took notes and later incorporated his observations in *Wildfire*.

They also crossed Monument Valley, then almost unknown; indeed, it was Zane Grey who years later conducted Jesse Lasky, the picture producer, to the valley, with the result that it became one of the most photographed areas in all Arizona.

The country was a land of a thousand canyons, in any one of which a man could be lost. Wetherill, who had made the trip twice, was bewildered for a time, but the Indian guide led them unerringly up the right canyon.

No better description of the trip and Nonnezosche can be given than the one Grey gave in *The Rainbow Trail*, the sequel to *Riders of the Purple Sage*. He wrote it during the following year, although it was not published until 1915.

Grey called Nonnezosche one of the greatest natural wonders in the world, and it apparently made a tremendous impression on him, for he wrote several articles about it.

Returning to Flagstaff, Grey set out with his guide and

entourage on a trip into the southern part of Arizona, which he was to use so often in later novels.

The trip was a satisfying one, and when Grey returned to Lackawaxen he learned that the editors of both *Munsey's* and *Popular* magazines were clamoring for a new serial. *Desert Gold* had been running in *Popular* at the same time that *The Light of Western Stars* was appearing in *Munsey's*.

Grey had never been to Texas, but around the campfires in Arizona there was talk about the Texas Rangers, and Grey had become intrigued with the story of Captain McNelly, who had been appointed to the command of the newly reorganized Texas Rangers in 1875. At that time Texas had within its borders eight thousand known outlaws, most of them fugitives from other states.

Grey read every available historical account of Captain McNelly, but as he studied his subject, Grey became impressed with the Texas Ranger, often a man who had been an outlaw before taking the star. Such a character appealed to Grey, and soon he was writing the story of Buck Duane, the outlaw-gunfighter, the most sought-after man in Texas, who finally became a Ranger and accepted the most dangerous assignments that Captain McNelly could give him.

The editors of *Popular* and *Munsey's* were both anxious to have the new story. Because *Popular* had published Grey's first serial, he was inclined to sell it to them, but Bob Davis's offer was so much higher that Grey sold *The Lone Star Ranger* to *Munsey's*.

The novel was published by Harper's early in 1915, and with it Zane Grey moved into the golden circle—the best-seller list. *The Lone Star Ranger* was ninth on the list of best-selling novels of the year. *The Rainbow Trail*, published the same year, barely missed the list.

The Rainbow Trail, under the title *The Desert Crucible*, was published in *Argosy*, a Munsey magazine. Later that year Grey wrote *The Border Legion* and sold it to *Munsey's*, where it began in the January 13, 1916, issue.

But the best-seller list had done its work. Aside from one more sale later in 1917, Grey was through with the pulp magazines. M. R. Currie, the editor of *The Country Gentleman*, the large-circulation farm magazine published by the company that put out *The Saturday Evening Post* and *The Ladies' Home Journal*, asked to see Zane Grey's next work.

That fateful story was *Wildfire. The Country Gentleman* read it and published it, and when it appeared in book form in 1917, it wound up as the number-three best-seller of the year.

Zane Grey's love of horses dated back to his first Western trip in 1907. Several wild-horse hunters joined Buffalo Jones's troupe for a few days, and Grey drew from them some of their adventures and their way of life.

In *Riders of the Purple Sage* he created three memorable equines in Black Star, Night, and Wrangle, but in *Wildfire* the horse theme is dominant and the human actors in the drama are secondary.

Wildfire is one of Zane Grey's best stories, and it was the book that marked the author's first appearance in a "slick" magazine rather than the "pulps" in which his work had previously appeared.

CHAPTER **20**

In *The Border Legion*, written in 1915, Grey moved into country that he did not know first-hand, the Idaho-Montana territory. It was a story that he knew well, however, having researched it thoroughly.

The story of Henry Plummer and his road agents, who numbered more than one hundred, was a fascinating one. Plummer, which was not his real name, was said to have originated in Indiana, and had gone to the gold fields of California in the rush of 1849. He had been unlucky there and became filled with bitterness. An educated man, he saw illiterate former farmers make rich gold strikes, but fortune eluded him, no matter how he tried. He drifted in with the lawless crowd, became involved in a few robberies and killings, then skipped the country, heading north for Oregon and Washington. He moved gradually eastward and was in eastern Washington when news of the gold strikes in Idaho caused most of the eastern Washington population to stampede for the new fields. Plummer went with them.

The best claims in Alder Gulch were already staked out when Plummer arrived. Plummer actually tried to work a claim, but he had become unused to hard labor. He had a good appearance, was an excellent talker, and when the thirteen-mile-long community decided to organize, he was elected sheriff.

He was a popular sheriff, but soon robberies and murders were the talk of the day. Stagecoaches scarcely ventured to leave Alder Gulch. Miners were robbed in their shacks and brutally murdered. No one knew who the outlaws were, but that they were organized soon became apparent.

Driven to desperation, the miners formed a vigilante organization, headed by X. Bieder, a butcher, and an attorney named Sanders, who later became the first U.S. senator from Montana, when the territory became a state.

One of the first men captured, even though he knew he was doomed, gave a roster of more than fifty names of outlaws, naming Plummer, the sheriff, as the leader. Within a matter of a few days the vigilantes hanged thirty-five outlaws, including Plummer, and all outlawry ceased.

One of the executed men was a fantastic savage named Boone Helm. He had been a guerrilla under Quantrell in western Missouri and boasted that he had twice turned cannibal. His last words before stepping into space were, "Hurray for Jefferson Davis!"

In Zane Grey's novel, Plummer became Kells; the characterization was true to Kells's prototype, Henry Plummer, a hunted, yet vicious killer, but he was not a sheriff in Zane Grey's story, merely the organizer and leader of a legion of outlaws.

Possibly the most fearsome and sanguinary villain ever portrayed in a Zane Grey novel is Gulden, drawn very freely from his counterpart, Boone Helm.

The final chapter, in which Kells kills seven of his chief lieutenants, including Gulden, is the most vicious and savage fight ever portrayed by any writer, yet Grey has written it in a way that is entirely believable.

The Border Legion must rate as one of the four or five best novels ever written by Zane Grey. The subject matter has been used by numerous writers since, but it has never been done as well.

In 1916 Zane Grey wrote *The U.P. Trail* and sold serial rights to *Blue Book* in 1917. *Blue Book* was a pulp magazine, but during this period it was considered a very superior magazine, had an unusually large circulation, and was able to pay the high rate that Zane Grey was now getting. It was the best investment *Blue. Book* ever made, for *The U.P. Trail*, when published in 1918, raised Zane Grey to the number-one spot on the best-seller list.

The U.P. Trail is Zane Grey's most ambitious novel, and if it is not the best book he ever wrote, it certainly cannot be rated far behind *Riders of the Purple Sage*.

In his dedication to Harper editor Ripley Hitchcock, Grey tells how he first became interested in the subject. His guide on several occasions had been Al Doyle, who had worked on the Union Pacific as a young man. Around the campfires Doyle had talked about those days. Grey had also come across a fascinating account of the building of the Union Pacific, written by the English author Robert Louis Stevenson. These accounts had inspired Grey to do extensive research on the subject, which is revealed throughout the book.

The story is an extremely complicated one, for Grey had to tell not only the involved story of the actual building of the railroad but also the personal stories of his leading characters.

The story opens in 1865 with a small wagon train headed eastward in Wyoming. The leader of the train is Bill Horn, who is returning east with a considerable amount of gold that he wrested from the ground in California. With the wagon train are Mrs. Durade and her fifteen-year-old daughter, Allie.

When they are about to be attacked by Indians, Mrs. Durade tells her miserable story to her daughter. She had been married to a man named Allison Lee, and Allie is actually Lee's daughter. She left her husband when Allie was very young to run off with a handsome gambler named Durade, who had treated her as a virtual slave, even forcing her to use her body to mulct victims. She had fled from Durade recently in California because of his growing interest in her daughter.

The Indians attack, and everyone in the wagon is killed with the exception of Allie, who crawled into a clump of brush.

A party of engineers surveying for the proposed railroad is not far away. It is under the command of General Dodge, late of the Union Army, who has been given the job of building the railroad. In the group are young Warren Neale; his trusted friend, the fugitive Texas gunfighter Larry Red King; and Casey, the Irish immigrant, with whom we will become better acquainted later.

To the camp comes Slingerland, an old trapper-plainsman who had encountered the wagon train before it was attacked by Indians. He has come to get the cavalry detachment that is with the surveyors.

It is too late to save the wagon train, but they find Allie Lee, unconscious from the shock of seeing her mother killed and scalped by the Indians. She regains consciousness but is out of her mind. They take her to Slingerland's cabin and leave her with the old trapper.

Neale and King visit Slingerland and Allie several times. The girl recovers slowly.

The railroad has already started building west from Omaha, and Neale's job requires him to go east and leave Allie in the Wyoming cabin.

All of the intrigue and the scandals of building the railroad are touched upon. Contractors with padded bills and payrolls are exposed. Sections of track are poorly laid and have to be relaid. Lurking among the crooked politicians and contractors is the vague, sinister figure of a financier named Allison Lee. Neale encounters him and antagonizes him, but Lee becomes more prominent and has several further encounters with Neale. Neale knows that he is the father of Allie Lee but does not reveal that knowledge.

The railroad moves west, and Neale from time to time goes ahead and sees Allie, who recovers. They fall in love.

The difficulties of the railroad seem insurmountable; the financing becomes a national scandal. But the road progresses in spite of the skulduggery that accompanies it. Frequently the Irish workers lay track with their rifles near at hand. Over and over they are attacked by Indians.

The gamblers, the sycophants, move along with the railroad, become more numerous, more daring as the rails move west. Finally things reach a climax in Benton, Wyoming, when the large tent city that has sprung up becomes a hell-hole.

Durade traces Allie Lee to the mountain cabin, abducts her when Slingerland is away. He takes her to Benton, where he establishes a gambling place and intends to use Allie as a lure.

In a smashing, climactic scene, Reddy King rescues Allie from the gambling place and loses his own life doing so, but it is Neale who finally has to save her from Durade.

There are subplots of the workers, chief among them the two fabulous Irishmen, Casey and McDermott, who, in miniature, tell the entire story of the ten thousand men who were brought from Ireland to do the back-breaking labor of building the railroad. Many of them lost their lives.

Finally, when the railroad joins the Central Pacific at Promontory Point, Pat asks the Irishman McDermott, "Tell me, who built the U.P.?"

And McDermott gives the perfect answer: "Me fr'ind Casey did." It is Casey's monument, for he has given his life for the U.P.

The U.P. Trail sold more copies than any other book published in 1918.

CHAPTER **21** ————————————————

After years of privation, of living on borrowed money, Zane Grey found himself a comparatively rich man in 1913. *Riders of the Purple Sage* had earned him more than fifty thousand dollars in 1912 and promised to bring in almost that much in 1913. In 1913 *Desert Gold* was published, and the way it began to sell indicated that it might well earn Grey as much as *Riders of the Purple Sage*.

His total income in 1913 was close to one hundred thousand dollars, and the new federal income tax was an infinitesimal amount.

A hundred thousand dollars in 1913 was the equivalent of a million dollars in the 1960's, at least in purchasing power. The house at Lackawaxen was remodeled, refurnished. Domestic help was employed, and a nurse for Romer, now four, and one-year-old Betty Zane.

New fishing tackle, of course, was bought from time to time. Grey installed a rowing machine on the porch of his home, on which he practiced faithfully every day to strengthen his arm and shoulder muscles.

Having become friendly with Bob Davis of Munsey's, who was no mean fisherman himself, Grey spent an occasional weekend fishing with Davis off the coasts of New Jersey and Long Island.

During Bob Davis' summer vacation, taken a bit late in the season, Zane and R. C. went with Davis to Nova Scotia, and there in the fishing banks the Greys whetted their taste for fishing in new and strange waters; Zane himself had already fished for tarpon off Florida and the coast of Mexico, but his brother had not been with him on those occasions.

The following spring, shortly after his return to Arizona, Zane Grey went back to Catalina Island and Avalon. As newlyweds the Greys had spent a few days at Avalon, where Grey had tried to catch some big fish. He had been unsuccessful but had secretly vowed to return someday. Through the years the fame of Avalon had grown, and it was only a matter of time before Grey returned there. The challenge of the Pacific sword-fish had to be met. They were the most difficult of all game fish to hook and work and finally bring aboard. Only the really expert fishermen of big game had ever accomplished the feat.

Zane Grey counted himself an expert fisherman, and he wanted that first swordfish. He traveled to Los Angeles, then crossed to the island that was the haven for all the big-game fishermen of the West Coast and the frequent port of call of Eastern fishermen.

The harbor at Avalon teemed with fishermen; the shops in the town catered to the fishermen, and the hotels were filled with them. It was a touch of paradise for Zane Grey.

On the day of his arrival Grey met the local taxidermist and told him that he wanted his swordfish mounted. The taxidermist snorted his disgust and told him to catch his swordfish first.

A tuna fisherman told him that if he fished steadily for perhaps two weeks he might strike a swordfish. But Captain Danielson—Captain Dan—was more optimistic, and Zane Grey engaged him to take him out in his boat. They went to Clem-ente Island, thirty-six miles from Catalina, and for twenty-one days trolled back and forth, covering a distance of more than fifteen hundred miles. During that period they sighted nineteen of the great swordfish, but Grey did not get a hook into a single one of them. On the twenty-fifth day victory seemed certain, for Grey finally hooked a giant swordfish, but lost him.

He had to give up the hunt, but promised Captain Dan that he would be back early the next year to try again. Captain Dan was skeptical, but in the summer of 1915 Zane Grey returned to Catalina and Clemente Island and within a few days had hooked and landed three swordfish, the largest weigh-ing one hundred and forty-five pounds.

Zane Grey was hooked by the swordfish. The big, fighting fish were a constant challenge to him. A few days later he finally made the strike that kept him an ardent fisherman of big fish for the rest of his life.

His hook was taken by an enormous fish, and after hours of playing the monster back and forth, up and down, the swordfish was lassoed and tugged onto the boat. Captain Dan estimated him at three hundred and sixty pounds, perhaps a record, but when the fish was loaded onto the wharf in Avalon two days later, the shrinking and drying-out process had reduced the weight of the fish to a little more than three hundred pounds.

Later Grey hooked an even bigger fish, which Captain Dan estimated might be twice the size of the previous big one, but after working him for hours, during which time their boat was pulled more than six miles by the big fish, the monster got away.

Grey left Catalina and Avalon, but he would be back the next year and the next, and soon he would establish a home in Avalon, which would be his home away from home.

Loren, the third and last child of the Greys, was born in 1915. Romer, born in 1909, was now six and Betty, born in 1912, the year of *Riders of the Purple Sage*, was three.

In 1916 Grey was in New York City and was told by his publishers that a motion-picture mogul, William K. Fox, was interested in acquiring rights to *Riders of the Purple Sage*. He wanted to talk to the author.

Zane Grey had barely been aware of the growing motion-picture business. He had been too busy with his writing, with his numerous hunting and fishing trips, to spend much time watching motion pictures during the brief time he had in the cities where there were theaters.

The business was still in its swaddling clothes. Audiences had become surfeited with the short five- and ten-minute pictures that were mere travelogues or comedy skits. Pictures had been made with stories after 1902, but they were hit-and-miss things; still the public seemed to enjoy them. The producers themselves were mere promoters, but in 1912 three men in New York got together and decided to make a worthwhile picture. Rights to a Broadway success, *The Squaw Man*, were acquired by Jesse L. Lasky. He engaged the services of a prominent young play director, Cecil B. De Mille, by promising him a small salary and a percentage of the picture's profits.

De Mille had never directed a motion picture, but he had already begun to believe that the sources of the new medium had barely been tapped. A glove salesman named Samuel Goldfish, who later changed his name to Goldwyn, was able to borrow two thousand dollars from a relative willing to take a gamble. Lasky himself had only a few thousand dollars, but the three men were able to acquire the services of one of Broadway's leading actors, Dustin Farnum. They now had the ingredients for making a motion picture. The pictures had mostly been made in the Palisades of New Jersey, but it was winter there now and the entrepreneurs could not wait until summer. It was decided that De Mille and the star would go to Arizona, where it was always summer, and there engage local talent and make the picture.

The train reached Flagstaff in a blinding snowstorm, and De Mille and his actor got back on the train and continued on to Los Angeles, where the sun was shining.

De Mille rented a barn in the midst of an orange grove, and the film was shot. It was the first motion picture to be made in Hollywood.

Made for a few thousand dollars, *The Squaw Man* made fortunes for all involved in its production, and it established California as the center of the budding motion-picture business. Then Carl Laemmle established Universal Pictures. William Fox was soon in Hollywood, as were many other producers and promoters, some of whom became famous. Lasky and a group established the studio that became known as Paramount. Goldwyn went in with a group, then withdrew, but his partners continued to use his name in Metro-Goldwyn-Mayer Studios.

In 1915 a picture was made for approximately sixty thousand dollars, which was eventually to earn forty million. The picture was *The Birth of a Nation*. Under its original title, *The Clansman*, the book had sold well since its publication in 1905.

William Fox, later frozen out of the business by a combination of his rivals, was one of the foresighted pioneers of the industry. He decided that if a successful book could be made into a successful motion picture, then the thing to do was to buy a successful book.

However, if one successful book could be bought, two could be bought just as readily. He saw Zane Grey in New York and offered him twenty-five hundred dollars for the picture rights to *Riders of the Purple Sage*. When Grey hesitated, Fox offered him an additional twenty-five hundred for a second book, *The Light of Western Stars*. Grey accepted the offer.

The two pictures were made in 1917 and released early in 1918. Immediately Grey had an offer for *Desert Gold* from Jesse Lasky. He held out—and finally got—the fantastic price of twenty-five thousand dollars for the book. He never accepted less than that for a book from that time on, and he established something else that no other author was able to get for many, many years. The sale was not an outright purchase, merely a seven-year lease. At the end of that time Grey could sell the property again to anyone who met his price.

Other motion-picture offers were made in 1917, but Grey would not budge from his asking price and no additional sales were completed.

It was the motion-picture business as much as his love for Catalina and its surrounding waters that influenced Grey to make the momentous decision in 1918 to pull up stakes in Lackawaxen and move to California. He was already making two or three trips a year to the Southwest. Each trip meant five days on the train each way. He was away from home too much.

His roots had been solidly implanted in Lackawaxen, and the decision to move was not an easy one. His mother had died the previous year, but his moving to California meant that his brothers, Romer and Ellsworth, and Ida, his sister, would also move. It was still a very close family group.

Zane Grey put the five-acre point of land, with its buildings, on sale, but then withdrew it. He could not bear to see the property pass into strange hands. Things might not work out in California. He was rich enough to keep two homes. Three. Even four. He soon had them all.

He had found a large house for rent in Hollywood. Dolly, aided by her husband's relatives, would get the family established in Hollywood, while Zane and R. C. would stop off in Arizona and initiate the young Romer, now nine, in the outdoor world.

A family quarrel broke out over that. Dolly thought Romer far too young for such a rigorous trip and insisted that he should go back into school as soon as possible. But Zane knew that Romer was ahead of his class. R. C. thought the experience would be good for his nephew. The men of the family finally won out, and with misgivings Dolly Grey permitted her elder son to go with his father and uncle to Arizona.

Zane Grey was one of the wealthiest authors in America. His books had been best-sellers since 1915. In 1918 *The U.P. Trail* headed the list during the entire year. Grey's income since 1914 had been nearly one hundred thousand dollars a year. He had just sold *Desert Gold* to pictures, and if he could hold his price there was no reason that he could not increase his annual income by fifty or even one hundred percent. He had many good years left. At forty-six he looked years younger, and he was in perfect health.

He took with him to Arizona a Japanese chef he had recently employed, Takahashi, who, even though he was too short to get his feet into stirrups no matter how high they were raised, proved to be an indomitable rider and an outdoorsman. He never seemed to tire, and no matter how hard the day's riding, Takahashi prepared an excellent meal, even under camp conditions.

Young Romer had been presented with a twenty-gauge shotgun and was soon blazing away at turkeys, squirrels, and rabbits. He was quite willing to shoot at the bears they encountered, but the older men drew the line at that.

With the Greys on this trip was the redoubtable Sievert Nielsen. Three years before, Harper's had forwarded a letter to Grey from the Norwegian, who said that he had read *Desert Gold* and assumed that the lost treasure described in it was a real one. Nielsen asked Grey to give him as much information as he could, after which he, Nielsen, would search for the treasure. If successful, he would split fifty-fifty with Grey.

Nielsen gave his background in the letter; he was a seaman but had left the sea a few years ago to turn prospector. He knew his business, having already taken four trips alone into the desert of Sonora.

Grey was about to leave for Catalina, but he wrote to the sailor-prospector and asked him to come to Avalon. Grey had hardly arrived in Avalon when Sievert Nielsen showed up. He turned out to be a man of thirty-five, with a magnificent physique. He was a well-educated man and apparently came from a substantial family in Norway; he was an adventurer by choice, not necessity. His calm coolness, courtesy, and intelligence appealed to Grey, and he took Nielsen on a few fishing trips. The man handled himself so well that Grey asked him to go with him on every succeeding expedition.

The next trip was to Arizona, and Nielsen was a member of the party. While they were there Grey purchased three acres on the rim of the Grand Canyon and ordered a cabin to be built on it. When the Grey entourage returned to California, Grey decided that the house into which the family had settled was not adequate, so he rented a furnished mansion on the corner of Adams and Western avenues.

At just about the same time, the filming of *Desert Gold* was to start in the desert near Palm Springs, a tiny hamlet at this time. Grey spent a few days at Palm Springs watching the filming. Nielsen accompanied him on the short trip.

CHAPTER **22** ━━━━━━━━━━━━━━━━━━━━

The desert had always fascinated Zane Grey.

It was now January, 1919, and the desert was livable at that time of the year. Grey and Nielsen traveled around the desert for a while, then decided to visit Death Valley. They boarded their horses and equipment on the Santa Fe and got off at Death Valley Junction, a stopping point within fifty miles of Death Valley.

Death Valley Junction existed mainly because of a borax mill that had been located there a few years before. There was a dingy little store where the desert men gathered in the evening. This was the kind of gathering that Grey always enjoyed, and that evening he listened to talk about float-surface gold and high-grade ores of zinc, copper, lead, and manganese. He heard, too, about the borax that had been hauled out of Death Valley by mule teams as recently as thirty years ago.

Nothing could now have kept Grey from going into Death Valley.

In the morning, while Nielsen checked their equipment and made additional purchases, Grey visited the borax mill. It was the property of an English company, and the work of hauling, grinding, and roasting borax ore went on night and day.

The ore was brought from Death Valley to the railroad twenty miles away; then the cars were put on a siding to the mill, where the ore was dumped from a high trestle into chutes that fed the grinders.

The mill was as dusty and filled with powder as an old-fashioned flour mill. Grey watched a chalk-faced operator at the grinders, who told him that the mill was producing twenty-five hundred sacks of borax a day. Grey, already choking from the borax powder, learned that the workers in the mill, whom he already pitied, could not exist for more than six months in these terrible conditions. He left the mill depressed, but once he and Nielsen left Death Valley Junction, his spirits were quickly restored.

Ahead of him now lay perhaps the greatest physical experience of his life, the conquest of Death Valley.

Driving the mules ahead of them, they slowly ascended a long gravel and greasewood slope, and by noon looked back and saw the borax mill, only a smoky blot on the desert floor.

They reached the pass between Black Mountain and the Funeral Mountains and felt a vast relief. Nielsen, a talkative man, had stopped talking except for an occasional word to the mules.

The blunt end of the Funeral range was as remarkable as its name. It sheered up high, a saw-toothed range with colored strata at an angle of forty-five degrees. Veins of black and red and yellow ran through the great drab-gray mass. The peak of the mountain was draped in streaky veils of rain from low-dropping clouds that seemed to be lodged there. All below lay clear and cold in the sunlight.

Their direction was westward, and at that altitude, three thousand feet, the sun was pleasant, for the wind was cold. The shallow wash leading down from the pass deepened, widened, and then spread out until its proportions were striking. It was a gully where the gravel washed down during rains, where a scant vegetation of greasewood, a few low cacti, and scrubby sage struggled for existence. Not a bird or lizard or any living creature was seen.

Walking in the loose gravel was as hard as trudging through sand, and after about fifteen miles, Grey's feet were like lead. But ahead of him strode Nielsen with his long wonderful stride.

Grey called to the Norwegian to stop and rest awhile, and Nielsen complied cheerfully. Then, to cheer Grey, he related one of his own adventures. On the eastern slope of the Sierra Madre range, in Mexico, his burros had been killed by lions, and Nielsen found it imperative to strike for the nearest ranch below the border, which he knew to be a hundred and fifty miles. He could carry only so much with him, so he discarded

his entire equipment, keeping only a few biscuits and a canteen of water. Resting an hour or two, now and then, and
without sleeping, Nielsen walked the distance of one hundred
and fifty miles in three days and nights.

Grey did not disbelieve the big man, for he was already
aware of his tremendous strength and endurance.

Rested, they continued on, and when it was almost
sundown, they rounded a sharp curve and saw before them a
sight that filled Grey with awe.

Between a white-mantled mountain on the left and the
dark-striped lofty range on the right was a gulf, a lazy void, a
vast stark valley that seemed streaked and ridged and canyoned.

It was Death Valley.

The sight before them oppressed Grey, but the Norwegian, absorbed for only a moment, strode on, and Grey
followed.

A red haze, sinister and somber, hung over the eastern
ramparts of the valley. As the sun began to set and storm
clouds moved across the sky, the scene changed, brightened,
grew full of luminous red light and then streaked by golden
gleams. The tips of the Panamint Mountains became silver
above purple clouds. At sunset the moment was glorious, dark,
forbidding, dim, weird, dismal, yet tinged with gold.

Nielsen, going ahead, had selected for their camp a pro-
tected nook where the canyon floor bore some patches of sage,
the stalks and roots of which would serve for firewood. The
two men unpacked, fed the mules some grain, then pitched
their little tent and made their bed. It was dark long before
they had their supper. During the meal the men talked a little,
but afterward, when the chores were done and the mules had
become quiet, a thick silence settled down upon them and they
did not talk at all.

The night was black, with the sky mostly obscured by
clouds. Zane Grey strolled away in the darkness and sat down
on a stone. The silence was intense. He strained his ears for
the sound of an insect or the rustle of sage or the drop of a
weathered rock. The soft, cool desert wind was soundless.

When Grey returned to the camp, Nielsen had gone to bed and the fire had burned low. He threw some branches of sage on it and the fire blazed up. But it seemed different from other campfires. There was no cheer, no glow, no sparkle.

The sadness, the loneliness, the desolation of the place seemed to weigh upon the campfire as it did on Zane Grey himself.

Grey and Nielsen were up at five-thirty. The sky was a cold, leaden gray with dull gold and rose in the east. A hard wind blew up the canyon.

An hour later they broke camp. Traveling in the early morning was pleasant, and they made good time down the winding canyon, arriving at Furnace Creek about noon. This stream of warm water flowed down from a gully that began in the Funeral Mountains. It had a disagreeable taste, acrid and slightly soapy. There was a green thicket of brush along the creek, consisting of a coarse grass, arrowood mesquite, and tamarack. The tamarack bore a pink fuzzy blossom, not unlike the common pussy willow.

On a ridge above Furnace Creek, Grey and Nielsen came upon a spring of posionous water. It was clear and sparkling, with a greenish cast and a white crust on the margin. Nielsen, kicking at the sand, uncovered a human skull.

They scouted about the vicinity of the creek for several hours, then in the late afternoon proceeded leisurely along the creek through an atmosphere that grew warmer and denser, to the floor of the valley. At dusk they made camp under some cottonwood trees on the west slope of the valley.

A warm gale blew all night. Grey lay awake for a while, then slept without any covering. Toward dawn the gale died away. Grey was up again at five-thirty. It was a clear, balmy morning.

Beyond their camp were green and pink thickets of tamarack and some velvety green alfalfa fields, irrigated by the spreading of Furnace Creek over the valley slope. A man lived there, raising alfalfa for the mules of the borax miners.

His was a lonely, terrible existence. At this season a few

Shoshone Indians were camped nearby, helping the man with the haying. The rancher's name was Denton.

He told Grey and Nielsen about Death Valley, about the wanderers and prospectors he had rescued from starvation and thirst, about the terrific noonday heat in summer, of the incredible and horrible midnight furnace gales that swept down the valley. With the mercury at one hundred and twenty-five degrees at midnight, below sea level, it was all a man could do just to live. No man could spend many summers there; Death Valley was fatal to all. The Indians themselves left the valley during July and August, moving up into the mountains. Denton claimed that meat-eaters and alcohol drinkers could not survive; a perfect heart and lungs were necessary to stand the heat and density of the atmosphere at two hundred feet below sea level.

Denton told of a man who had left his cabin early in the morning, strong and healthy. A few hours later he was found near the oasis unable to walk, crawling on hands and knees, dragging a canteen of water.

Another man, young, of heavy and powerful build, lost seventy pounds in two days.

Grey and Nielsen told Denton that they intended to walk across Death Valley. Denton advised against it, not because the heat was too much at this season, but because of other dangers—the brittle, salty crust of the sinkhole.

The two adventurers were determined to make the trip, and with a few biscuits in their pockets and plenty of water in their canteens, they set out.

A long sandy slope of mesquite extended down to the bare, crinkly floor of the valley, and the descent to a lower level was barely perceptible. The walking was difficult. Little mounds in the salty crust made it difficult to place a foot on the level. The crust appeared fairly strong, but it rang hollow under their boots, and they proceeded cautiously.

The difficult walking and the heaviness of the air tired Grey. He sat down on the ground and took out his notebook and began writing in it, so that Nielsen would not know how tired he was. The ground was now flat, salty alkali or borax ground, crusted and cracked. The glare hurt Grey's eyes. He felt moist, hot, oppressed, in spite of a rather stiff wind.

Grey was reluctant to get to his feet, but Nielsen was waiting, and they continued. Soon they reached a white, winding plain that resembled a frozen river. They found it to be a perfectly smooth stratum of salt, glistening as if powdered. It was not solid. At the pressure of a foot it shook like jelly. Under the white crust was a yellow, wet substance. It was an obstacle they had not counted upon. Nielsen ventured out onto it, and his feet sank in several inches. Grey went out and found that he did not sink in as deeply as Nielsen.

They returned to the solid ground and deliberated. Nielsen said that by stepping quickly they could cross without any great risk, though it appeared reasonable that if they stood still they would sink out of sight into the soft substance.

More frightened than he had ever been in his life, Grey started after Nielsen across the soft white field, moving swiftly but stepping lightly. They made it safely and reached a long flat of upheaved crusts of salt and mud, full of holes and pitfalls, a toilsome and painful place to cross. They finally negotiated it with difficulty and reached a gravel slope.

Denton had told them that it was seven miles across the valley, but it had taken Grey and Nielsen many hours to cross.

Turning, they now faced the afternoon sun and found the return trip even more formidable. It was as hot as Zane Grey wanted it to be, yet this was a comparatively cool winter day. What it would have been like in summer, he could not imagine.

On the return trip, Grey, trying to go too swiftly, stepped into a couple of holes, ruining both boots. His endurance was taxed as it had never been before, but when they had finally crossed the salt flat, he saw with relief that Nielsen drank a full quart of water, seemingly in one gulp. The big man's strength had also been used up.

Their camp that night was a welcome relief, and Zane Grey, lying awake, knew then that he would write a novel of Death Valley.

CHAPTER **23** _____

Grey plunged into the work as soon as he got home. He kept a diary at this period, and in it he recorded his progress day by day. It is one of the most remarkable documents ever written by a writer about the actual creation and production of a work. Grey, always susceptible to fits of black depression, suffered more during the writing of *Wanderer of the Wasteland* than at any time before or after. The book itself is his moodiest piece of writing, precisely what it should have been. Even though *Riders of the Purple Sage* had a greater success and is considered by most to be his best novel, many readers of Zane Grey prefer *Wanderer of the Wasteland*.

Grey spent five months in the actual writing of *Wanderer of the Wasteland*, more time than he had spent on any previous novel.

The record of these five months is taken verbatim from his diary:

January 19, 1919:

Today, after years of plan and months of thought and weeks of travel, reading, I began the novel that I have determined to be great.

It was with singular fire, sweetness, life, and joy that I began to write. None of that poignant worry, pain, fuss, or vacillation so characteristic of me at the outset of work! I have made a plan.

This novel will not be great unless I have absolute control and restraint; and I am absolutely determined that it will be a great novel.

I must look out for nervous strain.

I must not hurry.

I must not try to do too much in a short time.

I must have quiet and freedom from interruption.

On the other hand, there must be hours when I must force the novel out of my mind and be interested in the children and in pleasure and duties.

This means cheerfulness and responsiveness.

I must keep ever before me the long, long task, and the present laborsome moments that make for the far-distant result.

I must be prepared to expect depressions and to understand them, and to meet them with intelligence and counteraction, with change, and will.

The task I have set myself is tremendous, since it is one of sustained faith, power, and passion.

January 20:

I had a hard time writing today.

A start was rendered difficult by worry over the fact that my brother's wife has influenza and is threatened with pneumonia. Then R. C. protested against our plan of sending Romer to the Glendora School, saying he might get the influenza and be quarantined away from his home and parents. Lastly, Romer carried on high jinks with a party of six of his young friends, all full of the devil, and the climax came when I went down to encounter Romer and one of them fighting. Romer was the smaller, and his antagonist was threatening him with a stone. To my chagrin, I kicked them both, and my temper contributed to my nervousness.

It was a bad day, but I congratulate myself that it was not infinitely worse. I bore up under all these trials, till the last, then lost my temper momentarily.

I wrote seven pages of manuscript and it was hard work. The ideas did not flow, the pleasure in creating did not operate, the sense of power was aloof.

January 21:

Could not work this morning. Climax of annoying circumstances. But did not submit to discouragement. Finally wrote one page. Would have written more tonight, but had a caller on a motion-picture matter.

January 22:

No writing today! I have been tremendously excited all day by a motion-picture conference. We talked incessantly. The result seemed eminently satisfactory to me. I am very enthusiastic and hopeful about Z.G. *Motion Pictures, Inc.* It makes more work for me, which, however, I am satisfied to do.

About tomorrow I will reread my notes and plans and then go back to writing.

January 23–24:

Motion-picture councils.

January 25:

Wrote seven hours. Did not have any great trouble, but the subject matter was scarcely emotional, being merely progress. I find difficulty, however, in restraint and in fighting the sense of hurry. Always this need to hurry has driven me. But it must be a false feeling. I do not need to write fast. I can control this mood, and it is essential to learn to do it before I come to vital parts of my story.

January 26, Sunday:

All morning I tried to get started. No rain! The nurse ill—Dolly sick—the children wild to romp and play, and I grew nervous. At two-thirty I sat down determined to write. I got started, and all was well.

This evening I wrote two more hours. At night I find my mind works freer, and I am not interrupted. It behooves me to take advantage of the night hours.

Dolly read the first chapter, and her praise made me exultant and happy and full of inspiration.

January 27:

I managed to write four pages today. But I was too excited by outward influence. I must get away from them again, get back to the mood of writing. This period of interruption will pass.

January 28:

Sick this morning. Bad cold in head and rheumatism in my shoulder. Miserable dragging feeling. I had to fight off depression and fix mind sternly upon hopeful things, even though I was steeped in gloom.

I wrote six hours.

Tonight I wrote a couple of hours, just long enough to feel my power come back. It takes work to get into the right mood. I want to test my strength, my power, my latent and unplumbed depths in this novel. But now I need restraint. But on the whole today is encouraging. I seem to understand my task, even if I have not yet buckled down to it.

January 29:

At two o'clock this morning I awoke, hot and restless, and could not go to sleep again. My cold was worse. This worried D. I could not eat any breakfast, and during the afternoon I developed a temperature of $99\frac{4}{10}$.

January 30:

Sick and unable to write.

January 31. Birthday:

Today I felt better. Managed to write seven pages, which were done slowly and laboriously. Did not have any fire or inspiration. This is another birthday for me. How fast they come and go! We had a fine dinner and then played poker, my boy Romer taking part in the game. He was very much excited for the few moments that he played. I had great luck and won eight dollars.

My friend Duneka of Harper's died the other day. I had just received a beautiful letter from him, a tribute to my books, a fine inspiring word that I shall never forget. And now he is dead!

February 1:
I wrote eleven pages and felt fairly easy at it.

February 2:
Today was cloudy, rainy, cold, and disagreeable. The house was damp, and as we had only one fire going, I could not shut myself in any room to write and let everyone else be uncomfortable. So I wasted the day, and as a consequence I do not feel well tonight. My aches seem augmented. It is hard for a writer to learn the need of a stern exclusion of himself from everything pertaining to family and social life when he writes. I must do this thing. No one connected intimately with a writer has any appreciation of his temperament, except to think him overdoing everything.

February 3:
Wrote seven pages. It was a rather hard day.

February 4:
Today began bad! Romer was to go away to school, and this fact had stewed Dolly and me all up and made us feel so badly that everything went bad. My boy was excited and wild to go, yet sorry to leave. Finally I went to work and wrote hard and hard and hard. I don't know whether or not it is good. But it seems my bad moods do not greatly influence my work, except in keeping me from it. I wrote four hours and forgot my troubles.

February 5:
Bad day!!!

February 6. Five-thirty p.m.:
I have done no writing yet today and hardly expect to. Conditions have been against me and I was not yet strong enough to overcome them at once.
This was Dolly's birthday and I hate birthdays.

February 7:

I brooded and pondered and vacillated an hour this morning before I could accept the stab of starting to write. But at last I began and wrote for nearly six hours. When I stopped, the dark mood, as if by magic, had folded its cloak and gone away.

It is well to know this and to remember it constantly. I must not waste my substance in wild dreams and anticipations while I have this book to write.

February 13. Twelve-thirty a.m.:

Have been busy with motion-picture business for five days. Tonight at eleven o'clock I began to write and wrote two pages. I am amazed at the suddenness of the return of power and passion. Perhaps a lapse of time is good for my work. I feel that I can write best in the silence and solitude of the night, when everyone has retired. There is a bigness, a glory about the approach to the Wasteland Wanderer novel. I shall put myself into it as I have never done before.

Saturday a terrible accident happened here. The driver of my car ran over a little Japanese baby girl and killed her. I was sick, horrified, furious . . . and today she was buried. I can see her toddling around the yard, a strange little tot, cute, bizarre, human. I shall not soon forget that image. . . . I do not care for automobiles. They're dangerous and menacing. How tragic life is! It might have been my baby Loren. He is no better than the little Japanese girl. Someone might be careless and run over him. And, oh, the difference to me!

February 13. Night:

Wrote hard and well today—twelve pages, seven hours. Then I read Tagore, Ruskin, Arnold, and rhetoric. I am feeling well again and gaining strength and power and inspiration for the big book. It grows upon me day by day. I am beginning to understand the nonessentials even if I do not give them up.

February 15:

Have written twenty-four pages in the last two days. Have read Ruskin, Tagore, Arnold, and studied style. Every once in a while I feel the tremendous force of the novel. But it does not stay with me. I have too many distractions and interruptions. I am not yet deeply into it. Nevertheless I am not straining myself, or worrying about that. I shall take time with this great book. It grows and grows. It will be my best novel, I am sure. I shall utterly spend myself, my passion and soul and strength on it before I finish.

February 16. Sunday:

At nine o'clock last night I began to write. I had a good fire burning and my feet were wrapped in a blanket. The house was quiet. I became absorbed. The time flies, and at four-fifteen I had finished fifteen pages and the end of that passage. This was work I thrilled over. At three o'clock I felt fine, renewed, as if I had tapped a reserve force. But today I am tired and sleepy. I had only three hours' sleep.

February 19:

I have written only six pages in two days. My work and worry have been too much for me of late. Too much on my mind. Too much to decide. This motion-picture muddle had distracted me from my writing. Today I am sore, angry, bitter, and hopeless. The mood lingers. I have not yet dropped into that old black hell, and I shall not, but the danger was near.

I had the most trying time, sitting here, making scratches on my manuscript. All morning! It fills me with despair sometimes. But I must go on.

February 22:

Yesterday, February 21, was a bad day! I could not write! I went downtown and then out to the studio. Today I am better but irritable, strained, nervous. I cannot get a good hard grip on myself at once, as the worst will come.

February 22. Evening:

Today my boy Romer came home. Never was there such a time! He seemed absolutely changed. That school must be blessed by good teachers.

February 27:

I missed three days of writing. Restless and worried and distressed. Wasted days! Then I began to write again, five pages, after hours of idle scratching, and eleven the next day and today ten more. The novel grips me when I begin to write, and presently I am full of fire and passion. I am not ready yet for great concentration and passion.

March 1:

I have got back my fine spirits again!

Finished the seventh chapter. The book seems to have a big start, and that is all I need. I want to write and write and write. But this week I go to the desert again, and after that to Death Valley. There I will be able to write with the fire of a living flame. This novel obsesses me. It is wonderful, beautiful, terrible. I shall lose myself in love of the writing. Now I seem to think and think and think. And then write slowly. Restraint! Revision!

Today I had inspiring news. I met Mr. P.—the salesman for Harper & Brothers—and he told me *The Desert of Wheat* was selling remarkably well—far more than *The U.P. Trail*. The reorders, coming right after publication, are large. The novel has had a fine start. Mr. P. says they will go over the hundred thousand mark. All this is in order with the news of my book. Oh, it fills me with elation, hope, inspiration, and unquenchable spirit to go on and on and ON. . . ! ! !

March 2:

What a change can come over a man's mind in one short day! Tonight I am unhappy again—burdened over this motion-picture deal. It absolutely must be stopped! I will not let anything hinder my work; that I swear.

They tell some good stories about Romer, Loren, and Betty. The nurse tried to teach Romer to give the larger half of anything away when he divided it. She reminded him of this recently and he said, "Here, Betty, *you* divide it!"

March 12:

I had a fine rest at Palm Springs. Camped out under the mountains. Sat around the fire—walked in the moonlight, watched the desert, and profited exceedingly.

On the way out, I stopped at Glendora where Romer was attending school. It was great to see him there. I received a letter from him since then, and it is a masterpiece. He made known his dire necessities in a most subtle wording, and his postscript was this: "*P.S. I need the candy!*"

March 15:

We have had two days of storm and rain. Yesterday was the coldest, rainiest day I ever saw in California. Beautiful California!

March 29:

I have returned from Death Valley. It was a hard but wonderful trip. I walked across that ghastly place and back again. There has been much delay and abstraction in the course of my writing *Wanderer of the Wasteland*, some of it necessary and much of it needless.

It was good to get back to wife and babies. Betty grows prettier all the time.

March 31:

Today I began writing again, and without effort and strain. I have spent nearly a month in gathering material and in bothering with this motion-picturization of my book. It is time now to get down gradually to harder work than ever before. That I mean to do.

April 4:

Have been writing again for several days, in spite of illness. It is desperately hard to begin again after a long detachment. But I succeeded, and now it is growing easier. . . .

April 6, Sunday:

This morning a dust storm was blowing. I worked this morning after great difficulty in starting; and had to talk to an interviewer this afternoon. Then tonight I wrote some more, making in all a fair day's work.

April 9:

I read galleys all morning. My book *Tales of Fishes* is in preparation. I confess that reading proofs is a pleasure, at least of that book. It stimulates and inspires me.

Then, hard upon that task, I wrote twenty pages of my novel—seven hours of forgetfulness. Today I really got started. My wife came to me flushed and tearful with some of my ms. in hand, and she cried out, "Oh, it's great —great! I always felt you were going to do great things in this work!" It is seldom that Dolly shows any feeling like this. And to me it is more than inspiration.

April 12:

Yesterday was a lost day. I idled and dreamed and vacillated all morning. I sat with pencil in hand for three hours and did not write.

April 14:

Yesterday I wrote a little and rode horseback. I enjoyed it, but it played havoc with my legs. I'm stiff today, and I have not written a line. What an ordeal I went under to do the real work. Yet, I feel that I will do it.

April 17:

Yesterday I worked (fifteen pages), and some the day before, but today I did not want to write. I shirked it.

April 20. Midnight:

I have written eight hours today. The work is coming slowly. I feel the drive behind my spirit. Yesterday was idle. The day before I had to force myself.

April 26:

Having bad time again. Yesterday I could not write, so packed to send stuff to Avalon. Day before only eight pages. But before that I wrote twenty-six pages in one day.

This morning bad news in letters and telegrams threw me off. I fumed and fretted. It is so difficult to make these business decisions. I do not know what is good, or what is wrong. I have got to make a great effort to drive away the spell of blackness or sink into it. So I will go to writing!

April 27:

I did go, and wrote eighteen pages. It was a sort of triumph. Surely yesterday I was slated for the blues. But I determined not to succumb. I have established a fact. Many years has this been coming. Work is my salvation. It changes my moods.

Today I wrote twenty-three pages up to six o'clock, and tonight I shall write more. It's a tremendous emotional strain. I seem to live what I write. But the difficulty, the ordeal, is to start. That sense of immediacy, of hurry, of driving passion, is a dreadful thing to combat.

May 2:

Avalon again!

I was ill when we got here. The day before, I suffered severe pain in my breast. Could hardly breathe or stand erect. A doctor friend said I had neuritis.

May 6:

I am feeling much better and have begun to work again. And I'm beginning to climb the hills. This morning I climbed up the steep grassy slope back of my cottage to the road. How I panted! I could scarcely get my breath.

My legs were weak. Alas, for the old vigor. I wonder if I will ever get it back.

May 11:

Went to Los Angeles for several days to write the titles for motion picture. Lost five days from my novel and tired myself in the bargain.

I must now work as never before and am full of the zeal and force and passion to go at it. The next ten days or two weeks must be tremendous effort for me—sustained and controlled. I also must look out that I get proper exercise and rest. It will be a severe task upon my strength. I have never yet gone my limit, and I am curious to see just what I can do.

May 12. Evening:

What pitfalls await all our hopes and resolves!

This morning I got up at six-thirty and climbed the mountain. It was foggy, but the hills and slopes were clear. I was elated. I thrilled. I felt it all so poignantly, and I came back with the intention of working hard.

Then I got a telegram. It spoiled my cherished plans. And I grew disappointed, then angry, then bitter, and finally wretched. All morning I fumed and fretted about what to do. Then the mail came, and it had letters that angered and distressed me.

May 13:

Bad night. Got up loggy and tired and cramped with gloomy mind, tending toward dark and morbit imaginations. I fought. I climbed the mountain and walked far on the road. I fought as I walked, and when I got back I was in a sweat.

Doggedly I sat down to write, and the way was like a rough, painful road. I worked eight hours. And now my bitter black mood is lifting. The way is still long and steep and beset with pitfalls.

May 14:

Another disrupting telegram put me off this morning.
It took me hours to get to work, but at last I prevailed,
and from one till nine I did not know the passing of time.

May 17:

More agony! Another hopeless, black, terrible day. All
because I tried to write two letters and because I received
another. I believe I had been badly dealt with. My wishes
have been disregarded, and I have been affronted. No use
to try to write or rest or work or read.

May 18:

Yesterday I worked till my eyes gave out and my hand
was numb. Today I wrote nineteen pages and was tired
out after eight hours. I have fought desperately to conquer
my depression and misery. It seems to be fading.

May 20:

Worked hard today again, eight hours, twenty-three
pages. The novel grows apace. I shall be lost presently.
I feel the gathering weight of passion. I shall write like a
white flame.

May 22:

I have worked harder for two days. My eyes ache, my
hand is numbed, my arm feels dead.

May 23:

Events march on. I am in receipt of the largest offer
ever made by an American publisher to an American author. This seems incredible. I can't believe it—not yet.

Also I have received a telegram from Mr. Long of
Cosmopolitan that he is sending a man out to make me
an important proposition. This can mean only one thing.
He wants my novels. Incredible is this also. But I seem
to be on a slowly rising swell. I am going up. After all
these years of effort, agony, study, reading, reading, reading Arnold, Tennyson, Ruskin, Hudson, Poe, Stevenson,

Hamilton, James, and writing about the great outdoors, I am to come into my own. It looks well. But yet it is hard to believe. I can still afford to deal, to go on, to go on.

We have our ups and downs. I have been down for weeks. Perhaps I shall rise again.

May 24:

After breakfast I began to write. It came hard today. I labored and tortured my brain. Some things I could not do. I wrote for eight hours and then was unsatisfied. To-night I will try again. The climax is forming in my mind, and to give it birth will take heroic toil. I love my work but do not know how I write it.

May 27. Evening:

I slaved all day. Gradually got better. But writing was like digging coal. Loren was fascinated by sight and sound of an airplane today. He could not be dragged away. The buzz and roar simply delighted him. I never saw him so captivated.

May 29:

It is midnight. I have just ended my novel, *Wanderer of the Wasteland.* Twelve hours today—twenty-eight pages —and I sweat blood. Yet at this moment, I feel strong, keen, passionate, still unspent. The spell is in me yet. I do not know what it is that I have written. But I have never worked so hard on any book, never suffered so much or so long. Eight hundred and thirty-eight pages. One hundred and seventy thousand words. I have been long in getting the material, and five months in the writing. The only agony I feel now is the agony of reward. Have I written what I have yearned to write?

The two publishing offers Grey refers to were indeed fine ones. The head of one of the largest companies in New York had made a personal trip to California to try to talk Zane Grey into leaving Harper's and signing up with him. Grey, although flattered, would not hear of it.

His loyalty to Harper & Brothers was again tested by the emissary from Ray Long, of *Cosmopolitan*. Long was willing to pay one hundred thousand dollars for the serial rights to any novels that Grey was willing to give to him. It was an unheard-of price in 1920, but there was a string to the offer. *Cosmopolitan* was owned by the Hearst enterprises, which also had a flourishing book-company subsidiary. The book would have to be published by the Hearst company. Grey may have been tempted by the flattering offer, but he did not even give it a second thought.

Harper & Brothers had made him the best-selling author in America; he would not leave them, no matter what the offers were from other publishing companies. The offers may have been in the back of Grey's mind, however, the following spring when he asked Harper's to renegotiate his publishing contract.

CHAPTER **24**

People who did not know Zane Grey too well often talked about him and frequently remarked about his numerous lengthy trips away from home. The same was true about Dolly Grey; people who knew her only casually or through business wondered how she could see her husband go off on a six-month trip and make no protest about it.

There was speculation—and gossip—about it. Year after year, there were rumors that all was not well with the Zane Greys. They were separated, they were on the verge of divorce.

The large immediate family of the Greys and their few really intimate friends knew the true situation. They, like the Greys, refused to discuss it with others. They knew the facts, and that was all that mattered.

Zane Grey's was a complex character. His spirits were up, they were down. The "down" part of him dominated and grew even stronger with the passage of time. He was an extremely sensitive person. People who heard him talk sometimes thought him a complete extrovert. Nothing could be farther from the truth. He was painfully shy; when he talked, it was to cover up his embarrassment or to conceal the fact that he had been stung or was suffering from one of his black moods.

These black moods descended upon him even in his early youth. When he played baseball or engaged in a sport of some kind, he was at his best. But his long periods of fishing and his virtual seclusion at times, when he would remain in the house reading or just brooding, were not noticed by his family or his friends when he was a boy.

It was the introspective side of his character that made him a writer and that kept him one for so many years. Zane Grey was usually happy when he was working on his books, but the black mood could envelop him at any time.

One has only to read his diary entries to realize how deep and how frequent these black moods of depression were and what he did to combat them. He met Lina Roth on August 28, 1900. By March of 1901 they were already exchanging avowals of love—and had already had their first quarrel. Dr. Grey wrote a note of apology to Lina, and she wrote in reply, accepting his apology.

In April they quarreled again, and Dr. Grey told her of his black moods. In June, 1901, Lina returned Dr. Grey's letters and broke off with him. He wrote to her begging for an opportunity to plead his case, and the plea was apparently successful, for they were again corresponding two weeks later, and there is no mention of the breakup in their letters. There were never any later recriminations from Dolly.

But the black moods continued. Grey wrote to Dolly that it was best that he not see her for three or four days because he was suffering from one of his moods and he would probably start a quarrel with her. Lina was fully aware of these periods by now and sympathized with him.

The spells were not as frequent in 1903, but he still had them. In 1904 they seem to have lessened even more, and in 1905, the year they finally got married, there are no references

to them at all. Grey is now the ardent, perfect suitor. His letters are eloquent and emotional; his love for Lina Roth is the
most important thing in his existence.

There are only a few letters in 1906, for they were separated for only two or three days at a time. But the few letters
from this year are cheerful ones, very light in tone.

Toward the end of the year a slight note of desperation
is apparent. Zane Grey has been writing for a full year since
their marriage and has had no success whatever. There is a hint
of recurring spells of depression.

There are a number of letters in 1907 with references to
depression in the early part of the year. But the trip with Buffalo Jones in Arizona saved Zane Grey. His letters become
triumphant; they could even be considered boastful had they
not been written to his wife.

The year 1908 was a very bad one for Zane Grey, even
though he was beginning to have a semblance of literary success. By 1909, when his efforts were somewhat more successful, when he was thinking about and working on the book
that would make him famous, the black moods returned. He
had several severe attacks of depression.

He found a certain amount of relief in working, but writing also kept him completely alone for many hours of every
day. In the midst of a long fruitful session with his writing,
the depression would hit him without any apparent cause, and
then he would have to escape, by tramping the fields furiously,
by hunting and fishing, almost in desperation. When he was
physically exhausted, the depression faded, and he was able
to get back to his writing again.

The black moods did not decrease when success came; if
anything, they became even greater—and more frequent. In
1919 he was at the top of his career, not in earning power, but
in literary success. In 1918 his novel *The U.P. Trail*, was the
number-one best-seller of all books. He was number three in
1919 and would again be number one in 1920.

But read his diary closely for the five months during
which he wrote *Wanderer of the Wasteland*. He endured more

emotional torment during this period than at any other time in his writing career. He was compelled in the middle of the work to take off for three weeks and go back to Death Valley. Returning, he wrote with more zest, and the tone of his diary seems to improve considerably.

With the exception of the one three-week break, Grey was at home during the entire period of five months.

In 1922 it was Dolly Grey who left their home; she went east and spent several weeks in Lackawaxen. Grey wrote to her daily, and she replied as often. The letters from both are warm and tender, and there is virtually no hint that Zane Grey was having fits of depression.

Again, in 1923, Dolly went east and then to Europe. She was gone for several months, and the many letters that were exchanged are tender or bantering.

The love story of Dolly and Zane Grey is a truly remarkable one. It endured for thirty-nine years, from directly after their first meeting in 1900 until Zane Grey's death in October, 1939, and on Dolly's part it continued until her own death in 1957. Two years after her husband's death, Dolly notes poignantly in her diary, "Things are not right around here without Z.G."

In spite of the vicissitudes of fortune, the love between Dolly and Zane Grey was deep, passionate, and enduring. It was unabashed, open, and ardent. He never wrote a letter to her in which he did not express his love for her; this was as true in 1902, three years before they were married, as it was in the 1930's. In all their letters, even when Zane is stung by a letter of hers, there is always the final declaration of love, and it is virtually always more than just a casual signature.

There are endearing terms of affection, sometimes a long paragraph or more of his need for her, her need for him. Zane Grey wrote to her in his diaries, and he wrote with gratitude and devotion. In his moods of depression he refers to her, says that he knows he is hurting her, but he knows too that she will forgive him.

This deep love, this need for each other, is what held them

together through the trying periods, during the long periods of separation. Each always knew that the devotion of the other was steadfast, constant, that they would always be together again.

In the very early years Dolly was not altogether happy about his trips away from home, but she began to realize the true nature of them, the real need for them, and after about 1914 she no longer protested or chided him because of his absences. She accepted them as a part of their love for each other. Perhaps the separations were the principal cause of their long, constant romance. Certainly they were important. Had he stayed at home, Zane Grey would not have written half as much. It is doubtful that he could have endured through the long years without undergoing a complete emotional breakdown.

Although there was evidence of his depression in the diary of the writing of *Wanderer of the Wasteland*, the following year when Grey went to Long Key, Florida, and wrote *Code of the West* in five weeks, he did not have one black spell. He did not lose one day of writing. He went out and fished for ten hours a day and still managed to do his full stint of writing, in addition to writing daily letters to Dolly Grey.

To continue his writing career, Zane Grey *had* to take the many trips. He had to take them because of his physical health, because of his mental condition, and Dolly who was fully cognizant of her husband's complex character, nurtured and loved him throughout the long, long years. She was a remarkable woman.

CHAPTER **25** ━━━━━━━━━━━━━━━━━━

In 1920 Romer Grey was eleven, Elizabeth eight, and Loren five; they needed room to play, and Zane Grey found, at last, the home that he had sought since coming to California.

It was a big, three-story house on Mariposa Avenue in Altadena. It had large, spacious rooms and plenty of shade trees and gardens. It was on a five-acre tract of land. From the third-floor study Grey could see the peak of Mount Wilson in the north.

It was a restful place. Dolly Grey furnished it in keeping with the Spanish architectural style of the house. The huge living room had bearskin rugs on the floor, from animals that Grey had shot in Arizona.

Beyond the living room was the library, with wicker furniture and bookshelves around the entire room. On the floor were Navajo rugs Grey had bought in New Mexico and Arizona.

The many rooms of the large house became crammed with trophies and mementos of Grey's travels, and in 1928 Grey decided to do something about them. He measured off an area at right angles to the house; it was forty-eight feet by seventy-five. He told Dolly Grey that he wanted a study built there by the time he returned from the trip to New Zealand on which he was about to embark.

Dolly took him at his word. When Grey returned there was a two-story wing of the specified size. His trophies and mementos had been moved into the lower floor. The upper story was to be his working quarters. It could be entered from a passageway on the second floor of the house.

The entry room from the house was about one-third of the entire vast floor. It was a separate room, yet really a part of the whole, for only low bookshelves separated it from Grey's study—and a two-step stair down to the main part.

His huge Morris chair was in position. On it was the large plywood cutout board on which Grey did his writing. On a table within reach were stacks of paper and sharpened pencils.

From 1928 to 1939 Grey did his writing in this room. It has been preserved as it was in 1939, the shelves filled with the books that Zane Grey read and those he wrote, in the many, many editions, including twenty translations.

The writing board is still in position, resting on the arms of the Morris chair. Lina Elise Grey lived in this house until her death in 1957. It is occupied today by Romer Grey, who uses the former library downstairs to conduct the business of Zane Grey, Inc., a thriving company that deals in the books and the subsidiary rights.

The smaller part of the second floor was used by Zane Grey's secretary, who typed the manuscripts after they were corrected by Dolly Grey and answered the voluminous correspondence.

There was never any telephone in the new wing. Zane Grey did not want to be interrupted by its ringing when he was working. When a really important call came for him, it was taken in the main part of the house, and he went there to speak on the phone.

The Zane Grey family had left Zanesville, Ohio, in 1890. The last year there had not been a happy one, and when they moved to Columbus they had cut off all ties with Zanesville.

Zanesville had not forgotten the Greys, however. When Pearl Zane Gray became a famous college baseball star, his exploits were recorded in the Zanesville newspaper. R. C.'s major-league baseball records were dutifully reported in Zanesville, and the young author of *Betty Zane* himself sent a copy of his first book to the Zanesville paper and a short time later an announcement of his marriage to Lina Elise Roth, this a clipping from a New York City newspaper.

Later, when Zane Grey became famous, the Zanesville newspaper proudly hailed him as Zanesville's own.

Another of Zanesville's native sons, Sam Jenkins, who had delivered newspapers as a boy and had graduated to operating a newsstand and bookstore where the young Pearl Gray bought —and stole—so many dime novels, left Zanesville and went to New York to become a book salesman for Grosset & Dunlap, the company that had been reprinting the Zane Grey books in the cheaper editions and selling them by the hundreds of thousands.

Sam Jenkins had never forgotten Pearl Gray, who had been such an avid reader and customer of his little store. He had watched the spectacular rise of Zane Grey, the author, after his first success with *The Heritage of the Desert* in 1910, and when his company began publishing the reprint editions, he always did his best to sell his books. He made frequent trips to Zanesville, where he had maintained his contacts. Some of his old acquaintances were now members of the Zanesville Rotary Club, and in 1921 they thought of a plan to bring its most famous citizen back to Zanesville.

A motion picture had just been made of *The Desert of Wheat*, and the members of the Rotary Club thought that the local premiere of the motion picture was an excellent time to have a "Zane Grey Homecoming Week."

The entire city of Zanesville became participants in the event and turned out to pay its respects to Zane Grey. Schools were closed to enable the three thousand Zanesville children of school age to see *The Desert of Wheat* at the Weller Theatre and hear their favorite author speak to them.

The theater was jammed, and there were some thousands of people on the sidewalks waiting for Zane Grey to appear so that they could get a glimpse of him.

After the picture had been shown and Grey stepped on the stage, the children cheered him so wildly that he became choked with emotion and found it difficult to speak.

The Rotary Club gave a luncheon for Grey, and the city of Zanesville held a banquet for him at the new Masonic Temple.

It was difficult for Zane Grey. Articulate in the presence of friends and very small groups, Grey was shy before crowds and disliked making speeches. He was overwhelmed by his reception in his native city, but as soon as he was able, he slipped away from the crowds and found his way alone to Convers Avenue. The old house was still there, but the number had been changed from 363 to 705. The house was now owned by Henry Danker, and Grey reminisced with him, then went behind the house and located the spot of the old "cave" in which he had written his first story, "Jim of the Cave." He recalled the disastrous consequence of that first literary effort.

The succeeding years were too full for Zane Grey to return again to Zanesville, but he never forgot the tumultuous welcome in 1921, just as he always remembered the bittersweet days of his youth.

Zane Grey's diary reports his visit to Zanesville thus:

On March 23 I took the Pennsylvania train west, my destination being my old home, Zanesville, Ohio, that I had not really seen for over twenty-five years.

I was met at the station by an old friend—an old sweetheart (on my side if not hers)—and the trend of my memories was diverted. We rode uptown, past the old courthouse and out Sixth Street, across the bridge into Putnam, to her house on Woodlawn Avenue opposite the old seminary where my sister went to school. Then I returned to my old home and realized that I was in for a poignant experience.

Next afternoon I walked up by the old Third Street bridge and around the road under Putnam Hill. Memories thronged quick and fast. How beautiful the meeting place of the two rivers. Falls of Muskingum, it was called in early days, when my great-grandfather, Colonel Ebenezer Zane, and his brother Jonathan and others blazed a trail from Wheeling to Marysville, Kentucky. The trail was called Zane's Trace, and is now Main Street in Zanesville.

I went past the old Eighth Ward School, where I used to toil over my lessons and be in endless conflict with my teachers. It now was a deserted, bleak building with windows broken and falling into decay. But to stand there and look at it swelled my heart.

Then I went up to the McIntire Terrace. The streets did not seem the same. Many houses stood just as I remembered them. But they were smaller, and the grounds had shrunk and the trees had grown. All was changed.

I went to my old home and stood stunned at its plain,

small, drab appearance. My home! Two old trees were still standing, an oak and a walnut, both of which I had climbed a hundred times. Inside the house, changes had been made. I stood in the hall were Mother used to shut us children in during thunderstorms. Ah, it was as yesterday! I peeped into the room where my brother Romer and I used to go to bed in the cold and dark, afraid and shivering. We used to warm each other's backs. I stood in strange awe in the room where I was born. I remember that here my father was ill, and in hot days I had to stay in to fan the flies off him, and when he fell asleep I would put newspapers on his face and run away.

Then I took the road to Dillon's Falls. The old cabin of the Coffees stood, and I was told that they had lived there until recently.

My old camping and fishing grounds were now a summer resort. The old plank-enclosed bridge where I used to stub my toes and peep through knotholes was gone. In its place stood a hideous iron structure.

My stay there was brief, sad, and yet sweet.

. . . And so on through a week of tremendous mental stress. I was sought, praised, flattered, entertained, as never before in my life. I belonged to Zanesville. I was a Zane, and these, my people, my old friends and many new ones, were proud of me. The reception filled me with awe, wonder, sadness, and gratitude. It enchanted me. It almost directed my purpose in writing. It made me humble.

. . . While in Zanesville there came news concerning my publishing affairs in New York. My last book was the best-seller in all the U.S., and the Curtis Publishing Company planned a campaign for advertising my book.

Hard on that came a poisonous attack on my last novel by a writer in the *San Francisco Chronicle*. It was so bitter, so hateful, so amazingly unjust that it made me ill. From the heights I plunged to the depths. And so my last two days in Zanesville were not happy.

CHAPTER **26** ————————————————

Throughout his entire thirty-year career as a writer Zane Grey suffered from the barbs of the critics. He never got over their attacks on him. Over and over he swore he would not read the reviews of his books, but when one was published he found himself unable to resist reading them. Always they upset him. Sometimes he became actually physically ill. After reading a bad review he would find himself unable to write for days at a time.

In the middle 1920's, when he was America's best-selling author, when his annual income from writing exceeded that of any other American writer, Zane Grey was so hurt by the criticisms of his books that he wrote a twenty-page article that was a defense of his books and style of writing, at the same time that it was an attack on the critics who had always flayed him so mercilessly.

He was all for publishing the article, even though he knew that it might make the critics attack him even harder, but Dolly Grey protested, and in the end she won out. The original manuscript survives, however, and the reading of it is impressive if for no other reason than that it reveals some of the secret chambers of his mind. In it Grey is surprisingly humble in his evaluation of his own work. Even in his denunciation of the critics he shows remarkable restraint. They had flayed him with whips of rawhide; he retaliated with whips of soft velvet. Where they had denounced him with stinging, vitriolic words, he replied in soft metaphors.

The portly Heywood Broun had written that the substance of any two Zane Grey books could be written upon the back of a postage stamp. Grey merely says of this, ". . . It was not a kind or a brilliant thing to say about a hard-working, honest author."

Possibly the most influential literary critic of the day was the brilliant Burton Rascoe, whose vocabulary and the use of it were the envy of his contemporaries. With the publication in 1923 of *Wanderer of the Wasteland,* which the author considered his best work up to that time, Grey had pleaded that the critics should read the book honestly and not merely denounce it on the basis of his past work. He said that he would stand or fall on it. Burton Rascoe took him at his word. He read the book carefully and wrote a long review. Grey read it and thought it seemed to repay him for all the stings and arrows of the past outrageous criticisms, and then he came to the very last sentence, in which Rascoe destroyed all that he had said in what seemed to be a careless afterthought. He, Burton Rascoe, could not believe in purple cows. Grey was appalled and went about for days in a stunned condition.

In his reply to the critics Grey relates a scene that had taken place shortly before. While fishing at Long Key, Florida, he had seen the anchored yacht of the great merchant prince John Wanamaker, owner of the Wanamaker department stores. Grey was well known at Long Key, where he was president of the Long Key Fishing Club and its best fisherman. He was startled, however, when he received a summons to come to Wanamanker's yacht.

He entered the cabin of the yacht, where he saw a copy of his *Tales of Fishes.* Wanamaker then entered the cabin. He was in his eighties.

He placed his hand on Grey's shoulder. "Grey," he said, "I like your books. I have given away thousands of them, and sold hundreds of thousands. You have no conception of the force for good you are in our national life. It is the people who define your status. You cannot abandon your ideals. You have chosen the West as a field for fiction. But your appeal is universal. Never lay down your pen!"

Grey then addresses the critics in general. If the critics are right, he tells them, then he has no business bringing out idealistic romances in a world where ideals and romance are no more. But perhaps it is the critics who are wrong. He asks them who reads his books in such huge quantities; he says the critics should ask janitors, plumbers, salesgirls, librarians, firemen, engineers, carpenters, lawyers, preachers, schoolgirls, nurses, farmers, baseball players, actors (he mentions John Barrymore, who was a great fan of Zane Grey books), the millions of people who supported the motion-picture industry, for Hollywood was making more pictures of Zane Grey's books than of any other writer's works.

Zane Grey's answer to his critics is a revealing document, but its publication at the time would not have helped him. Dolly Grey was wise in persuading her husband to put the manuscript aside. It makes interesting reading today, but it would not have served to advance the career of Zane Grey himself.

Besides, the best answer to the critics was the steadily increasing popularity of Zane Grey's books and magazine serials.

The criticism of Zane Grey's writing was widespread and unrelenting. It began with his earliest books and rose to a crescendo as the sales of his books went up, up, and up. When he was America's best-selling author, the criticism was so widespread and universal that it condemned not only the writing of Zane Grey but also his publishers for printing such worthless trash and even the general public for reading and liking the works.

The critics who condemned Zane Grey did so from their citadels in Boston, New York, and Philadelphia, from their penthouses on Riverside Drive, their hall bedrooms. Few had ever seen a horse except on a bridle path in New York, or those patient equines that were attached to milk wagons.

Zane Grey did not write of the West until he had been there. When he first visited Arizona in 1907 he fell in love with the country, and until his death in 1939 he spent from one-quarter to one-half of his time in the West. He *lived* in the West for years. He saw the places he wrote about; he did the things his characters did. He rode horses; he hunted buffalo, mountain lions, bear, deer, elk. He climbed mountains in the wildest, most inaccessible places. He crossed rivers, swimming his horse; he rode invisible trails in the rain, in blinding snowstorms, in 110-degree heat. He camped at night in rainstorms, in below-zero weather. He knew the country of which he wrote as no other writer has ever known his backgrounds.

He knew the *people*. He talked with Indians—Comanches, Paiutes, Navajos, Apaches. He knew the taciturn Mormons, the Indian traders, the cowboys, and the ranchers. He knew Texas Rangers, gunfighters, gamblers, dance-hall girls.

He knew the young men and the old, the men who had taken part in the epic events of the roaring 1870's and 1880's.

Al Doyle, his frequent guide, had worked on the Union Pacific during its building between 1865 and 1869. He had been in the Kansas trail towns when they were wild and raw. Zane Grey knew personally dozens of men who had known Wyatt Earp, Billy the Kid, Jesse James, and General George Armstrong Custer. He knew Texas Rangers who had served under the great Captain McNelly. He got the stories from these people firsthand.

He was the most copious note-taker of all writers. When in camp he spent hours every evening writing down things he had seen or heard during the day. Nothing was too trivial for him. If he saw a plant or a flower he had never seen before, he wrote down its description, after ascertaining its name from the people he was with.

He wrote the actual *dialogue* of his companions. Sometimes his spelling had to be phonetic because of the way the words had been pronounced, but he wrote down the way it *sounded*. He was a faithful recorder; the way the people talked was the way he wrote it down. The people he wrote about *did* talk the way Grey had them talk.

It was said over and over that things that happened in Zane Grey's books had never happened in the West and *could* never have happened. That is not true. The fictional events in Western books have never been as wild as the things that actually happened in the years when the West was being conquered.

Cannibalism, a subject so abhorrent that fiction writers have shied away from it, was much more prevalent than has

ever been written about. More than forty persons were eaten
by the survivors of the Donner party. Quantrill, the infamous
Civil War guerrilla, was a hanger-on of the Albert Sidney Johnston expedition to Utah. He went prospecting in the Idaho
mountains with five companions in the fall of 1857. Early in
the spring he was found wandering in the mountains by a
detachment of dragoons. He carried the leg of a man wrapped
in a piece of burlap. His companions were never heard of again.
The soldiers were so revolted that they drove Quantrill out of
Utah. He returned to Kansas, where he taught a term of school
the following year!

In 1875 the adjutant-general of Texas published *The
Crime Book*, which listed by name eight thousand known outlaws then in Texas. Within two years more than half of these
men were eliminated—most of them by the Texas Rangers,
who seldom took prisoners. The Rangers became so feared
that a rumor of *one* of them being in the vicinity was sufficient
to disperse any gathering of outlaws.

No gunfighter ever depicted by Zane Grey or other writers
of Westerns was deadlier than the real-life John Wesley Hardin,
who was the inventor of the shoulder holster, the border shift,
the road agent's spin, and the other tricks of the gunfighters.
Hardin killed more than thirty-five *armed* men in his short
gunfighting career.

In the fight at Beecher's Island in Nebraska, forty plainsmen and soldiers held off two thousand Indians for almost two
weeks. At the fight at Adobe Walls in the Texas Panhandle,
twenty-one buffalo hunters, including the later well-known Bat
Masterson, withstood the repeated attacks of fifteen hundred
Arapahoes and Comanches, the Comanches led by the famous
Quanah Parker.

These were hardy men, the plainsmen and frontiersmen.
Given good weapons and ample ammunition and a reasonable
shelter, they were formidable opponents to any number of
savage attackers.

Custer and two hundred and three cavalrymen were
wiped out at the Little Big Horn—but the Indians who com-

mitted this massacre numbered well over ten thousand, perhaps as many as twenty thousand. The following day they repeatedly assaulted fewer than three hundred cavalrymen who had a good position, and they could not break through. Custer was caught in an exposed, indefensible position by a horde of well-armed Indians fighting on their own ground.

Zane Grey, aside from his perpetual note-taking, was a scholar of no mean ability. What he did not know, he researched. He never wrote on any subject until he had studied all the available material on it.

CHAPTER **27** ———————————

In 1920 Zane Grey spent some weeks fishing at Long Key, Florida. Dolly was in Lackawaxen during this time, where she became ill, and Grey's concern in his letters to her is apparent. When Dolly recovered she went to California, and Grey went to New York. The reason for this trip was that a new contract with Harper's was due.

Both Dolly and Zane Grey were well aware of the popularity of his books, and both believed strongly that the author should reap the rewards. Negotiations had been going on by mail to better the royalty terms that Grey was then receiving. The negotiations had been inconclusive, so when Grey arrived in New York he engaged the services of an attorney. The result is given in his letter, written on Sunday, April 10, from Lackawaxen, where he had gone immediately after the agreement had been reached. The letter reads:

Dear Old Dolly!

This morning I was awakened by song sparrows and robins. Made three fires. Packed wood. Pumped the pump. The air was keen and cold, exhilarating and sweet; the

valleys of the mountains were purple; the black summits
tinged with rose.

All the past came flooding back, and what I wanted
most and longed for with a pang in my breast was the
woman who fought and strove with me here in this hard,
barren, lonely place. You! This is home. This will
always be home for you and me. We ought to live here
some of every year and be buried here! I have half a
notion to wire you to come home. But I'll wait till I
see how I feel in a week or so.

There is a strike on the railroads and tubes and
ferryboats. Glad I am here with my baggage. No news
yet that you do not know.

Were the $8,000 and $500 checks all you received? I
sent several more, one for $3,000. Now, honey, don't
disobey your master!

Rome and Mr. Stern [Grey's lawyer] and I went down
to Harper to have it out. That was quite a conference.
But I will not tell you in detail until I see you. Suffice to
say that I could have gotten a check for $75,000 or
$100,000 advance on new contract, and I refused it
because Mr. Stern said the income tax on it would be
$48,000.

We gave in to Harper a little, and they met us, with the
result that Mr. Stern will draw up a contract very
satisfactory to me. Fifteen percent up to ten thousand—
twenty percent over that. Seven cents on cheap editions.
Ten thousand dollars' advance on delivery of novels.
Adequate foreign royalties. Four cents a volume on book
sets. The magazine will be open to me. Some victory!
There will be a tremendous push back of my work now.

So cheer up, honey, and try to deserve your loving
hubby. I will write you often.

> Yours,
> Doc

Zane Grey was a lifelong opponent of the Internal Revenue Service. Taxpayers of the 1960's sigh about the "good old days" of the 1920's and 1930's, when the income taxes were negligible. The truth of the matter is that the taxes were low during those years for the low-income groups, but they were quite substantial for those in the upper brackets.

Zane Grey's income in 1919 was close to one hundred thousand dollars. Both he and Dolly made numerous trips that year that were certainly connected with business and were therefore deductible. Grey also spent a considerable amount on his fishing and hunting equipment. He records in one letter that he spent over a thousand dollars on guns for his hunting trips, and certainly his tackle and gear for fishing cost him several times that. And his travel fares and cost of staying at the fishing resorts ran into large sums.

The Internal Revenue Service held a dim view of these deductions. That Zane Grey was then one of the world's best-known fishermen, that he published a book on fishing in 1919 and another in 1920, that he wrote eight long fishing articles for magazines like *The Country Gentleman,* and that a considerable part of his income came from these should certainly have made the Internal Revenue Service consider fishing a part of his profession and permit him to deduct the expenses accordingly. They did not, however.

In 1922 Grey's income required a payment of forty-four thousand dollars in income taxes. In 1924 Grey's income taxes amounted to fifty-four thousand dollars, but he was becoming somewhat reconciled by that time, and his journal entry when he paid the tax is not too scorching.

But he howled in 1925—and kept on carping about it— when Internal Revenue assessed him $1750 on the value of his schooner, *Fisherman.* He would not talk to the tax people for fear of losing his temper. The amount was finally reduced to $1500, which Grey paid, but very, very reluctantly.

The running feud that had existed between Zane Grey and the Internal Revenue Service since 1922 was still going on

in 1931, and had reached a point where Zane Grey and Dolly
thought it necessary for them to go to Washington, D.C., and
talk to someone who was above the local California I.R.S.
level. They took the train to Washington late in 1931, and
Dolly records in her diary that they had scarcely reached their
hotel when a message came from the White House. President
Herbert Hoover had read some of Grey's books and wanted to
send his regards. Later in the day came an invitation to have
lunch with the President and Mrs. Hoover the following day.

Dolly duly records the luncheon. The talk between them
and the President and his wife continued until four o'clock in
the afternoon.

The fact that Zane Grey and his wife had had lunch with
the President of the United States apparently did not impress
the people at the I.R.S., for in the following weeks Dolly refers several times in her diary to calls from I.R.S. people in
Altadena. The case was finally resolved, but not to Zane Grey's
satisfaction. He was, like virtually every other American, a
lifelong foe of the Internal Revenue Service.

One of Zane Grey's finest letters to his wife, written from
Long Key, Florida, on February 21, 1922, shows the close
relationship between them.

Dearest Dolly,

Yours of a week ago at hand. Dear girl, I despair of
answering this wonderful letter. I can't even try. At
best I can tell you that I shall trace every word you wrote
in lead pencil over with ink so that I can treasure your
letter always.

Honey, don't change! Be always as you are. My heaven,
if you get any nobler, any more wonderful—how can I
stand it? Please be bad. Please be selfish. Do something
terribly human so that I can hold up my head.

I welcome all you said about your life henceforth

and bless you for it, and love you more than you know.
And I will *do* more.

On March 17, 1922, he wrote to Dolly:

Dearest Dolly,

Am sending synopsis of *The Vanishing American,* also
copies of letters mailed to Lasky. At your leisure read
them all, so you will be posted as to my angle and also on
what I wrote to Lasky.
I am hopeful that you will think the synopsis great.
I think Lasky was surprised.
Mr. Crowell wired today that the article you sent was a
knockout. I presume you will take all the credit, for
you said you worked over it. Very well, I shall have you do
publicity work for me hereafter.
You sure are there, Dolly dear, when it comes to a
thing. To me you are simply a marvel, and all my
property, too.

Another letter, two days later, to Dolly: "That income-tax
robber made me ill."

And two days later, a telegram:

Troubles multiplied. Second income tax disallowed.
Claims bill for year 1920 over ten thousand dollars and
interest. I refuse to pay it. Please advise what legal steps
necessary.

CHAPTER **28** ————————————

In April, 1921, Dolly Grey took her first overland trip by automobile. She had with her the
two younger children, Loren and Betty; Hildred, a governess;

and two drivers. She wrote a daily report to Zane Grey, which reads like a travelogue. She reported on the condition of the roads (very bad in those days), the sort of places she stayed at night, and every incident that happened along the way. Her observations of the country are sharp, and the account, written every evening and mailed to Zane Grey, runs to eighty pages. They are excellently written and show a gift for description that would have been a credit to her husband.

They reached Lackawaxen in the middle of May, and Dolly promptly reported the fact to Zane, and in the letter expressed her love of the Lackawaxen place, regretting that they had ever gone west.

Zane Grey, meanwhile, had gone to Oregon to try the fishing in the Rogue River, and he had written Dolly to join him there. He had also written her daily while she was traveling eastward, addressing his letters to General Delivery at various cities along the way. Dolly did not get all of them.

In July, Dolly started westward, but this time she took the northern route and went to Oregon. It was another month of traveling over roads even more primitive than those in the South and Southwest. She wrote a similar daily chronicle of the return trip.

They were at home only two or three weeks when Grey left to go hunting in Colorado.

It was a rather good writing year for him. During Dolly's trip east he fished at Avalon for several weeks and wrote *To the Last Man*, one of his best and most successful motion-picture books. Filming was started even before the story began to appear serially in *The Country Gentleman*. He also wrote *Call of the Canyon*, beginning the story in Avalon, working on it in Oregon, then completing it just before his departure on the Colorado trip.

When he returned from Colorado he resumed work on a novel that he had actually begun more than a year before and put aside. Dolly had never been enthusiastic about this story, but Grey was determined to write it. There are two journal entries regarding the story:

Nov. 29, 1921:

Today I began rewriting *Shores of Lethe*. This makes
the fifth time I have undertaken that novel. I wonder—
has it always been a mistake? However that may be, the
start was one of unusual strain, and tonight I find myself at low ebb of spirit.

The intention to embody in this novel all the license
of the modern day—all the freedom of the young people,
the jazz and dance and ridicule, and their rotten sensual
stuff—has aroused in me the need to read the magazines
on present-day morals. And the effect has been to depress
and sadden and hurt me terribly. I see so much more than
I used to see. It may not be too late to write the novel.

Dec. 17, 1921:

Off and on and I have been writing *Shores of Lethe*.
Today I tortured myself back to writing. After all, what
is writing but an expression of my own life? These critics
who crucify me do not guess the littlest part of my
sincerity. They must be burned by a blaze. I cannot learn
from them.

The editors of *The Country Gentleman* had some qualms
about *Shores of Lethe* but were loath to reject any story of
Grey's and decided to publish it immediately. The title was
changed to *The Day of the Beast*. It is Zane Grey's one and only
"Eastern" story, and was not well received by the critics—and
not too well by the readers. It sold thirty thousand copies in
the Harper editions, a good sale for anyone else, but a very
poor sale for Zane Grey, who had never sold that few copies
since his very first book.

Grey was greatly disappointed in the reception, but he had
been well paid for the time involved in the writing of it and
reconciled himself with that.

Dolly Grey's cross-country trip in 1921 had been a strenuous one, but in 1922 she decided to repeat it. She started east
in May, with only a secretary and the driver. She left all the

children with her husband. She had scarcely gone when Zane wrote her on May 30, addressing the letter to Trinidad, Colorado, and expressing some concern regarding the driver:

> ... I have been concerned to hear from Rome [R. C.], Cookie, and others how Ken runs your cars and why he smashes so many springs, tires, etc. He is a fine driver, but like most Californians he has the speed mania. I will absolutely forbid him to run a car in L.A. over twenty-five miles an hour. Cookie says she has been with him when he ran forty. Ida also, but Rome says that that was the trouble when we crossed the Mojave. I like Ken, and he's O.K., but nothing doing on the speed stuff anymore. Do you get that, beloved? Not over thirty miles on any road, at any time. Otherwise I will fire this driver and scrap the cars.

Just before Dolly's departure Zane had begun work on *The Vanishing American*. He has several entries in his diary that report progress on this work. At the same time, he was writing long letters to Dolly every day.

In June he wrote Dolly to meet him in Oregon again, as in the previous year, and she dutifully made the return trip via the northern route.

Diary excerpts from 1922:

June 7:
I am writing my Indian story, the material for which I have been seeking for ten years and more. It is well started now and has tremendously gripped me. I feel the surge of the great tragic moments and believe I shall live up to them. It is a responsibility, this novel. I do not want to miss anything of my splendid opportunity. The Indian story has never been written. Maybe I am the man to do it. I must go deeper and even stronger into my treasure mine and stint nothing of time, toil, or torture.

June 9:

Loren came to my study today. He was important and bursting with news. He thrust his school report in my hand. "There," he said. "What do I get?" It was a good report, and I made him happy by giving him a dollar.

Betty's report was not so good, and when I did not offer her anything, she cried. Then I studied over the report again and found justification for fifty cents. She beamed.

They went to see the animal picture in the movies. Loren was wild to tell all he saw. He raved about the "crack—the crack-oo-crackodile." And Betty, in her recital of the impressions, told of the "oorang-ootang swanging on the branches of trees."

June 22:

I have finished *The Vanishing American*—my novel on the Indian. The idea had been long in my mind, as well as some of the material. In April I took a hard and trying trip across the Painted Desert, Paiute Canyon, and Uplands country to Nonnezosche. It was most productive. On May 5 I began writing, and I finished the novel June 8, with only two breaks in continuous work. I did not have one bad spell during the writing—an unprecedented record. Always I have had spells of depression.

This establishes the fact that I do not have to have them, and then my work is better and certainly my health.

Dec. 3, 1922. Sunday:

Romer tore the house to pieces today. He teased Betty and Loren until they ran wild. The living room, Indian room and library, and D.'s room were all in a mess. He wrote letters like a madman and altogether quite bewildered us. When he left to go back to the academy, D. and I fell upon each other's necks and breathed simultaneously: "He's gone. . . . Dear little man!" He wanted to emulate his father. He wants to write stories and fish and hunt and photograph and spend money as I do. It is a terrible thing. He is so dynamic, so compellingly energetic and vital, that he takes my breath. How the months slip into years! He talks of Harvard College to study literature.

CHAPTER **29** ━━━━━━━━━━━━━━━━━━━

Zane Grey was in New York on New Year's Day of 1923. He wrote to Dolly:

I wrote fifteen pages today. It's some day. Rained cats and dogs early, now at five P.M. it is blowing great guns and stormy but clear.

I saw the New Year in. It was a decent New Year's for a change, but it took a million officers to make it so. I got into the big ballroom here and was disgusted, but it was a strange, garish, colorful moving picture. I'll say people have gone crazy over eating, drinking, dancing and—

On January 7 he writes to Dolly again: "Harper sent a check out west, $27,500, I think."

Continuing the financial discussion, he wrote again on January 11:

I think I can see $480,000 in the next two years. Don't you think you had better stick to me? Of course, I can win you back by bribes and don't mean it that way. But isn't it nice?

I sent you another check to deposit for me. English royalties, $19,300 odd. Isn't that grand?

He left for Long Key, Florida, a few days later and on January 17 wrote to Dolly:

Began to work this morning. I will soon be the livest hubby you ever had. There's a great deal to accomplish.

I want to do some more work equal to *Tappan's Burro.*
Currie (*Ladies' Home Journal*) says that's a great story,
and commanded the top price ever paid. It will be
published in one issue, with two wonderful paintings.

My beloved, I have not had a single bad spell this
year. Lots of provocation, too. Let's make it a wonderful
year for work and achievement. I need your— Oh, all that
I went on record for in the dedication to the *Wanderer.*
And, Dolly dear, I don't want to be wholly selfish. I want
you to know I understand, and I surely think you the
most adorable and wonderful of women.

In February Grey finished *Code of the West,* writing
forty-seven pages the last day, which he reported to Dolly. *The
Country Gentleman* sent a check to him for thirty thousand
dollars, which he promptly mailed to Dolly. A letter from John
Pickett of *The Country Gentleman* adds this interesting
comment:

> I have been noticing splendid reviews you have gotten
> on *Wanderer of the Wasteland* and am delighted to hear
> that the sales are doing so well. At last you seem to have
> broken through the reserve of that New York bunch
> who scratch each other's backs and who look upon the
> country west of the Hudson as largely waste territories
> from a literary standpoint.

In January Grey had sent two checks to Dolly for $27,500
and $19,330, and this $30,000 brought his income to over
$76,800—during the first two months of 1923.

Grey left Long Key on April 1 and went to New York to
continue some negotiations with publishers. He had come to a
tentative agreement to do two novels a year for *The Ladies'
Home Journal* at thirty thousand dollars each, and he agreed
to do two for *The Country Gentleman* at the same price.

He returned to California, to be greeted with the news
that Dolly had decided to take a long vacation. He thought

she was entitled to it, but what Dolly had in mind was a leisurely drive across the country, a stay in Lackawaxen of a few
weeks, and then—a trip to Europe. She would be gone altogether for more than four months, and that disconcerted him.
He was already hard at work on *The Thundering Herd*, for
which he had high hopes.

Dolly started east early in May, and he began writing
her the daily letters from Avalon, where he had gone for fishing and to work on the new novel. On May 5 he had more
than three hundred longhand pages written.

Several diary entries of this period are of interest:

April 29, 1923:
  Florida for ten weeks was, as always, good for my spirit
and health. I wrote most of the romance *Code of the
West* and several outdoor stories, and fifty pages in. another book.

  I was in New York December 30 till January 14, and
I had a busy, exciting time. Then New York again from
April 2 to April 8.

  Dolly is fine, well, cheerful, full of her great plans, alert
to all the manifold angles of my work and surely the
grandest wife and helpmeet any man ever had the good
fortune to possess.

  Here I begin again to write.

April 30:
  I have begun to write again. Another romance! The
epic of the buffalo. *The Thundering Herd.* Where do I
find these romances? That query has been promulgated
by critics and reviewers who have never been west. I see
these romances, and I believe them. Somewhere, some-
time, they happened. My reward and my faith in myself
come from the many letters I get from simple readers—
old women, and young girls and boys, to all with hearts
full of romance, all true to the children in them.

June 4–5

It is now far into the night. I can hear the wash of the surf on the beach and the melancholy chirp of crickets. The night seems dark, cold, lonely. I have just finished *The Thundering Herd*, after writing all day and up to now. I am tired. May arm aches. My head boils. My feet are cold. But I am not aware of any weakness.

I do not feel that I have done well in the writing of this romance of the buffalo. Always I have that feeling at the end of work. I seem to have failed in the great epic strife I set out to picture. But the story went on of itself and was not what I planned. And now it must stand or fall.

Dolly spent a month in Lackawaxen and took a short trip or two to New York to take care of pressing publishing matters, and a week before sailing time she moved into the Hotel McAlpin, which was Zane Grey's favorite hotel in New York.

Grey wrote continuously, and when the *Mauretania* had sailed from New York, he addressed his letters to London, then to Paris, and finally to Italy and back to London. A flock of letters awaited Dolly upon her return to New York.

Although the trip was essentially a vacation, Grey kept writing Dolly to call upon the publishers in England, France, and Italy, and Dolly faithfully performed the service. Dolly enjoyed the trip thoroughly and several times hinted darkly about a mysterious Count who was pursuing her in Europe; this was sheer fiction and was in response to Grey's frequent suggestions that women were throwing themselves at him on his travels.

All of the children remained with Grey during Dolly's European trip. There was a nursemaid, a housekeeper, and other help in the home at Altadena, as well as in Avalon, where the family lived for part of the time Dolly was away.

When Dolly returned from Europe, she spent several weeks in New York and Lackawaxen, again taking care of business matters; then she began to drive back to California, making the trip of four weeks without mishap.

Grey felt the separation between himself and Dolly more keenly during this period than at any other time. Always she had been available to him, and he could run home within a matter of days to unload his problems on her. He could not very well send her his work, his business problems, while she was out of the country, but he told her of them.

He completed *The Thundering Herd* shortly after Dolly's departure, and Mr. Currie, the editor of *The Ladies' Home Journal*, did not like the story. It was the first in many years that had been submitted to an editor without Dolly's careful polishing, and when it was returned by Currie, Grey panicked. Currie's letter, however, was not a "rejection," merely a request for a rather extensive rewrite. Grey performed the revision with great effort and the manuscript was accepted. It was one of the few Zane Grey novels that did not have Dolly's touch in it somewhere.

CHAPTER **30** ━━━━━━━━━━━━━━━

In 1916 Zane Grey had become acquainted with a salmon fisherman of long experience, who extolled the fighting prowess of the steelhead trout that spawned in the Rogue River of Oregon. Grey soon took a trip to Oregon but found the swift waters of the Rogue River barren of fish.

Local fishermen expressed the opinion that the steelhead trout was a saltwater fish that went up the rivers only to spawn, but this was not until June, and they really did not appear in large numbers until July and August.

In 1922 Grey returned to the Rogue River with his brother R. C. and "Lone Angler" Wiborn, one of the most famous fishermen in the country. Grey had known Lone Angler from the University of Pennsylvania days, where Wiborn had been a track star. He met him again at Avalon in 1914. Wiborn had become a doctor but because of ill health had given up his practice and taken to the outdoor life. He was a quiet man and usually preferred to fish alone. His reputation as a nimrod was widely known.

Grey saw local fishermen all around him landing steelhead, but he could not seem to hook one. Two days went by, and then a fish took Grey's fly, and he had his first experience with a steelhead. The moment the fish was hooked he took off downstream, over the rapids, traveling at terrific speed. For his size the steelhead had more power and fight than any fish Grey had ever encountered. It was necessary to follow the fish through the rapids and fight him every foot of the way. It was almost impossible to reel him in, and the fish had to be maneuvered to the comparatively quiet waters near the shore.

On January 1, 1924, Dolly Grey again took to keeping a daily diary and continued more or less faithfully for the next five years, although there were occasional lapses when no record was kept for several days at a time. The diary records that she spent much time working on Zane Grey's income-tax return, beginning in early February and down to the March 15 deadline, when she records: "Tax over $44,000. Afraid to tell Z. G."

During the same period she spent one afternoon a week attending a class in novel-writing. She attended quite regularly and makes an occasional note about her progress. In 1925 she continued the novel class and added a course in short-story writing. She continued both courses for more than two years.

Z. G. was away, fishing at Long Key, and Dolly, in spite of the daily routine of working on his manuscripts, taking care of the huge house in Altadena, and working on his income-tax return (the I.R.S., at the same time, had requested a complete examination of all returns back to 1917), still found time for some entertaining, which she records, and going to the movies at least once and sometimes twice a week. She took the children to see *The Ten Commandments*, which greatly impressed young Loren. They also saw *The Covered Wagon*, which they liked, and *The Iron Horse*, which Dolly thought was a plagiarism of her husband's own *The U.P. Trail*.

In March and April Dolly drove into the desert, east of Indio, to spend several days talking to the large ranchers of date palms. This was at the request of Z. G., who was thinking of writing a book with a date-ranch background. She researched the background rather extensively, but apparently it did not appeal to Zane Grey, for he makes no later mention of it and never did use the background in any of his stories.

Not long after World War I, Zane Grey, while fishing off Nova Scotia, met Captain Laurie Mitchell. Mitchell was an English remittance man who had settled in Canada before the war. He married a French-Canadian girl and built a fine log cabin near the sea. He became an enthusiastic fisherman.

When the war came he enlisted in the Canadian Army and became a captain. He saw a great deal of action. When he returned to Nova Scotia after the war he found his home burned down, his wife gone. He remained in the area and became a great fisherman. When Grey met him, Mitchell held the world's record for tuna. They became close friends and went fishing together. After completing his tour of Long Key early in 1924, Grey went to Nova Scotia. There he heard that a schooner he had admired on a number of occasions was for sale at a ridiculously low price. He promptly went to examine the ship, *Marshal Foch*. She was one hundred and ninety feet overall, with a beam of thirty-five feet. She drew eleven feet, six inches of water and was equipped with three great masts.

The *Marshal Foch* was only five years old. She had been built in nearby Lunenberg. He located, one by one, the four skippers who had sailed the ship, and all were enthusiastic in their praise of her. She had crossed the Atlantic twice and had made a record run from Halifax to New York City. And, most important of all to Grey, she had never been used as a rum-runner.

Grey was able to buy the *Marshal Foch* for only seventeen thousand dollars. He wanted to have the ship converted to

engine power, and after discussing the work with Captain Sid
Boerstler, who had long been with him on expeditions, they
decided upon certain other changes. The work would take three
months, working with a maximum crew at top efficiency. Grey
could not wait for the work to be done and returned to California, leaving Captain Sid in charge, under the general super-
vision of Captain Laurie Mitchell. However, before he left
Nova Scotia Grey engaged a sailing master for the ship. Unfortunately, he did not investigate him as much as he should
have.

When Grey returned to California the season at Avalon
was on, and he moved the family to their home. He spent a
good part of his time fishing, but he also did much writing during this period, trying to get money ahead for the big venture
of the coming winter. He also went to Oregon for some steelhead fishing, then in September went briefly to Arizona on a
hunting trip. When he returned to Altadena he plunged into
his writing, to get ahead of schedule, in case he fell behind on
the long trip to the Southern Pacific waters.

He received a telegram from Captain Mitchell that the
ship, renamed *Fisherman*, was leaving Nova Scotia, and from
time to time cablegrams came, advising of the ship's progress.

The ship encountered heavy gales in the Atlantic but
made the run from Nova Scotia to Santiago, Cuba, in twelve
days. The *Fisherman* moved to Jamaica; then the sailing master set a course for Colón, Panama. On the second morning out,
despite protests by the officers, the sailing master took the boat
between some dangerous reefs and she ran aground.

While trying to work the *Fisherman* off, canoes full of
half-savage natives came out from an island to loot the ship.
Rifles were brought out to repel the attackers, but fortunately
the *Fisherman* was worked off before the natives could board
her.

The ship continued its journey to Colón, where it was
discovered the keel had been stripped off. Grey was advised of
the accident by cable and, responding, discharged the sailing
master and put Captain Sid in complete charge.

The *Fisherman* went through the Panama Canal and anchored at Balboa, to await Zane Grey, who was sailing from Los Angeles on the S.S. *Manchuria.*

With Zane Grey were R. C.; Romer Grey; the indispensable George Takahashi; Chester Wortley, a Hollywood cameraman; and Jess Smith, a cowboy and horse wrangler from Arizona. Smith's wife, an artist, and her sister, Mrs. Phillips Carlin, were with him. Johnny Shields, Romer's young friend from Avalon, had also come along.

It was a large list of passengers, in addition to the ship's crew and officers. At the last moment another passenger arrived, Grey's old fisherman friend from Florida, Bob King.

Zane Grey was well pleased with the reconditioned ship. He had paid only seventeen thousand dollars for her, but the reconditioning had added another forty thousand to the cost.

The newly christened *Fisherman* had been equipped with two driving engines, an engine to generate electricity for the lights and fans, another for the compressed air that forced water over the ship, and an emergency engine to use in case of accident to the generator. There were also pumps and other devices. The tanks were all built of steel and fitted into the sides of the vessel. There were tanks for five thousand gallons of crude oil, one for cylinder oil, and several for five thousand gallons of water and twenty-five hundred gallons of gasoline. In the forecastle was an engine to hoist sails and anchors; there were lathes, a tool bench, a carpenter shop.

The ship carried three launches, one swung over the stern and two cradled on the main deck between the main and mizzen masts. A great deal of care had gone into the design of these launches; they were between twenty-five and thirty-two feet in length and equipped with double motors and two propellers.

The ship was loaded with every conceivable kind of tackle money could buy. By the time the ship sailed from Balboa, Zane Grey had made a tremendous investment in her.

The *Fisherman* cleared from Balboa on the morning of January 30. Its first destination was to be Cocos Island, one of the least-known spots on earth. Without seeing another ship, the *Fisherman* reached Cocos Island, and the fishermen aboard swarmed into the launches and began fishing.

Two of the most eager and ambitious fishermen were young Romer and his friend Johnny Shields. They were also among the most successful. The waters teemed with fish, but even outnumbering the fish were the sharks. No one aboard had ever been in such a shark-infected area. A fish was hooked, and the sharks went for it. Reels could not be worked fast enough to haul the fish clear of the waters before the sharks caught them, and once there was blood in the water, the sharks swarmed toward the spot. It was useless to spear or shoot the sharks; that would only attract more of them.

It was the worst fishing area Zane Grey and his fishermen friends had ever been in; the fish were there but could not be landed.

The island itself was famous in history as a haven for pirates. Gold was supposed to be hidden on it; all the records indicated that, but the records also indicated that no one had ever found any of the pirate treasures.

Disgusted by the prevalence of the sharks, Zane Grey gave the order to haul up the anchors and sail to the Galápagos, six hundred miles off the coast of Peru.

Here islands were explored and new specimens of fish were encountered, tremendous fish at times. There were fewer sharks here, and the fishing was better, but Zane Grey began to worry. They had not seen another ship since leaving the Panama Canal Zone, and the responsibility for the many passengers and crew members preyed heavily upon him. If they had an accident or a fire aboard, there was no way to get help. The ship rolled heavily at anchor, and they had gone through several severe storms.

George Takahashi had stepped on sea porcupines, had sat on one. He was painfully bruised. Bob King had been bitten badly by a fish. Zane Grey had arranged for a doctor to sail with them, but at the last moment the doctor had been unable to come. Grey had to substitute for him.

He gave the order to sail north, going closer to the mainland. They traveled slowly, fishing at likely spots, but gradually neared the Panama Bay area.

The ship worked gradually northward, stopping at San
Lucas, at the tip of Baja California, then along the Mexican
coast, into the waters off California.

The *Fisherman* was anchored at Avalon three months
after the voyage had begun.

There had been much leisure time on the ship in spite of
the frequent stops for fishing. Zane Grey wrote continuously,
notes during the day, narrative in the evenings and mornings.
He completed most of the long documentary account of the
cruise before anchoring at Avalon. The book was called *Tales
of Fishing Virgin Seas,* and Harper's published it later that
year in a beautiful, large folio edition with a case. The book
contained more than one hundred full-page photographs, all
taken by Zane Grey and his associates.

Sievert Nielsen, who had made the Death Valley trip with
Zane Grey, had not accompanied him on his 1924 trip to Nova
Scotia. He had gone off on an expedition of his own. Returning
from the East, Grey expected to find a message from Nielsen.
When there was none, he made inquiries in some of Nielsen's
haunts. No one had seen him for weeks.

Grey went fishing off Avalon. No one there had seen or
heard of Nielsen. Someone mentioned that he had talked
about going to Baja California.

Nielsen had one weakness: periodically he went off by
himself and had a roaring binge. These drinking periods sometimes lasted for days, sometimes ran into weeks. Always,
however, Nielsen sobered up and returned and would not
touch whiskey for another long period.

Grey wrote to Nielsen's relatives in Norway. They had not
heard from him in months. Grey started a careful investiga-
tion. All he could determine was that Nielsen had gone to Baja
California. He employed investigators. They reported that a
man who fitted Nielsen's description had been in Tiajuana

briefly. He had been seen under the influence of liquor. Then he had disappeared, and no one had seen him again or could tell anything about him.

There were hints that Nielsen had become involved in a drunken brawl and that he had been killed, but the hints never became more than that. Nothing could be learned definitely; nothing could be proved.

Grey always believed that Nielsen had been killed in Tiajuana. He missed his loyal friend grievously. He had been greatly attached to him and several times in later years he recalled that Nielsen had twice saved his life at the risk of his own.

CHAPTER 31

Zane Grey's fame was at its height in 1925. A considerable number of his outdoor and hunting stories were published in magazines. A serial version of *The Deer Stalker* was published in *The Country Gentleman,* and *The Ladies' Home Journal* published *The Bee Hunter,* later called *Under the Tonto Rim* by Harper's.

Zane Grey's agreement with *The Ladies' Home Journal* expired with the publication of *The Bee Hunter.* Currie, the editor of the magazine, went to Europe that summer, assuming that all was well between him and Zane Grey, but Grey was irritated by Currie's failure to discuss a renewal of the agreement before going abroad, and when he was approached by *McCall's Magazine,* he sold them the serial rights to his newest book, *Desert Bound* (later called *Captives of the Desert*). Currie was greatly chagrined, but restrained himself, mostly as a result of Dolly Grey's placating.

Harper's published two of Zane Grey's books in 1925, *The Thundering Herd* and *The Vanishing American.* Both were very well received and had unusually large sales, but neither one made the charmed circle of the top ten on the year's best-seller list—chiefly because there were two of Grey's books pub-

lished within a single year. Harper's usually published only
one a year and put all of their promotion effort behind it. The
public, however, bought both books in large quantities, and
with three serials published that year and the numerous shorter
articles and stories, it was indeed a golden year for Zane Grey.

The Thundering Herd was a story about Buffalo Jones, one
of the hunters in the Panhandle of Texas who had practically
decimated the buffalo in the 1870's.

They were strictly hide hunters, receiving about three
dollars per hide. A small group of men would join together,
buy a couple of wagons and equipment, and set out for the flat
Panhandle, where herds estimated up to ten million abounded.

A good buffalo hunter earned sometimes as much as five
thousand dollars in a single season of hunting, which meant
that he had to kill at least two thousand buffalo. With virtually thousands of hunters scattered over the Panhandle, the
buffalo herds were wiped out within two or three years.

They were hard men, these buffalo hunters. They had to
be to endure their gruesome work, and they had to be resolute
to withstand the continual harassment of the Indians. The
Indian depended on the buffalo for his livelihood, and when
he saw the buffalo being extinguished, he rose in righteous
anger.

In *The Thundering Herd* Grey describes in considerable
detail the methods the hunters used and virtually every aspect
of their lives. It is one of Zane Grey's most rugged books, and
it is surprising that *The Ladies' Home Journal* bought the serial
rights. The realistic accounts of the killing and skinning of the
buffalo should have revolted the feminine readers. They did not:
the story proved to be one of Zane Grey's most popular serials.

More to the taste of the lady readers of *The Ladies' Home
Journal* was *The Vanishing American*, serialized in 1922 but
not brought out in book form until 1925.

This is one of Zane Grey's very best novels, and in it he
reveals his fondness for the American Indian and distaste for
his sad plight. The hero is a Navajo Indian who was picked
up by a party of whites when only seven years old. He was

brought up in a home of comfortable means, and his foster parents had him educated and sent to a large Eastern university. There he became an outstanding athlete, feted by the Easterners. (Zane Grey obviously patterned his hero after the great Indian athlete Jim Thorpe.)

In *The Vanishing American* Grey made a powerful appeal for understanding of the Indian and his problems, but the underlying mood is that the Indian is fighting a losing battle, that he will, in the end, be exterminated by the greed of the encroaching white man.

As a result of his success with these two books, Grey was able to plan the extended trip he had dreamed about for so long. He had received an invitation from the government of New Zealand; his fame as a novelist and fisherman had reached that country, and they believed that he would publicize the country if he once came to visit it. Zane Grey, of course, said that he would do exactly that, and with plenty of money coming in that year, he made his preparations for the longest fishing trip of his life.

CHAPTER **32**

Late in the summer of 1925 Grey returned to the Rogue River country. R. C. could not tear himself away from the swordfish at Catalina, so Captain Mitchell accompanied Grey.

While fishing for steelhead, Grey found that he could not take his mind off the big fish of the South Pacific, and around the campfires in the evening he talked with Captain Mitchell of a South Seas trip.

R. C. could not make the long trip to the South Seas, and Romer had lost too much time from school the winter before, so Grey decided to make the trip with Captain Mitchell.

They sailed from San Francisco on the Royal Mail S.S. *Makura* on December 30, 1925 and in good time reached

Papeete, Tahiti. Grey had read so much of Tahiti and had conjured up such a magical picture of the isles that he was greatly disappointed by the reality.

The romantic beachcombers of whom he had read turned out to be dirty, disgusting men. The businesses were all run by crafty Chinese who overcharged for everything. Everybody drank heavily, and Grey was a teetotaler. The resort hotel made famous in O'Brien's *White Shadows of the South Seas* was no more than a dive. The weather was moist and sticky, and Grey was glad when the *Makura* set sail and the cooling breezes again blew over the ship.

The ship stopped briefly at Raratonga, and two pearl traders came aboard. They told Grey of great game fish around Aitutaki Island.

On January 17 the coast of New Zealand was sighted, and the ship soon sailed into the harbor at Wellington, the destination of the Grey party. They remained only briefly in Wellington, however, then boarded a train for the fifteen-hour trip to Auckland, the commercial and business capital of New Zealand. Grey found his books in both cities and was warmly greeted by many who knew his name and had enjoyed his stories. Some of the New Zealanders were disappointed, however, when they saw that Grey did not wear sombrero, chaps, spurs, and guns.

From Auckland they embarked on another day's train ride to Russell, the fisherman's haven.

Russell turned out to be a beautiful little hamlet, and here were gathered fishermen from New Zealand, Australia, and many faraway countries. Grey was better known to these people as a great fisherman than as an author of Western novels.

Grey wanted to be independent, as always, and pitched a tent camp fifteen miles from Russell. The waters were new to Grey, the country was seven thousand miles from his home country, but fish were fish. There were swordfish off New Zealand, and they were mighty ones. After Grey landed a two-hundred-pound marlin he was hooked himself by the New Zealand fishing waters. He was soon after broadbill swordfish, mightier and gamier than those off Clemente, but the big event was seeing a ship with the fantastic name of *Desert Gold* and discovering that it had been named after Zane Grey's book of that title!

Before the trip was completed Zane Grey hooked the world's record striped marlin, weighing four hundred and fifty pounds. Captain Mitchell landed a nine-hundred-and-seventy-six-pound black marlin, a world's record.

Zane Grey and Captain Mitchell made a number of trips inland and fished the rivers and streams, and Grey, always interested in the new, became fascinated with the Maori tribesmen and found many of them in an extremely advanced stage of civilization.

An educated Maori took him to an inland village and introduced him to the chief of the villagers. The chief made a long speech, and the educated Maori translated it for Zane Grey. It turned out to be a tribute to the great American fisherman, Zane Grey, who had come from America to visit the New Zealanders.

Grey found his books everywhere, in the villages, in the rural farmhouses, in the homes of white New Zealanders, and in the huts of Maoris where the younger members of the family had attended school. Frequently the books were tattered from much handling and reading. He found that he was as famous in New Zealand as he was in America, and he was pleased.

Before he left New Zealand, Grey had already made up his mind to return aboard his own ship and spend more time there.

He did return to New Zealand in 1927 and again in 1928. R. C. and Romer were with him both times. Reports had been coming to him, however, of the huge swordfish to be found in the Tahiti waters, and he made plans to try his luck there.

In 1929, accompanied by Captain Mitchell and R. C., he went to Papeete and there met *Fisherman*. Reports of the big swordfish and marlin came from all sides, and they caught glimpses of the monsters now and then, but it was Zane Grey's worst fishing season. After eighty-three days of continual trolling and cruising about, he had not caught a single fish.

His friend Captain Mitchell hooked a monstrous twenty-foot broadbill swordfish but lost him. They sighted the huge fish frequently, but the swordfish were gamier than any Grey had ever fished for: they refused stale bait; they got hooked and threw the hook; they broke the lines.

It was a heartbreaking experience for a fisherman like Zane Grey, but he vowed to come back the following year.

Meanwhile he sold *Fisherman* to a wealthy copra planter. The cost of keeping it in operation was a vast one for the few months every year that he used it. He had been unfortunate in his selection of officers. His last captain knew the merchants of all the towns, made huge purchases at high prices, and grew wealthy from the kickbacks. Zane Grey was aware of it, but for a long time did nothing about it except that he began negotiations to sell the ship.

In Tahiti Zane Grey met two Americans who had settled there as the result of a strange pact they had made during World War I, when both were aviators in France. Charles Nordhoff had been with the Lafayette Escadrille and had already made a considerable reputation for himself, when he first met a young sergeant, who had been an automobile racer in America, Eddie Rickenbacker.

Nordhoff transferred to the American Army, where he became friendly with another American, James Hall. Both had literary ambitions, and they talked about what they would do if they survived the war. Neither of them expected to do that, since the mortality rate of the fliers was high. They decided that the civilization they knew, one that produced wars such as they were in, was too much for them. Having learned French, they decided to go to Tahiti after the war, settle down there, and live the simple life of the Polynesians.

They did just that and began writing books in collaboration; among them were *Mutiny on the Bounty* and *Pitcairn's Island*.

Both were excellent fishermen, but they fished essentially for fish to eat. Nordhoff, however, was interested in the big-game fish and had had some luck in fishing for swordfish.

He was already widely known in Papeete and the surrounding islands, which he had explored, and since he was able to talk to the natives, he inquired of them where and when they had seen big fish. He passed on much of this information to Zane Grey.

Nordhoff spent much time fishing with Grey. Hall joined them occasionally, but Grey became more intimate with Nordhoff. He learned from him that neither he nor his partner had any intention of returning to the civilized world. They were quite content with their quiet existence in the South Sea islands.

Some years later, when Hall died, Nordhoff did return to America, but he had lost touch with the world and did not remain very long. He soon returned to his beloved Tahiti.

Captain Mitchell remained in Tahiti and prepared a row of eight guest homes for the crew of the next year's fishing trip. Zane Grey, meanwhile, had some special ship's launches built and sent them to Tahiti.

He returned in 1930, and luck, or perhaps the knowledge that he had gained the previous year, stood him in good stead. Grey culminated the season with a record catch of a swordfish, although he and his crew had to fight off the sharks that threatened to eat the swordfish before it could be landed. The sharks bit out huge chunks, but when the swordfish was landed and taken to Papeete and weighed, it still tipped the scales at 1,024 pounds, a record catch for the area and for Zane Grey. Whole, the fish would have gone easily to 1,250 pounds, but Grey counted only what was weighed.

News of the record swordfish catch was flashed by radio to all the fishing centers of the world. It even reached Dolly Grey back in Altadena, and she cabled him: "What, ho, Ulysses! You hooked a better fish at home that might get away. Penelope."

It was time to go home.

CHAPTER **33** ━━━━━━━━━━━━━━━━━━━━━

Zane Grey had left in December, 1925, for his first trip to New Zealand, and while he was gone, Dolly Grey decided to make a second European trip. She made plans to leave by train for Indianapolis late in May, there to pick up a new car, a Stutz, and then drive to Lackawaxen with it. She would leave the car there and go to New York and board the steamship for the Atlantic crossing.

By cable she was notified that her husband had started on the return trip from New Zealand and would land in San Francisco on May 14. Dolly and the family drove to San Francisco in two cars and met Zane. Zane and Dolly decided to let the others drive back in one car, and the two of them drove alone from San Francisco. They stopped for two days at Pismo Beach.

When they returned to Altadena, Dolly worked frantically to get ready for her trip. The family would move to Avalon in her absence, and there was a continual rushing back and forth, but on May 26 Dolly boarded the train in Los Angeles. She did not like the train trip at all and commented on it in a letter written before she reached Indianapolis.

The big new Stutz was ready for her in Indianapolis, and she started out, driving to Zanesville, her husband's boyhood home. She stayed there overnight with the Andersons, whose friendship Zane had renewed when he visited the town in 1921.

She continued on to New York, spent a few days with her relatives, then boarded the ship on June 2. Her diary entries on the trip and in Europe are very sketchy; sometimes there are gaps for days at a time. Apparently she rented a car in Europe, for there is one cryptic entry, while in Italy: "Italian motorcyclist collided with us today." No reference is made to it the day after, so apparently there were no injuries.

She returned to New York aboard the S.S. *Berengaria* on August 21. She arrived back in Los Angeles on August 31.

Zane Grey had encouraged Dolly to take the European trip in 1923, and he made no objections when he heard of her plans for 1926, but after she had gone he began to fret about it. He lived at Avalon during the entire time she was away, but the routine of business details worried him. He made wrong decisions and wrote to Dolly continually, making references to her "second and *last*" trip to Europe; his remarks were facetious but now and then there was an undertone of seriousness. He simply did not like the business routine connected with being a successful author.

It was a good writing year for him. Dolly had made peace with *The Ladies' Home Journal,* and they serialized *Forlorn River* early in the year; but he later wrote a sequel, the very popular *Nevada,* and sold serial rights to the *American Magazine* for more money than he had ever received for a serial. He wrote shorter stories and articles for *Country Gentleman, American, McCall's,* and several other publications.

Harper's published *Under the Tonto Rim* in book form and also his book based on the first expedition to New Zealand, *Tales of an Angler's Eldorado.*

It was a good year for him, also, in motion pictures. Two older pictures were remade, bringing money into the Grey coffers, and he sold both *Forlorn River* and *Nevada.* The latter book was to be remade three times in the future, once as late as 1944.

Zane confined his fishing in 1926, after his return from New Zealand, to Avalon and the Rogue River, which he visited later in the year. He was making plans, meanwhile, for his third trip into the South Seas.

In 1926 Dolly Grey had given her husband a fine leather-bound book, on the flyleaf of which she wrote: "Dear Doc— Please keep a record of the precious things in this book."

"Doc" did not start the record in the little book until 1928, and then his entries were infrequent and sometimes very brief. Many times they are merely observations of the weather, nature, and little things he saw about him, like an account of a one-legged snipe.

He had missed two seasons at Long Key, but on January 30, when he begins his entries in his diary, he is at Long Key. His black moods have returned, and he comments on them; also he takes long walks and tries to tire himself with his fishing exertions. He makes notes of people: an old man of seventy-three who shows signs of mental aberration; a woman who sits beside a child in public, smoking a cigarette. (Grey shunned smoking as much as he did drinking.)

Returning to California, his mood lightened, he resumed work and then, on June 20, there comes this poignant entry:

I was in Avalon when Dr. G. [Dr. Greengo, the family doctor in Altadena] said it might be necessary to have an operation performed upon Dolly. That struck terror to my soul. But I could not believe it would have to be.

Nevertheless it *did* have to be. I knew it ten days ago. When I saw Dolly, I was reassured because she seemed well and strong and confident.

She went to the Good Samaritan Hospital in L.A. on June 18. I left her there. Next day I went back with R. C. and Romer. At nine o'clock I saw Dolly at the last moment. She was bright, cheerful, cool, game as a thoroughbred. Pride overcame my fears for a little. Then I saw her moved down the hall and into the elevator to go to the ward upstairs to take ether. She said, "I'm all right."

Somehow I got over that first hour, or through it. When the second began, the minutes dragged. I paced the gloomy hall. My mind whirled, yet outwardly I appeared calm. But I could not sit or stand still. Romer stood it well for a long while, but at last he weakened. He talked incessantly about everything except Mother.

When Dr. G. came down, it was about time to save me from collapse. He reported that the operation had been imperatively necessary and that it had been successful.

Something caved in in me, but I could thank God. My consciousness was such that I cannot now recall the thoughts I had, the prayers, the agonies.

There are several succeeding entries about Dolly's recovery. The final one, on July 4: "For some days Dolly has been out of danger and recovering slowly, but surely, so that the load is removed from my breast, and the inhibitions from my mind."

CHAPTER **34** _____

The years seemed to roll by too swiftly. In 1918, when Zane Grey had taken Romer on his first hunting trip, Loren was a baby. Grey had seen more of Romer through the years than of Loren, for he had taken Romer with him on a dozen or more trips. Romer had taken to the outdoor life with the same zest as his father. He enjoyed riding horses, hunting, and traveling through the wild country. Even more, he enjoyed fishing. He was a complete extrovert, tackling every new experience with complete exuberance.

Romer went twice with his father to New Zealand and twice to Tahiti. He took it for granted that he would make the long trips with his father. By 1930, when he was twenty-one, he was an excellent fisherman and landed about as many broadbill swordfish as his father and uncle, and sometimes he outdid them. He fished with more enthusiasm than the older men, and it was a clever fish who was able to get away from him once he had hooked it.

Loren, six years younger than his brother, was a completely different boy. Loren, too, seemed fond of the outdoors, but in an entirely different way from his brother. He was quiet and dreamy. Now and then he roused from his private dream world to do things that surprised those around him, but then he would lapse once more into his customary dreaminess.

Grey was in Avalon in the summer of 1924, when Loren, attending a boys' camp on Catalina, won first prize in a fishing contest, and Grey realized with a shock that the boy, in his way, was a chip off the old block. Loren was nine, the same age that Romer had been when he had been given his first gun and taken on the Arizona trip. Grey resolved to take Loren with him to Oregon that fall.

In September the gear and equipment were sent to Grant's Pass in southwestern Oregon. The Grey party, consisting of Zane, R. C., Captain Mitchell, and Loren, arrived at Grant's Pass and were met by Pettinger, a guide Grey had engaged beforehand.

There was a considerable amount of equipment, and Pettinger was ready with sixteen mules and eight saddle horses. He had three young men to help him.

They made a rather late start and would not reach Winkle Bar, their destination, before dark. It was a difficult three-hour trip up to the top of the mountain. Darkness fell when they were still five miles from the Rogue River.

As the pack train and the riders entered a forest, it was pitch dark, so that they could scarcely see their hands before their faces. R. C. and Zane got Loren in between them and tried their best to warn him of obstructing branches and bad spots on the trail. Loren could scarcely make out his father and uncle and kept calling to them to make sure that they were near.

The night trip took more than two hours, but Loren never complained about being saddle sore, although the older members of the party could scarcely climb down from their horses. Captain Mitchell, who was no horseman, actually fell off his mount when they reached the cabin at Winkle Bar. He swore that he would never ride another horse again as long as he lived.

Aside from being somewhat tired, Loren was no worse for the long, grueling ride.

Two boatmen had already been at the cabin for a month,

building a flume to bring water to the bar. They reported that the fishing had already been good for the past ten months, and the next morning, at an early hour, everyone was out, ready for the fishing.

Loren was given his first good rod and went off with one of the boatmen. He returned after a while with four small steelhead on a string and a broken fishing rod and complained that a big one had gotten away after breaking the rod.

The following year the entire family returned to Winkle Bar. There were R. C., Zane and Dolly, Romer, Betty, and Loren. And, of course, Captain Mitchell and the indefatigable Takahashi.

Dolly Grey caught a huge salmon, Romer as usual was one of the top fishermen in the group, and even Betty was able to hook and land a fish, but young Loren could not seem to hook a steelhead or any other kind of fish.

Grey had shown his younger son how to cast with flies, but Loren could not get the hang of it. Grey suggested more practice, and Loren said that if his father wanted him to learn fly-casting he should take him out alone on the river.

Grey promised to spend the following day with him.

Loren was up early the next day waiting for his father. They went down the river for a mile and began to fish. Loren cast the fly continuously and made some good casts, but the fish were not biting that day, and they continued farther down the river. The day passed, and neither one caught a single fish.

As they started back to camp, near sundown, Grey expressed his disappointment to his son, because it had been such a "bum" day.

Loren replied cheerfully, "It wasn't a bum day, Dad. You don't have to catch fish to have a good day."

In 1927 Zane Grey's fishing in New Zealand did not go too well; for forty-five days he could not catch a big fish, and he reported the failure regularly to Dolly Grey. He told her of his troubles, too. The government had given him a private railroad car to make the trip from Wellington to Auckland, but the *Fisherman* had to fight its way against heavy seas and was forced to use its motors all the way, which used up its entire fuel supply, which had to be replenished in Auckland. And in Auckland one of the mates stole the money that was in the captain's safe, went ashore, and got drunk. He then assaulted a New Zealand woman and wound up in jail.

The governor general of New Zealand came to call on Zane Grey. He told him that Grey's book and articles, written after his previous visit to New Zealand, had resulted in thousands of people coming to New Zealand. The Duke and Duchess of York were due to visit Auckland in a few days, and the governor asked Zane Grey to take them out for a day's fishing.

The news of this got around and created a furore in political circles. There were Zane Grey defenders and there were antagonists of his, and since Grey did not report further on the royal couple's visit, it can be assumed that the governor general, in the showdown, did not ask their majesties to fish with the American.

Lord Astor of England was in New Zealand, and he went fishing with Zane Grey. He was a prominent horse breeder in England, and they discussed horses; Zane told the Duke of his daughter Betty's love for horses, and the Duke promised to send her some pictures of some of his own steeplechase equines.

Late in 1927 Zane Grey was again in Arizona. In his letters to Betty, he tells her about riding her horse, Night—the horse he had bought in 1913 and kept for some years at Lackawaxen. He also wrote her about his own favorite horse, Brutus. On this trip Jesse Lasky, the Hollywood motion-picture producer, visited him, and Grey led him to places that Lasky later used in some of his films, among them the now well-photographed Monument Valley.

In 1927 Harper's published *Forlorn River* and *Tales of Swordfish and Tuna*, then in 1928 they went all out and published four Zane Grey books: *Nevada*; *Wild Horse Mesa*; a short novel in a gift edition, *Don, the Story of a Dog;* and *Tales of Fresh Water Fishing.*

The year 1928 was a good one for Zane Grey in the magazines. *Sunset Pass* appeared serially in *American; Collier's* published *The Sheep Herder (Shepherd of Guadalupe);* and *The Country Gentleman* finished the year with *Fighting Caravans.*

A new deal had been negotiated with the publishers of *Collier's* and *American.* They had paid $50,000 each for the last stories, but now Grey managed to increase the price to $175,000 for three stories, more than $58,000 for each book.

In 1930 Betty, seventeen, had been accepted at the University of Wisconsin, and Dolly drove her there.

Betty liked the university and a few weeks later wrote a twelve-page letter to her mother, discussing her life, her ambitions, her friends at school, and her opinions of her fiancé. She had been pledged by Pi Phi sorority and discussed that and other sororities.

The letter is an unusually well written one for a seventeen-year-old girl, revealing a surprising maturity. She had attended school more regularly than her older brother, Romer, who was ever ready to drop out of school for a few weeks—or months—to go on a trip or expedition with his father.

Both Dolly and Zane Grey were devoted to all three of the children; each was a distinct entity, each one had a personality entirely different from the other. Romer, as the eldest, had been indulged more than the others, but as Betty grew up, an extremely close relationship developed between her father and herself. Loren, in his turn, would also become very close to his father, especially after Romer was married and found outside interests.

Dolly spent much time with all of the children. Her diary references are studded with mentions of the children. When Romer began going around with his own friends, Dolly spent even more time with Betty and Loren, often taking them to movies. (Zane Grey once remarked that they were seeing too many movies for children between the ages of ten and twelve; however, later he himself took them to movies at least once a week when he was at home.)

CHAPTER **35** _____

In 1919 there were still no large motion-picture production companies. A producer bought a story or had one written—and sometimes he did not even have a story—and hired an actor and a crew. He rented stage space, which may have been an old warehouse, a barn, any place that was reasonably large and had a roof over it. An electrician or two were hired, and a cameraman, who carried his camera from place to place and set it up on a tripod. Sometimes the producer hired a director; sometimes he was his own director. He made a picture, spending ten or fifteen thousand dollars, or in the case of the really ambitious efforts, he might spend as much as one hundred thousand.

The producer sold the rights to a distributor, although sometimes he went out with the film himself and sold it to theaters. A producer was everything in those days. The public would pay their nickels and dimes and were satisfied with any type of picture. When they had the good fortune to see a really good one, they were enthralled.

Zane Grey heard of the money that producers were making from his books, and he thought he should be making all of the money instead of just receiving a small sum for the rights to one of his stories.

In 1919 he formed his own motion-picture company, Zane Grey Productions. He took into partnership with him a man named Ben H. Hampton. Grey came into their small office now and then and sometimes visited a set when the filming was going on, but Hampton was the actual picture-maker. Zane Grey had to write his books and go on his hunting and fishing trips.

The partnership did not work out. After three or four pictures, Zane Grey paid off his partner and sold Zane Grey Productions to Jesse Lasky, one of the real pioneers of the business, who had made *The Squaw Man*, the first motion picture ever filmed in Hollywood. Lasky had a company at this time that was very prosperous: Famous Players–Lasky. Adolph Zukor was a partner, and soon the company was to expand and become known as Paramount Pictures. The old Brunton Studio in which Zane Grey had rented space was enlarged and became the famous Paramount Studios; it is still in the same location.

From this time on, Grey remained aloof from the actual making of motion pictures, but his books were in great demand, especially at the new Paramount Studios. From 1921 until sound came in, in 1927–1928, Paramount never made fewer than two pictures a year from Zane Grey books; sometimes the number went up to five a year.

When talking pictures became the vogue, Paramount remade some of the old silent Zane Grey pictures and went on to make a long series of new ones. Gary Cooper played in one of the first talking pictures, *Fighting Caravans*. Richard Arlen, then Paramount's leading star, played in some of the Zane Grey pictures, but the real Zane Grey "hero" was Randolph Scott, who played in more than twenty Zane Grey films.

Scott's first picture was *Man of the Forest*. It was almost his last one. Scott was newly arrived in Hollywood in 1931 and was signed to a contract by Paramount to replace Jack Holt, who had just died.

Jack Holt had been in the silent version of *Man of the Forest*. To economize, Paramount wanted to use a few of the action scenes from the silent picture, so Randolph Scott had to wear clothes that matched Jack Holt's. In the first version there was a scene where the hero returns to his isolated forest home and a mountain lion pounces on him from a ledge and they wrestle for some time, the audience not knowing until the end of the scene that the mountain lion is "tame."

A new "trained" lion had been procured for the picture,

for it was necessary to show some close-ups of Randolph Scott wrestling with the lion. The trainer of the lion insisted that it was a milk-fed animal and had never tasted meat. He himself handled the lion beautifully, without any trouble.

When the scene opened, the mountain lion, on a cue from his trainer, pounced down on Scott and promptly sank its claws into Scott's back and its teeth into his shoulder. Scott, frightened as he had never been in his life, lay perfectly still. The trainer did not drag the lion away from Scott until the scene was finished.

While the doctor was patching him up, the actor asked the lion trainer why he had not come to his rescue immediately, and the trainer replied laconically, "It was a good take, and I didn't want to spoil the scene." The animal, on a chain, made a couple of furious lunges against Scott later; the actor was saved only because the chain was rather short.

The trainer, confronted later by the irate actor and director, admitted that the lion's principal diet was horse meat. Scott, riding horseback several hours a day, of course carried the smell of horse on his clothing, and that was the reason the lion had gone after him.

Scott relates another "Zane Grey story." In 1933 Paramount was doing a remake of To the Last Man. Gail Patrick was playing the mother of a three-year-old girl. It was a party scene. The little girl's pet pony was to enter, be slapped on the rump by the little girl, and then leave.

That was the way the scene was rehearsed, but when the camera rolled for the take, things did not work out that way. The pony entered, was slapped by the little girl, and promptly raised up its hind end and began kicking the tables and dishes to pieces. With the camera still rolling, the little girl dressed down the pony, and in clear, ad-libbed lines, told the animal how badly it was behaving and ordered it to leave the party.

The scene rolled to its conclusion and the entire cast and crew applauded the little girl for her excellent ad-libbed dialogue and handling of the scene.

Henry Hathaway, the director, saw the film the next day

and rushed to the studio to tell the executives of Paramount about the brilliant little girl. He insisted she should be signed to a long-term contract, as she most surely would become a great child star. One of the studio executives, however, was unimpressed, and the girl was not put under contract. Twentieth Century-Fox signed the little girl to a long-term contract.

Ninety days later Paramount had a script that required a small girl. They "borrowed" her from Fox, and had to pay thirty thousand dollars for her services. The picture in which they put the little girl was *Little Miss Marker*, which won an academy award, established its little heroine, Shirley Temple, on a long and illustrious career, and earned Twentieth Century-Fox millions of dollars.

Randolph Scott attributes his success as a motion-picture actor entirely to Zane Grey. He got his start in a Zane Grey picture, learned his trade through the long association with the pictures, and went on to fame and fortune in other pictures. *Time* magazine, in 1967, called Randolph Scott one of the wealthiest men in California, estimating his worth at three hundred million dollars. Most of this, of course, was because of good investments, but it must be noted that to make investments one must have some capital to invest, and Randolph Scott's fortune was founded on the money he earned in the long series of Zane Grey Western pictures.

Randolph Scott was always a great reader of books. He read the Zane Grey books from his early youth, and later, when he was playing the Zane Grey motion pictures, he reread most of them. He declares unhesitatingly that Zane Grey was the foremost writer of adventure stories of his own and any other time. His fondest memories are of the years that he was the "Zane Grey hero" in so many pictures.

Gail Patrick Jackson is one of Hollywood's most astute executives. As producer of the extremely successful *Perry Mason* television series she occupies a unique position, for Mrs. Jackson was for many years one of the industry's most beautiful and talented motion-picture stars.

She came to Hollywood in 1932 from Birmingham, Alabama, fresh out of college, where she had studied law. She was put under contract by Paramount Pictures and in 1933 was cast in one of Zane Grey's motion pictures. Grey rarely visited motion-picture studios, but happened to drop by on one occasion and was impressed with the young Gail Patrick's work. They became acquainted and remained friends until Grey's death in 1939. Gail Patrick visited at the Grey home many times, and in turn entertained both Mr. and Mrs. Zane Grey in Hollywood. Grey frequently told producers that Gail Patrick was the perfect Zane Grey "heroine."

"He was one of the finest men I ever met," says Gail Patrick Jackson. "He was an extremely shy man, but when you knew him well and talked of things he was really interested in, he was very articulate. He went out of his way to help me in my acting career, and on several occasions phoned studio executives and suggested that I was the right actress for specific roles in his pictures.

"Having been a baseball player when young, he remained an ardent baseball fan. I was married to Bob Cobb, who owned the Hollywood Stars, and when Mr. Grey attended a game he always sat in our private box. On a number of occasions, when an important game was scheduled we had dinner at the Brown Derby in Hollywood, which my husband also owned, then went together to the ball game.

"Zane Grey went out of his way to do things for people and was always thinking of ways to please his friends. He wrote many letters to me while on his fishing trips and usually brought back some small memento. One of my greatest treasures is a pair of opal earrings in a beautifully wrought native-workman box that he gave me after returning from his last trip to Australia, in 1938."

Gail Patrick's friendship with the Grey family continued even after Zane Grey's death. She says of Dolly Grey, "She was a patrician, down to the tips of her fingernails, and would have been described in my native South as a 'woman of quality.' She was completely dedicated to her husband and his work and carried on his business affairs while he was away on his hunting and fishing trips, which were so necessary to him."

Gail Patrick confesses that she had never read a Western book until after her first meeting with Zane Grey. She then bought one of his books and was charmed by it. "There was an air of graciousness in all of his work. His girls were ladies at all times, no matter in what predicament they were placed, and his heroes were courtly and stalwart, in the very tradition in which I had been brought up in the South. I eventually read all of Zane Grey's books and became a real Western fan as a result."

She still has the notes and letters written to her by Zane Grey and treasures them as her most valuable keepsakes.

Some of the actors who got their start playing in Zane Grey pictures were Gary Cooper, Randolph Scott, Richard Arlen, Richard Dix, Wallace Beery, Harry Carey, William Powell, Shirley Temple, Jack Holt, Jack LaRue, Billie Dove, Fay Wray, Lili Damita, Jean Arthur, Buster Crabbe, Gail Patrick, and Warner Baxter.

Victor Fleming directed a number of the early Zane Grey pictures at Paramount; he was later to direct *Gone with the Wind*.

Henry Hathaway, who is still directing some of Hollywood's biggest pictures, followed Fleming at Paramount and directed a dozen Zane Grey pictures. He knew Zane Grey personally and reveals a few forgotten facts about the writer's deals with motion-picture studios.

Grey wanted his pictures to be as authentic as his books and was strong enough during the 1920's to force a clause into his contracts that the films had to be made in the actual locations given in the books. Hathaway thus found himself filming *Wild Horse Mesa, The Heritage of the Desert,* and *Under the Tonto Rim* in northern Arizona. He recalls that he lived in Zane Grey's lodge on the rim of the Grand Canyon while filming these pictures.

Later Hathaway fished often on the Rogue River in Oregon, where Grey owned Winkle Bar. Hathaway himself bought a cabin at Rapid Riffles.

Hathaway recalls Grey as a quiet, easy-spoken man. "He didn't talk much," says Hathaway, "but he listened a lot, and he was always working on a new story. His books were marvelous. There was always something fresh and different about them."

Veteran Hollywood producer Harry Joe Brown made two motion pictures of Zane Grey books, *Western Union* for Twentieth Century-Fox and *Twin Sombreros* for the company he formed with Randolph Scott. "Grey was the most bankable author of the time," he says. "I leased the rights to *Twin Sombreros*, got Randolph Scott interested, and had no difficulty going to Columbia Pictures and making a releasing and financing deal. In fact, I'll add that this first property of Zane Grey's kept me in business for sixteen subsequent pictures with Randolph Scott and Columbia."

He could also have added that *Western Union*, which starred Robert Young and Randolph Scott, enabled him to interest Scott in an independent production company.

Sol Lesser, better known as the man who made the many Tarzan pictures, made one picture from a Zane Grey property, *Zane Grey's South Sea Adventures*. He bought the actual film from Zane Grey and showed it to an audience in Hollywood. It was well received, but exhibitors did not seem to want a picture that consisted of ninety minutes of fishing. Lesser went to New York City, rented a theater on West 42nd Street. The picture ran fourteen weeks at this theater and made enough to reimburse Lesser for his entire investment. It then went into general release.

Lesser made a number of pictures during this period based on Harold Bell Wright's books. Wright at the time was Grey's leading competitor on the best-seller lists. Lesser tried a number of times to buy Zane Grey books but always found that somebody had already purchased the picture rights, because Grey often sold books to pictures before they were published.

Lesser met Zane Grey on a number of occasions. "He was

a very modest man," he says in recollection. "He did not mix much with the Hollywood crowd. I had been a fan of his books long before I met him. He had a vivid writing style, and his books were highly moral in tone. He and Harold Bell Wright were my favorite authors."

Jack Karp, head of the legal department of Paramount Studios for many years and eventually vice-president in charge of production, had a considerable contact with the Zane Grey family because of the numerous sales to Paramount, but Karp himself never met Zane Grey. His dealings were entirely with Lina Elise Grey. They would discuss the terms of a contract over the telephone, and then, when the contracts were ready, Dolly Grey would go to the studio and sign them, since she held her husband's power of attorney.

Karp says that Dolly was an excellent businesswoman. He always found her to be fair and reasonable, and the relations between the studio and the Zane Greys was always an excellent one. Karp was a boyhood fan of the Zane Grey books. An ardent fisherman himself, he kept up with Zane Grey's fishing career and exploits in the newspapers and sportsman's magazines.

Karp says that Grey was away from Hollywood during many of the contract negotiations, but even when he knew that Grey was at home in Altadena, it was always with Mrs. Grey that he arranged matters. He confirms the fact that all of the Zane Grey deals with Paramount were leases, usually of seven years. Frequently they had to renew a lease, but there was never any quibbling about this.

After Zane Grey's death, when television became very big, the studio found that although they owned the negatives to the Zane Grey pictures they had made, they could not sell them to television because the Zane Grey contracts had stipulated theatrical release only. However, an arrangement was worked out by which the rights to the motion pictures were sold to a TV distributing company for a quarter of a million dollars.

The money was split evenly between Paramount Pictures and the Zane Grey estate, which at the time was being administered by Lina Elise Grey.

Jack Karp's memories of his association with the Zane Grey family are very warm.

Motion-picture actor James Cagney never played in a Zane Grey film, but he read his first Zane Grey book in 1912 —*Riders of the Purple Sage*. He remained a lifelong fan of Zane Grey's books.

Richard Arlen, Paramount's biggest star during the 1920's, played in a number of Zane Grey motion pictures, beginning when the studio was still called the Brunton Studio, under the direction of Jesse Lasky. In the late 1920's he played in remakes of *The Border Legion* with Jack Holt, *The Light of Western Stars*, with Mary Brian, and *Under the Tonto Rim*.

Arlen began reading the Zane Grey books as a boy in St. Paul, Minnesota. He came to Hollywood while still in his teens and went to work at the Brunton Studios as an "assistant" director, but he worked in that capacity for only a short time, when a director asked him to play a part in a picture. He was a star within a year or two.

Although he played in a number of Zane Grey pictures, Arlen said he never saw Zane Grey at the studio and might never have made his acquaintance, except for the fact that he had a sixty-five-foot ship at Avalon moored near Zane Grey's *Fisherman*. Arlen came along one day and saw Grey regarding Arlen's boat, *The Pagan*, with a shrewd, appraising look. They got to talking, and then Zane Grey introduced himself. They later became very friendly, and Arlen even went fishing with the famous writer in one of the Grey launches. He recalls that he felt awkward beside the greatest fisherman of the Avalon Club, but redeemed himself when he finally caught a small marlin.

Their friendship continued for a long time, although Arlen recalls that it was only around the fishing waters that they met. He says that Grey was a quiet, thoughtful man, very modest about his accomplishments as a writer.

Arlen says, "I wouldn't have had such a long run at Paramount if it hadn't been for Zane Grey stories. They were always tremendously successful at the box office, and as a result of being in them, my own salary increased a great deal."

Of the Zane Grey "hero" Arlen says: "He was always a direct man, without the slightest phoniness." Of the books in general: "Grey was the finest author of his time. I was then, and still am, a great fan of Zane Grey's novels." Then, as an afterthought, he adds, "He was a helluva fisherman, too!"

Erle Stanley Gardner, creator of Perry Mason, whose novels have sold one hundred and fifty million copies—more books than have been sold by any other author—was an early reader of Zane Grey. He says of him: "Zane Grey was a literary giant. He had the knack of tying his characters into the land, and the land into the story. There were other Western writers who had fast and furious action, but Zane Grey was the one who could make that action seem not only convincing but inevitable, and somehow you got the impression that the bigness of the country generated a bigness of character."

Erle Stanley Gardner is known today as the world's foremost writer of mystery novels; he not only read Westerns in his early writing days but also wrote a number of them for magazines. Several of these, featuring a character known as Black Bart, ran in the famous *Black Mask Magazine*.

CHAPTER **36** _____

In spite of the fact that Zane Grey spent so much time away from home on his many extended hunting and fishing trips, he was very much a family man.

A typical day at home saw Grey getting up shortly after six o'clock in the morning, never later than seven. He would have a substantial breakfast of cereal, fruit, hotcakes, and ham or sausages. After breakfast he walked to the post office in Altadena, which was a good mile and a half from his home on East Mariposa Avenue.

This morning walk was a ritual with him; he made it every weekday that he was at home, and it was more because he wanted the exercise than that he was anxious to see the morning mail.

When he returned, the fishing-tackle man had usually arrived. This was a man that he employed regularly when at home, an expert on tackle. Grey spent some time with him always. They went over the tackle, seeing which needed repair or replacement. They discussed new tackle and gear bulletins that Grey had received. At the height of his fame as a fisherman, manufacturers of fishing tackle frequently consulted him about proposed items, and many of the innovations were first suggested by Grey. At one time there were more than a dozen items named after him.

Like so many writers, it was difficult for Grey to get started on a new book or story. When he was fishing, the hours were precious. In order to spend as much time on the water as possible, he had to get up early and write, and he also wrote late in the evening, but when at home he was not so pressed for time, and he would keep putting off the inevitable moment when he had to go into his study, sit down with his writing board, and start putting down words on paper. Sometimes he would go for days on end without writing a single line, but always when the pressure built up, he would get at it, and then the pages poured forth at a rapid pace. He was capable of writing one hundred thousand words in a single month.

There was a tennis court behind the Mariposa house, and Grey was always ready to play tennis with some member of the family. While R. C. was alive, he came over frequently, and he was generally able to beat Zane Grey at tennis, but the keen rivalry between the two at any sport from fishing to tennis never abated.

As Romer grew up, he spent much time on the tennis court, and by the time he was in his early twenties he was able to give his father a good workout and was frequently able to beat him.

Betty disliked tennis. There was a stable on the property, and she spent much of her time with her horses or out on the streets and bridle paths nearby.

At times Grey was an ardent motion-picture fan, especially if one of his own pictures was playing, when he would take the entire family to see it. During the playing and afterward the family would have to listen to Grey's comments on the pictures, which were usually critical. As much as he strove for authenticity, the motion-picture people completely ignored it and did things in his pictures that made Grey cringe. But he was critical of pictures other than Westerns. He was old-fashioned in his views on the morality of the 1920's and 1930's.

Zane Grey was always an avid reader. He enjoyed research, and when he was interested in a subject he got everything available on it. He subscribed to every hunting and fishing magazine that was available, and he read them from cover to cover. He also subscribed to the general periodicals, and Dolly Grey bought most of the new novels of the day.

Grey usually spent the evenings quietly, reading in Dolly's room. He was not averse to reading the novels of his competitors. At one time he had a number of Max Brand's books on a shelf and a few by Ernest Haycox. However, he usually read Haycox's books when they ran as serials in the magazines during the 1930's.

As to be expected, Zane Grey was a lover of animals. He always had a dog or two at home, but he was especially fond of cats, and there were never fewer than two in the house, and sometimes there were as many as eight. They had the full run of the large place.

There were three cats aboard the *Fisherman* on its first cruise to the Galápagos. In his account of this trip, Grey mentions the cats several times. They all had names and were individuals to him. There were always cats in the Lackawaxen home, and the Altadena place was never without them.

His two favorite dogs, who lived to ripe old ages, were an

Airedale and a Paiute shepherd, the latter an animal he got from an Indian shepherd in Arizona. The Airedale was given to him as a puppy in Altadena and grew up to be an excellent dog.

When he worked in his huge study, there was always a cat in the room. Their laziness was restful to Grey.

Grey disliked the radio and would never have one in a room with him. He died before television was available, but he would surely not have liked it, except perhaps to watch a sporting game. He never got over his love of baseball and went frequently to Hollywood Park to watch the Hollywood Stars play visiting teams.

A. C. Lyles, a Hollywood producer of Western pictures, tells a story on himself. He came to Hollywood at the age of sixteen and got a job in the mail room at Paramount Studios. By the time he was twenty-one he had advanced himself to a job as press agent, and, in his spare time wrote a story that he sold to *Photoplay*. It was a great event to a twenty-one-year-old. He was acquainted with Bob Cobb, the owner of the Hollywood Stars, and Cobb took him to a baseball game at Hollywood Park one evening.

A middle-aged man was already seated in the box, cheering a play made by a Hollywood player. The exuberant Lyles missed the name on the introduction and after a while began talking to the baseball fan. He asked to be excused for his exuberance, as he had just sold his first story and asked if the man had ever had the thrill of writing a story.

The baseball fan admitted that he had. When Lyles asked him if he had published anything, the reply was, "Yes, I've had a few things published."

A short while later Lyles whispered to Cobb, to ask the name of the other man in the box.

"Why, he's Zane Grey," replied Cobb. Young A. C. Lyles was tongue-tied for the rest of the evening.

Zane Grey also enjoyed football and went to see many of the college games in California. One of his special diversions was going to the wrestling matches, usually accompanied by either Romer or Loren. He had no illusions about this "sport," but he enjoyed going to the Olympic Auditorium and yelling like everyone else when the "hero" finally vanquished the "villain." He knew many of the wrestlers personally.

There were few visitors to the great house on Mariposa. When Grey was home he insisted on devoting his time to his writing and to his family. Readers of his books learned of his address and called continually at the home, asking to see the famous author. They seldom got inside.

On Sunday nights the clan got together, Ellsworth, R. C., their wives. A poker game always got started, and by the time he was fifteen or sixteen, Romer was sitting in at these games; Loren's turn came later. The games were heated ones, the competitive spirit of the Greys extending even here.

The women played with the men. Dolly Grey loved poker, and she liked to win. The game was usually a twenty-five-cent limit, but they were hard-fought games. Grey had learned poker while at the University of Pennsylvania but had not improved his game until he sat in some of the games with the cowboys of Arizona, among the best poker players in the world. Grey liked to recall the games with the Westerners and always claimed that he had not really known anything about poker until he had played with the taciturn, patient players of the Southwest.

Zane Grey liked big cars, and during the 1920's he favored the Lincoln. A Pasadena dealer once telephoned to say that they had received a new model that was three or four inches longer than any previous one. Grey went down to see it and then looked over another of a different color. The salesman asked him which he preferred, and Grey replied that he liked them both and would take them both. He wrote a check for slightly more than ten thousand dollars, and the salesman never quite got over it.

Zane Grey remained a Hollywood figure but spent less and less time among the motion-picture people. He was spending much time every year making the grand tour of the fishing spots, Long Key in Florida, Nova Scotia, and certainly not

least, Avalon in California. He was writing fishing articles for
the magazines, and Harper was publishing his fishing books.
His fame as a fisherman became international. He held at one
time several world records: bluefin tuna, 758 pounds; yellow-
tail, 111 pounds; striped marlin, 450 pounds; dolphin, 63
pounds; silver marlin, 618 pounds; striped marlin, 1,040
pounds; tiger shark, 1,036 pounds; Allison's tuna, 318 pounds;
Pacific sailfish, 171 pounds; broadbill swordfish, 582 pounds.
He was called "the greatest fisherman America has ever produced."

All the time that he was fishing, Grey was also taking
inland trips. He fished in the mountain streams of Colorado,
Wyoming, California, Oregon, and Washington. He took pack
trips to his beloved Painted Desert, into every corner of Arizona and New Mexico.

Grey liked best the area of southern Utah and northern
Arizona. He had built his lodge on the rim of the Grand
Canyon in 1923, and he visited it for a few weeks every year
until 1930. It was the general background of many of his
stories.

Grey liked to visit novelty stores and buy trick gadgets.
On one of his trips to Tahiti, he would call a Polynesian and
ask him to pull a bandage tight about his arm. When the na-
tive did so, the bandage squirted warm water in his face: The
Polynesians were delighted with this trick and insisted that
Grey perform it on their friends.

On one of the Tahitian trips Grey took the entire family
along and rented a cottage. The women had some shopping to
do in Papeete, and Grey volunteered to baby-sit with Betty
Zane's two youngsters, aged two-and-a-half and four. He got
busy with his writing, and rousing himself after a while, discovered that the children were gone. He found them in the
bathroom, but they had locked the door on the inside and
either could not or would not unlock it. Grey went outside
to the bathroom window and climbed in. Dolly Grey usually
traveled with a small pharmacy and had piled a shelf with
lotions, medicines, pills, and what-not. The children had

dumped all of this into the bathtub and had squeezed toothpaste and shaving cream over everything.

Grey left the mess in the bathtub but attached a note to the tub. It was addressed to Dolly: "This mess was made by *your* grandchildren."

When they were living in Avalon during the summers, Zane Grey liked to take the children to a movie on Saturday afternoon. The usual fare on Saturday afternoons was a couple of serial installments. Betty Zane recalls being taken to a movie one Saturday when she was seven. Her younger brother, Loren, was along. Her father held her hand through the entire performance, which he seemed to enjoy as much as the children.

Zane Grey seldom identified himself to strangers on his trips, but Betty Zane recalls one occasion when he did so. The family had been fishing on the Rogue River, and arriving at the railroad station in Grant's Pass rather early, had to wait for a train. Grey's fishing rods, his equipment, and camping paraphernalia were deposited neatly on the platform of the depot, making a rather imposing array.

A stranger came along, saw the equipment, and remarked on it. "It ain't nothin' compared to what Zane Grey's got down on the river. I spent the summer with him, fishin', and man, you ought to see the stuff he's got."

Zane Grey gave the man a cold look and said, "You spent the summer with Zane Grey? I don't remember ever seeing you before. I happen to be Zane Grey." The stranger made a quick departure.

Zane Grey was fond of playing small practical jokes on his friends and fishing associates. He had gotten into this early, on his first trip to Arizona with Buffalo Jones. Frank and Jim, Buffalo Jones's two hands, were forever trying to frighten the "tenderfoot." One evening they talked loudly about having seen a huge rattlesnake dart under the floor of the cabin in which they were living.

Later Grey found a thin string spread across his sleeping bag. It led through a hole in the wall outside. Suspecting something, he pulled on the string. It was attached to a rope, which came slithering across the sleeping bag. If he had been awakened by that in the middle of the night, it could have been a frightening experience, particularly if he had gone to bed thinking of rattlesnakes.

Grey got the men out of the cabin and moved the coiled rope and string to the bedroll of one of the two hands. In the middle of the night he made a noise that he believed would awaken the pranksters, then began drawing in the string. When the rope began to slither across Frank's bedroll, there was a sudden, awful scream, and the man bounded out of his bed and burst out of the cabin, yelling that a rattlesnake had bitten him.

Zane Grey's elder brother, Ellsworth, or Cedar, as he was usually called, was eleven years older than Zane and fourteen years older than R. C. Zane had not gotten along with him too well when they were boys in Zanesville, but when the Greys all settled on the point of land at Lackawaxen, the three brothers frequently went fishing together. Ellsworth liked fishing but was never as passionately devoted to it as his younger brothers. Nor was he as athletic. He had injured his back while lifting a railroad tie as a boy and was never as strong as he should have been. By profession he was an artist and illustrator and was rather successful at it when he lived in New York, but when he moved to Lackawaxen he went into New York only occasionally, and his illustrating jobs became more infrequent.

He moved to Los Angeles with the family migration in 1918 and lived for many years in Hollywood.

R. C. was the best athlete of the family, and even in later years was a physical-culture advocate. He took excellent care of himself, but in the early 1930's, while running to catch a streetcar, he had a minor heart attack. He still continued his strenuous life, and in 1934, he suffered a heart attack from which he did not survive. Ellsworth, the least athletic of the Greys, died in 1931.

Zane Grey's elder sister, Ella, died while still a girl, but Ida lived until 1937. She remained a spinster throughout her life. She lived with her mother in the cottage at Lackawaxen. When her mother died she moved in with R. C.'s family. She lived with them until R. C.'s death, then moved in with Zane Grey's family. She developed cancer and died in 1937.

Zane Grey knew all the Hollywood luminaries of his time, but few ever visited the house on Mariposa; Zane Grey saw them in Hollywood at the studios or at restaurants. On occasion Grey dropped in at the Trocadero. These visits were rare, however, because when he was in and around Hollywood he spent his evenings at home.

Only occasionally did he entertain visiting New York publishers. The business with them was carried on by mail or on Grey's occasional trips to New York.

Grey had few friends among writers. His closest, perhaps, was Rupert Hughes, a popular author of the 1920's and early 1930's but today almost forgotten. His nephew, however, is exceedingly well known today—he is Howard Hughes.

Before he went to California, Zane Grey's best-loved fishing waters were off the keys of Florida. He joined the Long Key Fishing Club and eventually became its president, but once he discovered the broadbill swordfish off Clemente Island in the Pacific, he went less and less to Florida.

R. C. was with Zane on many of his swordfish expeditions. He went more to keep his brother company, for R. C. liked freshwater fishing best of all. But he became almost as adept at fishing for the huge swordfish, marlin, and tarpon as his older brother. Perhaps his indifference to whether or not he caught the big fish was of help to him. Zane took big-game fishing seriously and pursued it with all the ardor and zest with which he had attacked his writing and everything else. He wanted to excel in everything he did; he had to be best.

Zane Grey liked to have a member of his family with him on his many hunting and fishing trips. He took his son Romer to Arizona in 1918 when Romer was only nine years old. In

1919 Romer accompanied his father on a swordfish-hunting trip to Clemente Island. Romer went fishing to Clemente with his father again in 1920, 1921, and 1922. He accompanied his father to Arizona in 1920, and in 1923 went with him to the Northwest. In 1924 Zane Grey bought *Fisherman* in Nova Scotia but had the captain and the crew sail it to Panama. In Panama Grey, accompanied by Romer and R. C., boarded the ship, and they sailed to the Galápagos, six hundred miles off the coast of Peru. They returned to California, stopping off at Cape San Lucas at the tip of Baja California.

In 1926 Romer went with his father down the Rogue River in Oregon from Grant's Pass to Gold Beach.

In 1927 Romer was with his father on the New Zealand expedition. They were gone eight months this time. Yet, in 1928 Romer traveled alone to Tahiti to meet his father on *Fisherman*, and continued on with him to New Zealand. They did not return until June, 1929, but in the fall of 1929 Zane Grey took Romer to Green River, Utah, to visit the famous Robber's Roost, the inspiration for Grey's book of the same name. From Utah they traveled to Arizona and saw again the famous Rainbow Bridge.

In 1932 Zane Grey and Romer went to Oregon and Washington and to Vancouver Island to fish in the Campbell River for the famous Tyee salmon.They returned to Rogue River and fished for the first time in the North Umpqua River. They returned to this area yearly until 1937.

In 1937 Zane Grey and Romer went on a story-scouting expedition to Ft. Bridger in the Jackson Hole, Wyoming, country, also visiting Yellowstone Park.

The three-year-younger Loren does not remember his first trip with his father, but he was on many of the shorter fishing trips that Zane Grey took while living in his summer home at Avalon. Loren was nine years old in 1924, when he went on his first long trip with his father to Winkle Bar in Oregon. In 1931, when he was sixteen, he went with his father to the South Seas, and again in 1935 he went to Tahiti with him.

He repeated the trip to Tahiti in 1937, taking off a year from his college work to make the trip.

Dolly Grey, unlike her husband, was never an enthusiast of the outdoor life, but she went with him frequently, and the entire family then went along. She liked to cruise in the waters off Catalina Island and Clemente, but she did not care for the long trips. She did, however, go several times with the entire family to Oregon, and in 1926 she caught a record salmon on the Rogue River and for a time almost became an ardent fisherwoman. But there were too many things to do at home. There was always the problem of the children's schools, the work in the house, and the management of Zane Grey's complicated publishing affairs.

Zane Grey was interested in the writing but was annoyed with the business details of negotiating with magazines and book publishers. He left most of these to Dolly. For periods, R. C. tried to help with the business end, but it was usually Dolly who carried the burden, for R. C. was with his brother on most of the longer trips away from home.

Zane Grey's earnings between 1915 and 1932 were enormous at a time when income taxes were trivial by today's standards. One must remember also that the purchasing power of a dollar was much greater during those years.

A salesgirl earned from ten to fifteen dollars a week; a bookkeeper averaged twenty dollars a week and was an "accountant" when his salary was raised to twenty-five dollars a week.

A laborer in 1915 earned twelve to fifteen dollars a week. In the early 1920's he received twenty to twenty-five dollars a week. Executives of business firms drew fifty and sixty dollars a week; presidents of the companies received perhaps a hundred dollars a week. A physician or surgeon counted himself fortunate if his annual income went over ten thousand dollars. So did attorneys.

Zane Grey was earning more than $100,000 a year by 1920. During the 1920's his income soared to $300,000 and

$400,000 a year. He reached the half-million mark, and once, his biggest year, it went to $575,000.

Dolly Grey was an excellent businesswoman. She, more than anyone else, evaluated Zane Grey's writing. She sold his stories for him, and she always insisted on the top dollar. When *The Country Gentleman* did not protest too strongly over paying $35,000 for a serial, she raised the price of the next one to $40,000, then $45,000, and finally she established a price of $50,000 for *The Country Gentleman*. The *Ladies' Home Journal* paid $50,000 several times for Zane Grey stories. So did *McCall's*, and *American* went as high as $60,000. *Collier's* topped the list by paying $80,000 each for three serials.

Once, when the better-paying magazines demurred at paying the high prices for a particular story, Dolly, wanting to unload the story quickly, let *Cosmopolitan* have the serial rights for the "bargain" price of $50,000.

Dolly Grey was the "rich" member of the family. When the big serial and royalty checks began coming to the Grey home, Zane Grey made a deal with his wife. The checks were split evenly; Grey took half and Dolly got half. Dolly ran the house with her share and saved the rest. Zane Grey spent his on his expensive trips, his hunting lodges and ranches, his boats and ships. Dolly's money remained an anchor to windward, a bulwark against the leaner days—which came in the Depression years of the 1930's.

Then, perhaps, Dolly Grey erred. With the sudden drying up of the serial market in 1932, because of inability of the magazines to pay the high established rates for Zane Grey books, Dolly Grey remained firm. The books were as good as ever; the Depression could not last; the big prices would return.

Zane Grey protested to Dolly at times. He felt the magazines would buy his stories, if prices were cut. Dolly argued against it. It was the subject of many talks. Harper's had twenty books ahead, for which serial rights had been sold. These newer books could be held for the eventual return of the big magazine prices.

Zane Grey did not make an issue of it. It had been Dolly

who had engineered the sales of his stories into the fantastic prices of the 1920's. She had done well then; he would have to respect her judgment now.

Zane Grey had lost his zest for hunting. More and more he had become a conservationist in recent years as he saw the wildlife of the mountains becoming scarcer. The fall of 1929 was the last time he went hunting. He continued to visit the Western regions that he had loved so much, but after 1929 his hunting consisted of taking pictures of animals.

After he sold *Fisherman,* Zane Grey came to regret it, and in 1930, when he heard of a ship for sale in the East, he went there to look at it. The ship was the *Kallisto.* She had been made by Krupp of Germany, reportedly for Kaiser Wilhelm II before his abdication. She was a three-masted schooner and seemed like a superb ship to Grey. He bought her and engaged a captain and crew to bring her to California.

CHAPTER **37** ═══════════════════════════

In the summer of 1930, Zane Grey again began to write in his diary. The first entry is dated August 21, 1930. It reads:

Dolly and Betty are motoring east. Romer is in Oregon, Loren visiting. I am alone.

It is a big house to be alone in. What would it be to be alone forever? There is the past—of memories, of pictures, of letters and books, but these would soon kill me.

Love grows more tremendously full, swift, poignant, as the years multiply.

In the early dawn I awake to thinking, "So sad and sweet—the days that are no more." Nevertheless, I arise full of eagerness and energy, knowing well what achievement lies ahead of me, perhaps the best, if not the most.

Romer was married while I was in Tahiti, an elope-

ment. His bride is a young, beautiful, fine, and sensible
girl, studious, with nothing of the flapper about her. They
are nineteen and twenty years old. Betty's engaged at
eighteen. My wife is quite lightheaded with these hap-
penings. Loren made a great record at fishing in Avalon
this summer. So that's something.

Some pages have been cut out of the diary at this point,
and the next entry comes as a shock. It is:

July 10, 1931. Yacht, 550 miles off San Pedro:
    After six months of strife in the South Seas, I am near-
ing home, worn out in body, but still unquenchable in
spirit.
    This trip has been remarkable for trouble. Despite its
one great white light, it has ended in failure.
    My financial ruin appears certain. I am facing the crisis
of my life. I am prepared for the worst, and know my clear
stern resolve. I will not be crushed by all this disaster. . . .

The 1931 expedition to Tahiti was an ill-fated one from
its very inception. For seven years the association between
Captain Mitchell and Zane Grey had been a very close one.
The two men respected each other's fishing ability, but Zane
Grey was the celebrity, a famous, wealthy author. Captain
Mitchell's reputation was based solely upon his fishing experiences. He was completely without funds, the remittances from
England having ceased some years back. He became Zane
Grey's companion, but he was, in effect, an employee, a full-
time employee, for when Zane Grey left Tahiti each year,
Captain Mitchell remained behind to take care of the boats
and equipment. Grey paid him a salary of four hundred and
fifty dollars a month twelve months of the year, plus access to
the equipment and supplies that Grey left with him. For the
several months of every year when Grey was with Mitchell,
the captain's daily expenses were paid by Grey.

It was a substantial drain upon Grey, but he did not mind it. Until 1931.

This 1931 trip, which began late in 1930, was to be the one of which Zane Grey had long dreamed, a complete trip around the world, with stopovers at a few of his regular places and a few new ones. Grey wanted to try for big game fish in the Indian Ocean, off East Africa, near the island of Madagascar. The trip was planned for a full year, and Grey wanted to take Loren with him.

Grey paid forty thousand dollars for the *Kallisto* and had it sailed from the East Coast to San Pedro, California, where it was turned over to a shipbuilding company. In his usual freehanded way, Grey told the shipbuilders what changes he wanted made in the ship. He did not ask for bids from other builders, did not insist on a firm quoted price for the work. He only asked that the work be done as quickly as possible. He did not stop to think of the double shifts, the overtime required. He asked only that the ship be ready for sailing in December, 1930.

He left the provisioning and equipping of the ship entirely in the hands of the ship's officers.

The ship was completed on time, and it was supplied and equipped with everything that would be needed for the cruise of a year, plus some extras against emergencies. It was one of the most completely equipped ships that ever set off on a cruise. It was also one of the most expensively fitted ships. Of these costs Grey was oblivious. The final bills were not rendered before his departure.

But Grey had obviously had in mind about one hundred thousand dollars, a figure that would not have crippled him at the time, although it would have extended him somewhat. However, he knew that he would write a couple of books during the course of a year and that money would be coming in steadily. Although it was late 1930, the Depression had not yet caught up with the Greys.

While the ship was being prepared, Betty was married to Robert Carney, who had been Romer's closest friend for a couple of years. Betty and Carney had been engaged for some months, and both Zane and Dolly approved of the engagement and the marriage, although they had hoped that the marriage would not be so soon, for Betty had only that September entered the University of Wisconsin.

For a wedding present, Zane Grey proposed that Betty and her new husband join them in Tahiti and perhaps sail on with him around the world. The young couple thought well of the idea, for Carney was as devoted a fisherman as Romer, and Betty never wanted to pass up an opportunity to be with her father.

The ship sailed with Zane Grey and Loren aboard. They reached Tahiti after a miserable voyage. The *Fisherman II*, as the *Kallisto* had been renamed, was an abominable sailer. The slightest seas caused her to roll, and when they encountered a storm, everyone on board was sure that she would roll over and sink. Loren, not yet sixteen, was scared out of his growth, and Zane Grey, even though he was a good sailor, was in continual despair.

Fisherman II went off its course to Hawaii, where she was gone over thoroughly. It was discovered that she had lost her balance during the conversion work. The ballast had been moved and not distributed properly. Some minor changes were made in the ship, and she continued on into the South Seas but soon encountered another storm, worse than the previous one. *Fisherman II* acted as badly as it had in the first storm.

Although *Fisherman II* was equipped and supplied for a year's cruise, it was somehow discovered that purchases were required at every port of call and the prices for supplies kept getting higher and higher. The people who were buying the supplies were getting kickbacks from the island merchants, and sometimes they were selling things from *Fisherman II* and keeping all the money.

It was costing Zane Grey five thousand dollars a month to operate the ship, far more than he had counted on.

Fisherman II reached Tahiti and found mail from Dolly Grey. The bills from the shipbuilding company, the outfitters and purveyors, the ship's chandlers, had come in. They totaled more than three hundred thousand dollars, three times as much as Zane Grey had estimated. It was his fault, of course, for not getting estimates and firm prices.

The crew was one of the worst Grey had ever had on a ship. The officers were even worse.

Cables went back and forth between Grey and Dolly. Slowly he realized that he could not now afford to continue the trip around the world. He would, in fact, have to raise money even now to remain in Tahiti long enough for the honeymoon couple, Betty and Bob Carney, to join him.

Things had not been going too well between Grey and Captain Mitchell, and Grey, becoming suddenly angry at a report from one of his people about something that Captain Mitchell was supposed to have said, decided to discharge him.

Unfortunately, Grey confided in one of his people, and the next day Grey received a call from an attorney. Captain Mitchell had heard that he was going to be discharged and was starting suit against Zane Grey for four hundred and fifty dollars a month for the next eighteen months.

Grey was furious; he had no contract with Mitchell. Their agreement had been an offhand, handshake agreement. But now the chips were down, and Grey got his own attorney. He learned that under the French law, by which Tahiti operated, an "employee" could attach everything he owned in Tahiti. And Captain Mitchell had been an employee.

A compromise was worked out. Grey agreed to retain Mitchell in his employ for three hundred dollars a month. But the long friendship between them had been ruptured, and it was on a business basis that they now met. The old feeling that had existed between them for so long was gone.

Betty and Bob Carney arrived by steamer and were with *Fisherman II*, but back in California Dolly was finding herself

pressed in taking care of the immediate obligations incurred
by the rebuilding and outfitting of the ship.

A serial that had been accepted by a magazine for sixty
thousand dollars—and she had counted on the money—was
suddenly returned. She could not send any substantial sums to
Grey, who desperately needed money for operating costs of the
ship and the retinue that surrounded him. He decided to sell
twenty-five hundred gallons of gasoline that were surplus,
since he did not intend to continue around the world. He also
sold a launch. Then a rumor, fanned by some of those un-
friendly to him, spread quickly through Papeete and the nearby
islands: Zane Grey had to sell his equipment to pay his employees. Grey found that he could not even cash a check.

Sadly, Grey decided to return to California at once.

The personal and financial disasters that struck Grey on
this trip were the cause of the poignant entry in his diary when
only 550 miles from the coast of California.

There were still problems when he came home, but Dolly
Grey had been working to solve them during his absence, and
the sale of a serial for sixty thousand dollars—the one that had
been returned during his absence—helped to ameliorate the
immediate financial crisis.

Fisherman II continued to be a headache as long as he
held title to her, but with the ship in port, Zane Grey's ex-
penditures for her upkeep were small. He continued to send
his remittances to Captain Mitchell, still in Tahiti, but the
remittances were of short duration, for the Englishman died
within a year.

For the next two years Grey's fishing trips were nearer
home, at Avalon and in Oregon, where he owned the small
cabin at Winkle Bar. He did, however, take a trip to Idaho
late in the fall of 1931 to get material for a new novel.

CHAPTER **38** ─────────────────────

The stock-market crash of 1929 was a catastrophe to Zane Grey's colorful and faithful
retainer George Takahashi. Always a thrifty man, Takahashi
had saved his money and invested it in stocks. He had augmented his savings by acting as a loan shark for his compatriots
in Los Angeles, lending them money at interest of ten percent
a month. In 1929, while still working for Zane Grey as chef
and general factotum, Takahashi counted himself a wealthy
man, worth in excess of one hundred thousand dollars. The
stock-market crash wiped him out.

Zane Grey had little money in stocks. He had invested his
money in ships and people. He had taken his losses and had
not worried. His income in 1930 and 1931 was still very large.
Year by year his payment for serials had gone up. He was still
selling books to motion pictures at twenty-five thousand dollars each. His book sales had fallen off somewhat, but they
were still good, especially in the lower-priced editions.

In 1932 Harper's brought out *Arizona Ames* and *Robber's
Roost*, but serial rights had sold in previous years to these two
books, so Grey had only the book income from them.

In the early part of the year he sold serial rights to *The
Young Runaway* (later published as *Wyoming*) to *Pictorial
Review*, and shortly thereafter serial rights to *The Lost Wagon
Train* were bought by *Cosmopolitan* at a somewhat smaller
price than he was used to getting. But *Collier's* soon bought
Thunder Mountain.

And then the serial market for Zane Grey books dried up.
He spent months writing *Boulder Dam*, spending a great deal
of time on location where the huge dam was being constructed.
He researched every aspect of the giant project, and it showed
in his manuscript.

But *Collier's* declined the serial rights. So did *Cosmopol-*

itan, The Ladies' Home Journal, and even the faithful *Country Gentleman.*

The Depression had greatly affected the magazine business. Belts were tightened all along the line. Employees were dismissed from their jobs; salaries of those who remained were slashed. The magazines still sold well, but magazines do not make their money from subscriptions or newsstand sales; they earn it from advertising, and this income had decreased drastically.

Collier's, which had paid eighty thousand dollars within the past year for a Zane Grey serial, was now buying stories from other writers, not as well known as Zane Grey, but nevertheless good, who were very glad to accept the fifteen to twenty thousand dollars that the magazine could afford to pay.

The year 1933 was a complete blank for Zane Grey. He did not sell serial rights to a single book. He did not sell any short material to any magazine. The magazine editors told him that they could not afford his prices. When he offered to sell at a lower price, they still demurred. It was not low enough.

Zane Grey spent months of self-searching. Were the editors telling him the truth, or had he lost his touch? Was his writing falling off? He was sixty years old. He was still in excellent health and it seemed to him when he was at work that the writing came as easily as always. Perhaps he ought to work harder at it, try to make it better. He wrote *Western Union,* researching his subject with more than even his usual thoroughness. Harper's assured him that it was one of his finest books—but Grey could not sell serial rights to it.

He wrote *Shadow on the Trail, Thirty Thousand on the Hoof,* and *Stairs of Sand,* the long-awaited sequel to *Wanderer of the Wasteland.* They were offered to the magazines. All rejected them.

The Country Gentleman still wanted to use his name, but did not want a long serial. Perhaps a short one. Grey wrote *Outlaws of Palouse,* and *Country Gentleman* accepted it and

published it early in 1934. It was the last serial story Zane
Grey ever sold to a magazine.

R. C. Grey died in 1934, and his death affected Zane
Grey deeply. He had been so close to R. C. as a boy, as a
young man, in their maturity. R. C. had been his companion
on so many of his hunting and fishing trips; he had had the
same zest, the same enthusiasm for the adventurous life. R. C.
was only fifty-nine; Zane was sixty-two. He was still in excellent health, had known no serious illnesses. He was as vigorous
as a man ten or fifteen years younger. But then R. C. had been
vigorous almost to the end. His heart had simply given out
one day.

The children were growing up. Romer was twenty-five,
married, and had a child; Betty was twenty-two; and Loren
was nineteen and entering college. The house in Altadena was
quieter.

The trophies, the mementos, were all there, but something
had died in the house—the spirit of R. C. Zane could still plan
his fishing trips, but he had to plan them without R. C. His
brother would no longer go with him, would no longer join
him later on.

All he had left was his writing. It had to be done, of
course, but there was no longer the same urge that there had
been all these years. Harper's had fifteen books that were still
to be published. They would take the new ones, of course, but
there would be no immediate money from them. The money
that would come in from the yearly book that was published
was now but a dribble, where once it had been a golden
torrent.

A newspaper syndicate approached him; would he be interested in writing a daily comic strip? Grey was tempted to
refuse the offer with righteous indignation, but perhaps that
was the way things would be in the future. He needed a brand-
new interest, something that would take his mind from his
regular chores, that might open up a new source of income.

He discussed it with the syndicate people, and from the

talks a daily comic strip was born: *King of the Royal Mounted.*
Grey could not sustain his interest in it; Romer wrote many of
the continuities for the strip. They bore Grey's name, but the
content was totally different from anything he had done before.

Nevertheless, he had been a conscientious worker all his
life, and he could not now totally neglect this new project. He
wrote story outlines; Romer broke them down into daily con-
tinuity. The strip earned a fair amount of money, and then
the Whitman Publishing Company of Racine, Wisconsin,
issued the comic strip in a series of small hardbound books to
be sold for fifteen cents a copy in the cheaper outlets—drug-
stores and five-and-ten-cent stores. They bore Zane Grey's name,
but Grey hated to see them.

Franklin D. Roosevelt came into the Presidency in 1933,
and the myriad of government agencies tried to break the
long Depression. They eased things somewhat, but the Depression did not go away. The business recovery was slow, cautious.

CHAPTER **39**

What Zane Grey needed was a long fishing
voyage, but it had to be in new waters. New
Zealand and Tahiti would have too many memories, for R. C.
had been with him in both areas. There was only one more
unknown great fishing area for Zane Grey to see and conquer.
Australia.

He wrote to fishermen in Australia, to fishermen who
lived elsewhere but had fished in the waters off the great subcontinent. He gathered information for months and made his
plans, and finally, late in 1935, he set sail for Sydney, arriving
there on New Year's Eve.

A launch he had ordered made to his specifications in
Auckland, New Zealand, was waiting for him in Sydney, and

soon Grey moved on to the village of Bermagui, 275 miles down the coast from Sydney.

He had not lost his skill. Age had not weakened him for this sport of sports. He caught a black marlin weighing 480 pounds and a striped marlin of 324 pounds, then topped this by setting a new record in catching a tiger shark weighing 1,036 pounds.

The season, according to the Australians, was a bad one for fishing, but it was an excellent trip for Zane Grey. He caught his hoped-for quota of the big fish, and some to spare. He did not neglect other opportunities in Australia. He had been aware for years, from the unusually large number of letters that he received from Australia, that his books were big sellers there and had been received with unusual response.

Zane Grey spent a little more than seven months in Australia, and most of this time he was actually fishing, first at Bermagui, then at Sydney, and finally among the islands of the Great Barrier Reef. He was in the northern reef area more than three months. He could not have spent more than three or four weeks altogether on the mainland itself. Yet the background material he gathered during this visit for *The Wilderness Trek*, which he wrote during the coming months, is astonishing. The story concerns two American cowboys who go to Australia and throw in with a huge movement of cattle across the entire continent, a trip that takes two years and five months.

As in his Western novels, Zane Grey makes you feel that you are making this trip yourself. He identifies most of the animals and birds of the subcontinent's various areas; he describes the flora and fauna, the mountains, the rivers, the deserts, and the fertile areas that the cattle drive crosses.

His two American heroes speak the typical Western dialect of his previous books, but the native Australians all speak the dialogue and slang that is peculiar to Australia itself. He employed a number of Australian boatmen and guides, but since these were fishermen living in the coastal areas, he could not have gotten all of his background material from them. Quite obviously he read a great many books on Australia, but he must also have spent every available moment ashore, talking to people from the interior.

When *The Wilderness Trek* was finally published in 1944, it was well received by the Australians. It is one of Zane Grey's most interesting books because of its background and feeling of authenticity, but serial rights went begging.

He did, however, sell serial rights in that year. The two-million circulation *New York News* bought serial rights to *Knights of the Range*. The price paid, fifteen thousand dollars, was but a shadow of what Zane Grey had received in 1932 and the many years before, but it seemed to indicate to him that things were easing up. The Depression could not hold on much longer.

The Trail Driver and *The Lost Wagon Train*, written some years before, were brought out by Harper's in 1936, and both promptly sold to motion pictures. *West of the Pecos* sold early in 1937. *An American Angler in Australia*, Grey's account of his 1936 trip to the Antipodes, was also published by Harper's in 1937. Grey had enjoyed writing this book as much as he had enjoyed his trip to Australia, and he was already planning a second trip to Australia.

CHAPTER **40** _____

The grim warning came during the summer of 1937. With Romer and a guide, Grey went fishing to the North Umpqua River, his favorite of all the places in Oregon. He was trolling for steelhead when suddenly he fell over unconscious. Romer and the guide had to carry him to their automobile and rush him to a hospital. Grey did not recover consciousness until the next day, when it was discovered that he was completely paralyzed. A specialist was summoned from San Francisco, and after a few days Zane Grey was taken to a hospital in Los Angeles.

Speech returned slowly, but it was many days before Grey could move even a muscle. Dolly Grey records in her diary: "Z. G. was able to move a finger today."

His recovery was fairly rapid then, but it was several weeks before he recovered sufficiently so that he could sit up and finally move about.

The diagnosis of the specialists had been coronary thrombosis and stroke. He was sixty-five years old. A second attack might prove fatal, but there was no reason that he could not have some productive years if he would forgo the strenuous life he had been leading.

Zane Grey would have none of that. All his life he had believed in physical fitness, and all of his life he had exercised and indulged in outdoor activities. He refused to believe that he must now, at sixty-five, lead a sedentary life.

In 1922 and 1923 Zane Grey had come across a copy of Emile Coué's book, which had an enormous vogue for a time. It was a treatise on willpower and self-hypnotism, and a phrase taken from the book, "Every day, in every way, I shall become better," had become a household saying. Grey had written to Dolly several times extolling the book and its teachings, and he had applied them to himself. He returned to the theory now, and in spite of the admonitions of Dolly and his family, he began to exercise.

His physical condition improved almost immediately, and Grey plunged into exercise even more. He was soon working out on the rowing machine, and by early spring the casual observer would have thought him fully recovered. He was able to walk and move about in a normal fashion, but there were some sections of his body where the muscles still did not respond.

He had been corresponding with people in Australia; he had promised them that he would return and set some new fishing records.

Dolly protested and enlisted the aid of Dr. Greengo, who also advised against the trip, but Zane Grey would not heed their admonitions. He felt as fine as he ever had. The ocean trip would restore his health completely, and the exercise in the fishing banks off Australia would be better than his old rowing machine.

He was sixty-six, but he still had a few years left in him. Dolly, who knew that the greatest fear of his life had always been that of growing old—and admitting it—stilled her remonstrances.

Zane Grey's return trip to Australia in 1938 was one long accolade. Government officials sought him out, as did many of the Down Under Country's leading citizens. He was overwhelmed with invitations to speak at civic and private gatherings, but this was not for Zane Grey, and he fled to the fishing waters.

Australians still sought him out. A reef he had discovered on his previous trip was officially named the Zane Grey Reef and so went on the maps.

His book *An American Angler in Australia* had been published in 1937 and was widely publicized. It resulted in a huge influx of tourists to Australia and included many fishermen who now fished the waters that Zane Grey had made famous.

His heart attack of the previous year kept Zane Grey from strenuous exertions on this trip, and he did not try for any new fishing records. He fished chiefly for pleasure and went ashore several times to visit new and interesting places that he had heard about. He spent a considerable time shopping for gifts for his American friends, and in one shop bought out the entire stock of stuffed life-sized koala bears, which he later distributed among friends, both young and old.

Everyone he met knew of him; all, it seemed, had read his books. It was known that he had written an Australian "Western" novel, and he was asked continuously when it would be published so that it could be bought and read.

He enjoyed a triumphant success in Australia, but when he left the country he was very tired. He recovered somewhat during the trip back to California, and once he was home, he plunged into his usual activities; he fished off Catalina and went to Oregon and fished both the Rogue and North Umpqua Rivers.

He worked as hard as he had always worked. The Depression was still on, and book sales were down, but that fact did not lessen the quantity of Zane Grey's production of pages.

The family moved to Avalon in the spring of 1939, as they always did, and later in the summer Grey spent a short time in Oregon, but he had planned no long trips for that year and he did not make any. He tired sometimes after only an hour's fishing. Time was taking its toll, time and the paralyzing stroke of two years ago.

He spent a very quiet summer and fall at home in Altadena. Dolly and Romer took care of the business affairs. There was considerable activity in Hollywood with his books, where Paramount had remade a long series of his stories.

Romer took a trip to New York every now and then. In 1936 he sold serial rights of *Knights of the Range* to the New York News Syndicate for fifteen thousand dollars, and in 1939 he sold another serial to the same market for the same price. It was a far cry from the huge rates of the 1920's and early 1930's but was considered a good price under the existing circumstances.

Dolly Grey did not think so. She was always optimistic and every year expected conditions to become better. She thought that the books should be held for the big prices that she felt certain would soon come back. They never did, however.

Western Union was published by Harper's in October, 1939. On October 21 Zane went down to his favorite bookstore, Vroman's in Pasadena, and spent the afternoon autographing books. He was cheerful and joked with book buyers and signed the seventy-five-cent editions as pleasantly as he did the more expensive Harper editions.

All of the family were at the Altadena house on Sunday —Romer, Betty and her children, and Loren. It was a quiet day, and for some reason the Sunday-night poker game was passed up. Zane read in his wife's room for a while in the evening, then retired to his own room. The custom of separate bedrooms had been established some years before when Zane worked late at his writing and did not want to awaken Dolly when retiring.

Dolly was awakened early in the morning by a call from Zane. She hurried into his room. He was clutching his chest, gasping, and he cried out plaintively, "Don't ever leave me, Dolly!"

Dolly wanted to call the doctor, but Zane restrained her. The pain in his chest began to ease and after a while faded away. Zane decided that it had been a mere indigestion constriction. He went back to bed and to sleep.

On Monday morning he rose at seven, somewhat later than usual. He dressed, then sat down on the edge of the bed. Suddenly he gasped, cried out, and fell to the floor.

The family doctor could not immediately be reached, and Loren got into a car, raced down the street, and found a doctor, whom he took to the house. The doctor pronounced Zane Grey dead. He had never recovered consciousness.

Dolly Grey recorded it simply in her diary: "Z. G. died this morning at seven-thirty A.M."

CHAPTER **41**

At the time of Zane Grey's death, Dolly Grey was fifty-six years old, Romer thirty, Elizabeth twenty-seven, and Loren twenty-four. For a while it seemed that Loren might become as great a fisherman as his father, but in 1940 he enlisted in the U.S. Navy and served for fifteen months in the South Pacific. At the end of the war he was a lieutenant. He is today a professor of psychology at Valley State College in California.

Romer Grey lived for several years on the Grey ranch in Riverside County, where he raised cattle, but he came back more and more to Altadena to help with the administration of the Zane Grey books and properties, and when his mother died in 1957, he became president of Zane Grey, Inc.

Robert Carney drowned accidentally while swimming, and Elizabeth Grey lived in Southern California until she married George Grosso, a banker and horse breeder in northern California. Grass Valley, California, has been her home for many years.

The book that Zane Grey had been autographing at Vroman's bookstore only two days before his death, *Western Union*, was sold to Twentieth Century-Fox early in 1940 and starred Robert Young and Randolph Scott. The producer was Harry Joe Brown; as a result of this picture, Harry Joe Brown went into partnership with Randolph Scott. They filmed Grey's book *Twin Sombreros*, although the final motion-picture title was changed to *Gunfighters*. It began a long association between Brown and Scott, which lasted through the making of sixteen motion pictures.

At the time of his death, Zane Grey had several unfinished manuscripts. He had been writing his autobiography off and on for more than two years but had taken the story of his life only up to his first year at the University of Pennsylvania.

He was also working on a new Western novel, which he called tentatively *School for Cowboys*; he was about two-thirds finished with this.

While in Tahiti in the mid-1930's, Zane Grey wrote a long novel, which was totally unlike anything he had ever written. It was called *The Reef Girl*, a story of the South Seas, where he had spent so much time. His publishers were unenthusiastic about it, believing his reading public preferred to read his Western novels.

He had also written two historical novels, one a story of

the young George Washington, who was with the British General Braddock at the disastrous defeat of the British by the French and Indian forces. This story is titled *George Washington, Frontiersman*.

A third book was a story of Sam Houston. It was completed in a rough first draft but was never polished or rewritten because of the large backlog of books that Harper's already had at the time of Zane Grey's death.

The sales of Zane Grey's books held up steadily during the 1940's, and in the war years even increased. One of the first books published in the Armed Services Editions was a Zane Grey book. Soldiers, sailors, and marines, in every theater of the worldwide conflict, carried Zane Grey books with them, either in the small Armed Services Editions or the regular paperback editions.

In 1934 a Liberty ship, the *Zane Grey*, was launched, with Loren Grey, Betty Grey Carney, and their mother, Mrs. Zane Grey, taking part in the services.

A movement was started in the late 1940's at Zane Grey's home town, Zanesville, Ohio, to purchase the old Gray home on Convers Avenue and turn it into a Zane Grey Museum. This did not materialize, but a museum was finally established in downtown Zanesville and now has thousands of visitors annually. All of the Zane Grey material in it was furnished by the heirs of Zane Grey, including several of the original manuscripts of Zane Grey books. It includes much fishing tackle and many personal mementos.

At the time of Grey's death, the family owned the large estate at Altadena; a big house at Avalon on Catalina Island; the hunting lodge and ranch on the rim of the Tonto, in Arizona; the fishing lodge at Winkle Bar, Oregon, an area still referred to by real-estate people as "Zane Grey Country"; and a ranch in Riverside County, California. All of these properties were gradually disposed of, with the exception of the house at Altadena, where Romer Grey resides today and conducts the business of the estate.

The original cottage at Lackawaxen, Pennsylvania, which

grew into a massive structure through continual additions, is today an inn, called fittingly the Zane Grey Inn.

Because of Zane Grey's foresight during the 1920's, the motion-picture rights to his books were leased for only seven years, and all through the 1930's and 1940's motion-picture rights to the books continued to be sold. One was sold as recently as 1968.

At the time of Grey's death, Harper's had twenty of his books still unpublished. Some had appeared as serials in the 1920's and early 1930's, but some had not been published in any form. Harper continued to publish these, and two or three remain to be published in the near future, as well as a number of shorter stories of less than novel length.

Grosset & Dunlap, who published the cheaper reprint editions from the very early years, has continued to bring out the Zane Grey books. Their 1968 catalog lists sixty-one "active" Zane Grey book titles.

At the time of Zane Grey's death a total of twenty-seven million Zane Grey books had been sold. By 1968 the total had increased to more than forty million. This figure will become even larger, because new editions of the books are already under contract.

The Walter J. Black Company began publishing matched editions of Zane Grey books in the "Zane Grey Book Club" in 1950 and continues to sell more than three hundred thousand copies a year.

A new magazine, *Zane Grey Western,* is planned, as is a new line of paperback editions, "Zane Grey Westerns."

CHRONOLOGY

1872   Pearl Zane Gray is born at Zanesville, Ohio.

1875   Romer Carl Gray born.

1878   Pearl Gray enters Moore Street Grammar School.

1886   Pearl Gray enters Zanesville High School.

1890   Pearl Gray graduates from high school. Family moves from Zanesville to Columbus, Ohio. Pearl gets job as usher in theater. Romer goes to work as delivery boy for grocery store.

1891   Pearl Gray becomes traveling tooth puller, going to small towns. Plays baseball for Columbus team.

1892   Pearl pitches against Jacktown team, as "ringer." State dental board prohibits Pearl Gray from continuing as a tooth puller. Pearl receives offers from universities. Accepts conditional scholarship from University of Pennsylvania Dental School. Enters university.

1893   Pearl plays on varsity team as pitcher, is ruined when new rule lengthening distance from plate to pitcher's mound is put into effect. Kept on team in outfield because of hitting ability.

1896   Pearl Gray graduates from Penn. Goes to New York and opens dental office on West 74th Street.

1900   Pearl Gray meets Lina Elise Roth.

1902   Sells first article, "A Day on the Delaware."

1903   Completes first novel, *Betty Zane*, written during winter.
        Cannot find publisher who will accept. Borrows $600 from
        Lina Roth to pay for publishing of *Betty Zane*. Pearl now
        calls himself Zane Grey, dropping "Pearl."

1904   Writes *The Spirit of the Border*. Cannot get it published.

1905   Writes *The Last Trail*, cannot get it published, but places
        The Spirit of the Border with A. L. Burt & Company.
        Lina Roth's grandfather dies. Lina comes into inheri-
        tance. Zane buys home at Lackawaxen. Lina Roth and
        Zane Grey marry in New York and go to live at Lacka-
        waxen.

1906   *The Spirit of the Border* published by Burt. Zane Grey
        writes unsuccessfully.

1907   Zane Grey meets Buffalo Jones, borrows last of wife's
        money, and goes to Arizona to spend several weeks with
        Jones, hunting, catching mountain lions with lasso. Returns,
        writes *The Last of the Plainsmen*. Book rejected by Harper's;
        Zane told he shows no literary promise whatever. Sells three
        fishing articles to magazines.

1908   Writes juvenile book, *The Short Stop*, accepted by A. C.
        McClurg. Sells five articles to fishing magazines.

1909   Sells five articles to fishing magazines, begins long novel
        of the West. Romer Grey born October 1, 1909.

1910   Completes *The Heritage of the Desert*, sells serial rights
        to *Popular Magazine*. Book is accepted by Harper &
        Brothers, published in July. Sells juvenile book to Harper's,
        The Young Forester.

1911   Sells seven articles and short stories to magazines. Writes
        The Young Lion Hunter for Harper's. Writes *Riders of the
        Purple Sage*; serial rights rejected by *Popular* and other
        magazines. Grey takes trip to Mexico, fishes off Tampico,
        goes up Santa Rosa River. Writes juvenile, *Ken Ward in
        the Jungle*. Sells long article on same subject to *Field &
        Stream*.

1912   After *Riders of the Purple Sage* rejected by several maga-
        zines and by several readers at Harper's, Grey goes over head
        of editor and persuades vice-president to read it. Novel is

accepted and published and becomes huge success. Elizabeth Zane Grey born April 22, 1912.

1913 Writes *Desert Gold*, sells serial rights to *Popular Magazine*. Harper's publishes, and book very big seller. Writes *The Light of Western Stars* and sells serial rights to *Munsey's Magazine*.

1914 *The Light of Western Stars* published by Harper's. Huge success. Goes on extended fishing trips, first fishing for swordfish at Catalina. Fishes at Long Key, Florida; Nova Scotia; and New Jersey. Another trip to Arizona. Writes *The Lone Star Ranger*; sells serial rights to Munsey's *All Story*. Writes *The Rainbow Trail*; sells serial rights to *Munsey*.

1915 Both *The Lone Star Ranger* and *The Rainbow Trail* published by Harper's. *Ranger* hits best-seller list, *The Rainbow Trail* not far behind. Writes *The Border Legion*; sells serial rights to *All Story*. Loren Grey born November 20, 1915.

1916 Writes *Wildfire*; sells serial rights to *Country Gentleman* for large price. *The Border Legion* sells very well in Harper edition.

1917 *Wildfire* published by Harper's; appears on best-seller list. Writes *The U.P. Trail*; sells serial rights to *Blue Book*. Last pulp magazine sale. Writes *Man of the Forest*, sells serial rights to *Country Gentleman*.

1918 *The U.P. Trail* is published by Harper's. Is the top-selling book of the year. Three books made into motion pictures: *Riders of the Purple Sage*, *The Rainbow Trail*, and *The Border Legion*. Greys move to Hollywood, California. Grey takes Romer on first outdoor trip to Arizona. Writes *Desert of Wheat*; sells serial rights to *Country Gentleman*.

1919 Visits Death Valley. Writes *Wanderer of the Wasteland*; sells serial rights to *McClure's Magazine*.

1920 *Man of the Forest* published by Harper's. Is number one on best-seller list. Writes *The Mysterious Rider*; sells rights to *Country Gentleman*.

1921 Writes *To the Last Man*; sells serial rights to *Country Gentleman*. Writes *Call of the Canyon*; sells serial rights to *Ladies' Home Journal*. *The Mysterious Rider* published by Harper's. Again in top ten on best-seller list.

1922   *To the Last Man* published by Harper's. On best-seller list.
       The Day of the Beast also published by Harper's. Writes
       The Vanishing American; sells serial rights to *Ladies' Home
       Journal*.

1923   Writes many fishing articles. *Code of the West* sold to
       Country Gentleman, *The Thundering Herd* to *Ladies'
       Home Journal*.

1924   Buys *Fisherman* in Nova Scotia and has the ship recondi-
       tioned. Starts from Panama Canal for Galápagos Islands.
       Writes many articles.

1925   Adventures in Galápagos Islands. Biggest writing year. Sells
       many articles. Writes *The Bee Hunter* for *Ladies' Home
       Journal*, *The Deer Stalker* for *Country Gentleman*, *Don* for
       Harper's Magazine, *Captives of the Desert* for *McCall's
       Magazine*. Harper's publishes *The Thundering Herd* and
       The Vanishing American. Grey takes in $575,000 in 1925.
       Sails for New Zealand in December.

1926   Fishing in New Zealand. Sells *Forlorn River* to *Ladies'
       Home Journal*, *Nevada* to *American*.

1927   Fishing in New Zealand. Writes *Open Range* for *Country
       Gentleman*, *The Water Hole* for *Collier's*.

1928   Fishes at Tahiti. Writes *Sunset Pass* for *American Maga-
       zine*, *The Sheep Herder* for *Collier's*, and *Fighting Caravans*
       for *Country Gentleman*.

1929   Fishing at Tahiti. Writes *The Drift Fence* for *American*,
       The Yellow Jacket Feud for *Collier's*, and *Rustlers of Silver
       River* for *Country Gentleman*, plus shorter serials for high
       pay.

1930   Writes *The Dude Ranger* for *McCall's*, *Robber's Roost*
       for *Collier's*, short serial for *Ladies' Home Journal*. Fishes
       off Tahiti. Buys *Fisherman II*.

1931   Spends over $300,000 refitting *Fisherman II*; sails it to
       Fiji; runs out of money. Returns home. Writes *West
       of the Pecos* for *American*, *The Trail Driver* for *McCall's*,
       Raiders of Spanish Peaks for *Country Gentleman*.

1932   Writes *The Young Runaway* for *Pictorial Review*, *The Lost
       Wagon Train* for *Cosmopolitan*, *Thunder Mountain* for
       Collier's. Book sales fall off with Depression days.

1933   Writes *Boulder Dam*; cannot sell serial rights.

1934   Sells *Outlaws of Palouse*, short serial, to *Country Gentleman*.
        This is last story sold to magazines.
1935   Writes books; cannot sell serial rights.
1936   Sells serial rights of *Knights of the Range* to *New York News*
        for $15,000. In Australia for fishing.
1937   Sells serial rights of *Majesty's Rancho* to *New York News*.
        Suffers heart attack at North Umpqua River. Recovers at
        Altadena.
1938   Returns to Australia. Sells no serial rights.
1939   Dies at Altadena, California.

THE ZANE GREY SERIALS

TITLE	MAGAZINE
The Heritage of the Desert	Popular
Down an Unknown Jungle River	Field & Stream
Riders of the Purple Sage	Field & Stream
Ken Ward in the Jungle	American Boy
Desert Gold	Popular
The Light of Western Stars	Munsey's
The Lone Star Ranger	All-Story Cavalier
The Desert Crucible	Argosy
(*The Rainbow Trail*)	
The Border Legion	All-Story
Wildfire	Country Gentleman
The Roaring U.P. Trail	Blue Book
Man of the Forest	Country Gentleman
The Desert of Wheat	Country Gentleman
The Mysterious Rider	Country Gentleman
Wanderer of the Wasteland	McClure's
Arizona Bear	Country Gentleman
To the Last Man	Country Gentleman

TITLE	MAGAZINE
Call of the Canyon	Ladies' Home Journal
The Day of the Beast	Country Gentleman
Sea Angling	Izaak Walton Monthly
The Vanishing American	Ladies' Home Journal
Code of the West	Country Gentleman
The Thundering Herd	Ladies' Home Journal
Wild Horse Mesa	Country Gentleman
The Fisherman	Outdoor America
The Bee Hunter	Ladies' Home Journal
(*Under the Tonto Rim*)	
The Deer Stalker	Country Gentleman
Desert Bound	McCall's
(*Captives of the Desert*)	
Forlorn River	Ladies' Home Journal
Nevada	American
Rocky Riffle on the Rogue	Field & Stream
Shooting the Rogue	Country Gentleman
Open Range	Country Gentleman
(*Valley of Wild Horses*)	
The Water Hole	Collier's
(*Lost Pueblo*)	
Avalanche	Country Gentleman
Stairs of Sand	McCall's
Sunset Pass	American
The Sheep Herder	Collier's
(*The Shepherd of Guadaloupe*)	
Fighting Caravans	Country Gentleman
The Drift Fence	American
Amber's Mirage	Ladies' Home Journal
The Yellow Jacket Feud	Collier's
(*The Hash Knife Outfit*)	
The Ranger	Ladies' Home Journal
Rustlers of Silver River	Country Gentleman
(*Rogue River Feud*)	
Arizona Ames	McCall's
The Dude Ranger	McCall's
Canyon Walls	Ladies' Home Journal
Robber's Roost	Collier's

TITLE	MAGAZINE
Tales of the South Seas	Physical Culture
West of the Pecos	American
The Trail Driver	McCall's
Raiders of Spanish Peaks	Country Gentleman
The Young Runaway (Wyoming)	Pictorial Review
The Lost Wagon Train	Cosmopolitan
Thunder Mountain	Collier's
Outlaws of Palouse	Country Gentleman
Knights of the Range	New York News
Majesty's Rancho	New York News
Twin Sombreros	New York News

ZANE GREY MOTION-PICTURE FEATURES PRODUCED

BOOK TITLE	NUMBER OF TIMES PRODUCED
The Last Trail	4
The Heritage of the Desert	3
Riders of the Purple Sage	4
Desert Gold	3
The Light of Western Stars	4
The Lone Star Ranger	4
The Rainbow Trail	3
The Border Legion	3
Wildfire	3
The Desert of Wheat	1
Man of the Forest	3
The Mysterious Rider	3
To The Last Man	2
Wanderer of the Wasteland	3
The Call of the Canyon	1
The Thundering Herd	1
The Vanishing American	2

BOOK TITLE	NUMBER OF TIMES PRODUCED
Under the Tonto Rim	3
Forlorn River	2
Nevada	3
Wild Horse Mesa	2
Fighting Caravans	2
Sunset Pass	3
Arizona Ames	1
Robber's Roost	2
The Drift Fence	1
Code of the West	3
Thunder Mountain	3
West of the Pecos	2
Raiders of Spanish Peaks	1
Knights of the Range	1
Western Union	1
Twin Sombreros	1
Stairs of Sand	3
The Maverick Queen	1
The Dude Ranger	3
Lost Pueblo	1
The Ranger	2
Avalanche	1
Canyon Walls	2
From Missouri	2
The Horse Thief	2
Born to the West	2
Open Range	1
South Seas Adventures (Featuring Zane Grey himself)	1
White Death (Featuring Zane Grey himself)	1

SHORT SUBJECTS:

Fisherman's Pluck (Featuring Zane Grey)	1
Fighting Mako (Featuring Zane Grey)	1

THE BOOKS

The books listed carry only the original publishers' name and the first date of publication. Most of the books were reprinted many times, sometimes by more than one publisher.

1903
Betty Zane   Charles Francis Press
1906
The Spirit of the Border   A. L. Burt & Company
1908
The Last of the Plainsmen   Outing Publishing Co.
1909
The Last Trail   Outing Publishing Co.
The Short Stop   A. C. McClurg & Co.
1910
The Heritage of the Desert   Harper & Brothers
The Young Forester   Harper & Brothers
1911
The Young Pitcher   Harper & Brothers
The Young Lion Hunter   Harper & Brothers
1912
Riders of the Purple Sage   Harper & Brothers
Ken Ward in the Jungle   Harper & Brothers

1913
Desert Gold   Harper & Brothers
1914
The Light of Western Stars   Harper & Brothers
1915
The Lone Star Ranger   Harper & Brothers
The Rainbow Trail   Harper & Brothers
1916
The Border Legion   Harper & Brothers
1917
Wildfire   Harper & Brothers
1918
The U.P. Trail   Harper & Brothers
1919
The Desert of Wheat   Harper & Brothers
Tales of Fishes   Harper & Brothers
1920
Man of the Forest   Harper & Brothers
The Red-Headed Outfield   Grosset & Dunlap
  and Other Stories
1921
The Mysterious Rider   Harper & Brothers
1922
To the Last Man   Harper & Brothers
The Day of the Beast   Harper & Brothers
Tales of Lonely Trails   Harper & Brothers
1923
Wanderer of the Wasteland   Harper & Brothers
Tappan's Burro   Harper & Brothers
1924
Call of the Canyon   Harper & Brothers
Roping Lions in the Grand Canyon   Harper & Brothers
Tales of Southern Rivers   Harper & Brothers
1925
The Thundering Herd   Harper & Brothers
The Vanishing American   Harper & Brothers
Tales of Fishing Virgin Seas   Harper & Brothers
1926
Under the Tonto Rim   Harper & Brothers
Tales of an Angler's Eldorado   Harper & Brothers

1927
Forlorn River   Harper & Brothers
Tales of Swordfish and Tuna   Harper & Brothers

1928
Nevada   Harper & Brothers
Wild Horse Mesa   Harper & Brothers
Don, the Story of a Dog   Harper & Brothers
Tales of Fresh Water Fishing   Harper & Brothers

1929
Fighting Caravans   Harper & Brothers

1930
The Wolf Tracker   Harper & Brothers
The Shepherd of Guadaloupe   Harper & Brothers

1931
Sunset Pass   Harper & Brothers
Zane Grey's Book of Camps   Harper & Brothers
   and Trails

1932
Arizona Ames   Harper & Brothers
Robber's Roost   Harper & Brothers

1933
The Drift Fence   Harper & Brothers
The Hash Knife Outfit   Harper & Brothers

1934
Code of the West   Harper & Brothers

1935
Thunder Mountain   Harper & Brothers

1936
The Trail Driver   Harper & Brothers
The Lost Wagon Train   Harper & Brothers
King of the Royal Mounted   Whitman Publishing Co.

1937
West of the Pecos   Harper & Brothers
An American Angler in Australia   Harper & Brothers
Tex Thorne Comes out of the West   Whitman Publishing Co.
King of the Royal Mounted and   Whitman Publishing Co.
   the Northern Treasure

1938
Raiders of Spanish Peaks   Harper & Brothers

King of the Royal Mounted in the Far North	Whitman Publishing Co.
King of the Royal Mounted Gets His Man	Whitman Publishing Co.
King of the Royal Mounted Policing the Far North	Whitman Publishing Co.
King of the Royal Mounted and the Great Jewel Mystery	Whitman Publishing Co.

1939
| Western Union | Harper & Brothers |

1940
| Thirty Thousand on the Hoof | Harper & Brothers |

1941
| Twin Sombreros | Harper & Brothers |

1942
| Majesty's Rancho | Harper & Brothers |

1943
| Stairs of Sand | Harper & Brothers |

1944
| The Wilderness Trek | Harper & Brothers |

1946
| Shadow on the Trail | Harper & Brothers |

1947
| Valley of Wild Horses | Harper & Brothers |

1948
| Rogue River Feud | Harper & Brothers |

1949
| The Deer Stalker | Harper & Brothers |

1950
| The Maverick Queen | Harper & Brothers |

1951
| The Dude Ranger | Harper & Brothers |

1952
| Captives of the Desert | Harper & Brothers |
| Zane Grey's Adventures in Fishing | Harper & Brothers |

1953
| Wyoming | Harper & Brothers |

1954
| Lost Pueblo | Harper & Brothers |

1955
Black Mesa   Harper & Brothers
1956
Stranger from the Tonto   Harper & Brothers
1957
The Fugitive Trail   Harper & Brothers
1958
Arizona Clan   Harper & Brothers
1959
Horse Heaven Hill   Harper & Brothers
1960
The Ranger and Other Stories   Harper & Brothers
   Avalanche
   Canyon Walls
   From Missouri
1961
Blue Feather and Other Stories   Harper & Brothers
   The Horse Thief
   Quaking Asp Cabin
1963
Boulder Dam   Harper & Row

THE MAGAZINE STORIES

Many of Zane Grey's stories, novels, and articles on hunting and fishing appeared originally in magazines and were later included in books. When the book title is not that of the original magazine story, it is added in parentheses.

TITLE	MAGAZINE
1908	
Cruising in Mexican Waters	Field & Stream
	January, 1908
Lassoing Lions in the Siwasn	Everybody's
	June, 1908
Tige's Lion	Field & Stream
	June, 1908
1909	
Roping Lions	Field & Stream
	January, 1909
Lord of Lackawaxen Creek	Outing
(*Tales of Fresh Water Fishing*)	May 1, 1909
In Defense of Live Bait	Field & Stream
	June, 1909
Rabihorcados and the Boobies	Everybody's
(*Tales of Fishes*)	September, 1909
Nassau, Cuba and Mexico	N.Y. & Cuba Mail S.S. Co.
	October 25, 1909
1910	
Lightning	Outing
	March 21, 1910
A Trout Fisherman's Inferno	Field & Stream
	April, 1910
The Winning Ball	Popular
(*The Red-Headed Outfield*)	May 1, 1910
The Heritage of the Desert	Popular
	Serial beginning
	May 25, 1910
Accidents in Camp	Field & Stream
	June, 1910
False Colors	Popular
	June 1, 1910
Old Well-Well	Success
(*The Red-Headed Outfield*)	July, 1910
The Knocker	Success
(*The Red-Headed Outfield*)	August, 1910
The Rube	Success
(*The Red-Headed Outfield*)	October, 1910

TITLE	MAGAZINE
1911	
Down an Unknown Jungle River (*Tales of Southern Rivers*)	Field & Stream Serial beginning March, 1911
On the Trail of the Jaguar	Harper's Weekly May 6, 1911
The Rube's Nutty Nine (*The Red-Headed Outfield*)	National Post May 6, 1911
The Rube's Waterloo (*The Red-Headed Outfield*)	National Post May 20, 1911
The Rubber Hunter	Popular June 15, 1911
The Rube's Pennant (*The Red-Headed Outfield*)	National Post June 17, 1911
The Rube Breaks into Fast Company (*The Red-Headed Outfield*)	National Post July 1, 1911
Water Tigers of the Gulf Stream	Field & Stream December, 1911
1912	
Riders of the Purple Sage	Field & Stream Serial beginning January, 1912
Fighting Qualities of Black Bass	Field & Stream May, 1912
Ken Ward in the Jungle	American Boy Serial beginning May, 1912
Horses of Bostil's Ford	Munsey's June, 1912
Barracuda of Long Key	Field & Stream July, 1912
Tiger	Munsey's September, 1912
1913	
Phantoms of Peace	Munsey's January, 1913
Amberjack of Sombrero Reef	Field & Stream February, 1913

TITLE	MAGAZINE
Desert Gold	Popular Serial beginning March 1, 1913
The Light of Western Stars	Munsey's Serial beginning May, 1913
Following the Elusive Tuna	Field & Stream September, 1913

1914
The Lone Star Ranger	All-Story Cavalier Weekly Serial beginning May 9, 1914
The Last of the Duanes	Argosy September, 1914

1915
Nonnezosche, the Rainbow Bridge	Recreation February, 1915
Swordfish, the Royal Purple Game (*Tales of Fishes*)	Recreation February, 1915
A New Wonder—Nonnezosche	World February 14, 1915
The Desert Crucible (*The Rainbow Trail*)	Argosy Serial beginning May 1915 Field & Stream Serial 1915–1916

1916
The Border Legion	All-Story Weekly Serial beginning January 15, 1916
Wildfire	Country Gentleman Serial beginning April 8, 1916
Picture and Short Article	Recreation June, 1916
Some Rare Fish of the Sea (*Tales of Fishes*)	Recreation October, 1916
Sailfish (*Tales of Fishes*)	Recreation December, 1916

TITLE	MAGAZINE
1917	
The Roaring U.P. Trail	Blue Book
	Serial beginning
	June, 1917
Two Fights with Swordfish	Recreation
(*Tales of Fishes*)	October, 1917
Man of the Forest	Country Gentleman
	Serial beginning
	October 20, 1917
1918	
Catalina Tuna	Field & Stream
	March, 1918
Colorado Trails	Outdoor Life
	March–June, 1918
Gladiator of the Sea	Field & Stream
(*Tales of Fishes*)	April, 1918
Avalon the Beautiful	Field & Stream
(*Tales of Fishes*)	May, 1918
The Desert of Wheat	Country Gentleman
	Serial beginning
	May 4, 1918
Gulf Stream Fishing	Field & Stream
	July, 1918
1919	
Light Tackle	Field & Stream
	January, 1919
Swordfish of the Sea	Field & Stream
	March, 1919
Big Tuna	Field & Stream
	May, 1919
The Mysterious Rider	Country Gentleman
	Serial beginning
	June 7, 1919
1920	
Death Valley	Harper's
	April 22, 1920
Sport of Kings	California (L.A. Examiner)
	April, 1920
Fishing for Swordfish and Tuna	Country Gentleman
	May 1, 1920

TITLE	MAGAZINE
Crater Lake	Country Gentleman
(*Tales of Freshwater Fishing*)	May 15, 1920
Wanderer of the Wasteland	McClure's
	Serial beginning
	May, 1920
Pelican Bay	Country Gentleman
(*Tales of Freshwater Fishing*)	June 26, 1920
Record Fight with a Swordfish	Country Life
(*Tales of Swordfish and Tuna*)	August, 1920
Yaqui	Country Gentleman
	September 25–
	October 2, 1920
Arizona Bear	Country Gentleman
	Serial beginning
	November 13, 1920
The Great Slave	Ladies' Home Journal
	December, 1920
1921	
Why I Write Western Stories	American Newstrade Journal
	May, 1921
Zane Grey's Deep Sea Angling	Sportologue
	May, 1921
To the Last Man	Country Gentleman
	Serial beginning
	May 28, 1921
Call of the Canyon	Ladies' Home Journal
	Serial beginning
	November, 1921
1922	
The Day of the Beast	Country Gentleman
	Serial beginning
	April 1, 1922
Sea Angling	Izaak Walton Monthly
	Serial beginning
	August, 1922
The Vanishing American	Ladies' Home Journal
	Serial beginning
	November, 1922

TITLE	MAGAZINE
Bonefishing	Country Gentleman November 18–25, 1922
The Bonefish Brigade	Izaak Walton Monthly December, 1922
1923	
Blackfish and Swordfish Stories	Forestry
The Seventh Wave	Izaak Walton Monthly January, 1923

Tyee Salmon
  (*Tales of Freshwater Fishing*)
	Izaak Walton Monthly
	  February, 1923

Steelhead	Country Gentleman February 3, 1923
Bear Trails	Country Gentleman March 3–17, 1923
The Gladiator of the Sea	Outdoor America March–April, 1923

Code of the West	Country Gentleman
	  Serial beginning
	  April 28, 1923

The Ten Books I Have Enjoyed
  Most
	North American Newspaper
	Alliance
	  May 6, 1923

Tappan's Burro	Ladies' Home Journal June, 1923
The Whale Killers	Country Gentleman August 11, 1923
Roping Lions in the Grand Canyon	Boys' Life November, 1923
Fishing the Rogue	Country Gentleman November 17, 1923
1924	
Down into the Desert	Ladies' Home Journal January, 1924
Heavy Tackle for Heavy Fish	Catalina Islander January, 1924

At the Mouth of the Klamath
  (*Tales of Freshwater Fishing*)
	Outdoor America
	  January, 1924

Trails over the Glass Mountains	Outdoor America January, 1924

TITLE	MAGAZINE
The Thundering Herd	Ladies' Home Journal Serial beginning February, 1924
Three Broadbill Swordfish	Outdoor America February, 1924
Heavy Tackle for Heavy Fish	Outdoor America February, 1924
Xiphias Gladius (*Tales of Swordfish and Tuna*)	Country Gentleman February 9, 1924
Trees	Outdoor America March, 1924
One of the Wonders of the Deep	Outdoor America March, 1924
Tonto Bear	Country Gentleman March 1, 1924
Help Us Save Vanishing America	Success April, 1924
Monty Price's Nightingale	Success April, 1924
The Heights of Wild Horse Mesa	Country Gentleman April 12, 1924
Wild Horse Mesa	Country Gentleman Serial beginning April 19, 1924
Forest Fires, Automobiles, Good Roads	Outdoor America May, 1924
Birds of the Sea	Outdoor America June, 1924
Breaking Through	American July, 1924
The Fisherman	Outdoor America Serial beginning July, 1924
Surprise Valley	Outdoor America August–September, 1924
Gulf Stream Luck	Country Gentleman October 4, 1924
Everglade Tarpon	Country Gentleman October 11, 1924

TITLE	MAGAZINE
Desert Bound	McCall's
(*Captives of the Desert*)	Serial beginning
	December, 1925
Rooster Fish and Leaping Whales	Country Gentleman
	December, 1925

1926

Thrill of Striking Fish	Country Gentleman
	January, 1926
Southern California Out of Doors	Los Angeles Times
	January 1, 1926
Forlorn River	Ladies' Home Journal
	Serial beginning
	February, 1926
Rocky Riffle on the Rogue	Field & Stream
(*Tales of Freshwater Fishing*)	February–August, 1926
Breaking Through	New Zealand Tid-Bits
	February 10, 1926
Log of the Gladiator	Sunset
	March 15, 1926
My Adventures as a Fisherman	American
	April, 1926
Shooting the Rogue	Country Gentleman
	April–May, 1926
Will H. Dilg	Field & Stream
	June, 1926
From Missouri	McCall's
	July, 1926
The Man Who Influenced Me Most	American
	August, 1926
Sport in New Zealand Waters	Field & Stream
	September, 1926
Love Your Work, Says Zane Grey	Progressive Farmer
	September 13, 1926
Nevada	American
	Serial beginning
	November, 1926

1927

Sheep Raising in New Zealand	Country Gentleman
	January, 1927

TITLE	MAGAZINE
My Son's First Bear	Country Gentleman February, 1927
Open Range (*Valley of Wild Horses*)	Country Gentleman Serial beginning March, 1927
The Vanishing American	W. H. Dilg League Monthly July, 1927
The Water Hole (*Lost Pueblo*)	Collier's Serial beginning October 8, 1927
Grand Canyon	American Motorist December, 1927

1928

Naza	Golden Book February, 1928
Avalanche	Country Gentleman Serial beginning February, 1928
Stairs of Sand	McCall's Serial beginning March, 1928
Sunset Pass	American Serial beginning April, 1928
Big Game Fishing in New Zealand Seas	Scientific American August, 1928
The Sheep Herder (*The Shepherd of Guadaloupe*)	Collier's Serial beginning October 27, 1928
The Camp Robber	McCall's October, 1928
Fighting Caravans	Country Gentleman Serial beginning November 2, 1928

1929

The Drift Fence	American Serial beginning April, 1929

TITLE	MAGAZINE
Amber's Mirage	Ladies' Home Journal Serial beginning May, 1929
The Yellow Jacket Feud (*The Hash Knife Outfit*)	Collier's Serial beginning September 21, 1929
The Ranger	Ladies' Home Journal Serial beginning October, 1929
Arizona Ames	McCall's Serial beginning October, 1929
Rustlers of Silver River (*Rogue River Feud*)	Country Gentleman Serial beginning December, 1929

1930

Landing the World's Record Tuna	World January 26, 1930
Big Game Fishing	Outdoor Life April, 1930
Fishing	American Legion May, 1930
The Dude Ranger	McCall's Serial beginning October, 1930
Canyon Walls	Ladies' Home Journal Serial beginning October, 1930
Robber's Roost	Collier's Serial beginning October 11, 1930
Giant of the South Seas	Outdoor Life November, 1930

1931

Tales of the South Seas	Physical Culture Serial beginning February, 1931
Modern Sea Angling	Outdoor Life February, 1931

TITLE	MAGAZINE
West of the Pecos	American Serial beginning August, 1931
The Trail Driver	McCall's Serial beginning October, 1931
Raiders of Spanish Peaks	Country Gentleman Serial beginning December, 1931
1932 The Young Runaway (*Wyoming*)	Pictorial Review Serial beginning May, 1932
The Lost Wagon Train	Cosmopolitan Serial beginning July, 1932
Thunder Mountain	Collier's Serial beginning October 22, 1932
A Plea For Westerns	Modern Screen December, 1932
1934 Outlaws of Palouse	Country Gentleman Serial beginning May, 1934
1935 Lever Action Rifles	Sports Afield May, 1935
North Umpqua Steelheads	Sports Afield September, 1935
1936 Knights of the Range	New York Sunday News Serial beginning January 19, 1936
The Mako Shark	Field & Stream April, 1936
Fly Fishing	Horrocks-Ibbetson Co. December 28, 1936

TITLE	MAGAZINE
1937	
World Record Tiger Shark	Field & Stream February, 1937
Grey Nurse Sharks	Field & Stream April, 1937
Australian Angling	Field & Stream June, 1937
Marlin and Man Eaters	Field & Stream August, 1937
Majesty's Rancho	New York Sunday News Serial beginning September 26, 1937
1939	
They Came Tough in Tahiti	Southern Sportsman November, 1939
1940	
Twin Sombreros	New York Sunday News Serial beginning January 14, 1940
1954	
Mystery of Quaking Asp Cabin	American Weekly June 27, 1954
1955	
Whale Killers of Two-Fold Bay	American Weekly June, 1955

INDEX